MW01235865

Youth Peacebuilding

SUNY series, Praxis: Theory in Action
Nancy A. Naples, editor

Youth Peacebuilding

Music, Gender, and Change

Lesley J. Pruitt

Cover image © Mecaleha / iStockphoto.com

Published by State University of New York Press, Albany

Printed in the United States of America

For information, contact State University of New York Press, Albany, NY
www.sunypress.edu

Production by Diane Ganeles
Marketing by Anne M. Valentine

Library of Congress Cataloging-in-Publication Data

Pruitt, Lesley J.
Youth peacebuilding : music, gender, and change / Lesley J. Pruitt.
p. cm. — (SUNY series, praxis: theory in action)
Includes bibliographical references and index.
ISBN 978-1-4384-4655-4 (hardcover : alk. paper) 1. Youth and peace
2. Children and peace. 3. Peace-building. 4. Peace—Songs and music.
5. Youth—Political activity. I. Title.
JZ5579.P78 2013
303.6'6—dc23

2012023135

10 9 8 7 6 5 4 3 2 1

To the amazing, talented, awe-inducing young peacebuilders who inspired this study from the beginning: Thank you for letting me into your world, sharing your dreams with me, and making me believe this universe is a much better place than I could have envisioned. May your vision for a better tomorrow shine brighter than a thousand splendid suns!

Contents

Acknowledgments

Funding for this project was provided by a 2008 University of Queensland Graduate School International Travel Grant and by the University of Queensland School of Political Science and International Studies.

A modified version of some paragraphs from the following articles have been partially incorporated in chapters 3–7: "They Drop Beats, Not Bombs: A Brief Discussion of Issues Surrounding the Potential of Music and Dance in Youth Peace-building," *Australian Journal of Peace Studies* 3 (2008): 10–28; "Music, Youth and Peacebuilding in Northern Ireland," *Global Change, Peace & Security* 23, 2 (2011): 207–222; parts of an earlier version of chapter 4 appeared in "Creating a Musical Dialogue for Peace," *International Journal of Peace Studies*, 16, 2 (Autumn/Winter 2011): 85–106; some excerpts from chapter 7 appeared in the current or modified form in "'Fixing the Girls': Neoliberal Discourse and Girls' Participation in Peacebuilding," *International Feminist Journal of Politics* (2012).

I am thankful to the editors of these journals listed as well as the several anonymous reviewers for providing thoughtful and constructive feedback, which I hope is evident in the modified versions found in this book. I am also grateful for guidance and support I received from Barbara Sullivan, Roland Bleiker, and Anita Harris. Many thanks are also due to Siobhan McEvoy-Levy, Ross Marlay, and Mark Chou for their helpful engagement with my work over the past several years. Any and all errors that remain are my own.

Prelude

> What would you think if I sang out of tune, would you stand up and walk out on me? Lend me your ears and I'll sing you a song, and I'll try not to sing out of key.
>
> —John Lennon and Paul McCartney, "With a Little Help from My Friends"

It seems only right to begin this musical journey with a plea from a song. As I discuss throughout this book, music—as expression, as creation, as inspiration—can provide many unique insights into transforming conflicts, altering our understandings, and achieving change. Some of the unique capacities of music are found precisely in its difference from other forms of communication, such as writing and speaking. Therefore, I want to acknowledge that in some ways it is reductive to talk about music with only written words. Moreover, I am a scholar of peace studies, a social scientist rather than a trained musician, so my lack of technical knowledge around music also limits what I can say. Nevertheless, I humbly ask the reader to suspend disbelief long enough to engage with the ideas discussed here. Based on my experiences with the young people I had the pleasure to meet in researching this book, I truly believe that music is not only an accessible medium in its own right, but that it can also change the way we think and communicate in our day-to-day lives. So I invite you to put on a song that means something to you when you read this and let the rhythm lead your mind someplace new . . .

Introduction

In the peacebuilding arena, the United Nations (UN) has tended to focus on formal political processes such as peace negotiations, institution building, and elections. It is difficult, if not impossible, for young people to be actively engaged in many of these peacebuilding activities. However, it is clear that young people are not disengaged from peacebuilding work. Around the world we see young people involved in a range of activities that aim to build more peaceful societies. For example, many youth take part in programs that use popular culture as a medium for political engagement, are involved in political movements and activism, or participate in local peace education programs.

Despite this, research in the field rarely mentions youth; and their experiences and knowledge are often ignored, both in attempts at theory-building and in efforts at understanding peacebuilding practice at the grassroots level. This is important, as it does not account for peacebuilding practice through the eyes of those who experience it. However, there are some scholars of peacebuilding who have recently emphasized the importance of youth in the construction of effective peacebuilding.[1] Their scholarly contributions in particular offer a sound starting point for this investigation.

More attention is needed to how everyday activities of people, including young people, may be utilized in peacebuilding activities. One activity that young people are particularly involved in is music. Over the last few decades, the music industry has grown significantly and spread with globalization. Consequently, there is now a wider variety of music accessible to more people than at any time in history. Music is an integral part of youth culture around the world. Young people use it to express themselves, create new styles, make a statement, define their circle of friends, or set the mood for events. We see young people involved in a range of activities including listening to music, dancing, creating and performing their own music and dance, and participating in community music and dance programs.

For some of these young people, these practices are also involved in building a culture of peace—for example, by challenging racial and gender inequality, poverty, and community violence. These stories for the most part remain to be told. What I aim to do in this book is draw on the experiences of the young people I encountered in my research to share their stories and explore the many ways I think they can contribute to our understandings of peacebuilding, both in theory and in practice. I hope this will be of interest and useful to researchers of peacebuilding who have never considered youth or are looking to learn more about their experiences, as well as to policymakers and practitioners of peacebuilding who are interested in hearing more from youth and applying what they learn in their planning, implementation, and evaluation.

The Research Puzzle and Key Terms

My primary research question in this project is: *Can music be a useful tool for engaging young people in peacebuilding?*

I use the term "music" here to denote participation in a range of activities, including performance via singing, dancing, playing musical instruments, or otherwise appropriating existing music to forge new musical creations. This includes learning and practice of musical expression.

The definition of "youth" is highly contested in the contemporary world. The United Nations Population Fund (UNFPA) defines "youth" as the age group from 15–24 years old and young people as those in the range of "10–24" years. However, it is impractical to use rigid age categories to define youth in divided societies facing violent transformation.[2] After all, child soldiers may in some ways be adults and former combatants in their mid-30s may have lost their youth to the cause. In any case, the term "youth" is variable and context-specific, so it is reasonable to consider any definition both critically and flexibly.[3] I use the term "youth" to include young people who self-identify and/or are identified by their peers and mentors as youth.

In post-conflict societies, peacebuilding is often understood as a sequence of activities ranging from cease-fire to creating a new government and reconstructing the economy while bringing together former enemies.[4] However, peacebuilding is also needed in diverse contexts with different types and levels of conflict; thus, it more broadly includes grassroots processes that can: aid in restoring and healing relationships in communities affected by conflict; create institutions to prevent both social and political violence; and empower citizens working for social change across religious, ethnic, and political divides.[5] When looking at peacebuilding here, I refer to bottom-up approaches aimed at preventing, reducing, transforming, and assisting people with recovery from all forms of violence, including structural violence that has yet to result in widespread civil turbulence.[6] So my focus is on the building of positive peace. This is similar to what the UN calls a "culture of peace." Because they are synonymous, I use "positive peace" and "culture of peace" interchangeably throughout this book.

Positive peace has been advanced as a deeper, more just, and therefore more sustainable form of peace. Positive peace is not just the absence of war or direct violence; it involves much more, including gender justice, an assurance of fair political, economic, and social arrangements and the preservation of human rights.[7] Building peace thus requires a broad process of creating a societal environment to promote education on human rights, aid and development, and restoring community life.[8] From this perspective, positive peace can be understood as working from the ground up to eventually alter common cultural norms of managing violence.[9]

Pursuing a "culture of peace" is an integral part of peacebuilding. As Boulding suggests, a culture of peace includes promoting peaceful approaches to difference, both in behavior and institutions, and finding a successful balance between the needs for autonomy and relatedness.[10] Bush gives a more in-depth description, explaining that a culture of peace has many components, including breaking down the culture of war, taking into account armed conflict and physical violence more generally, both within and between cultures as well as within families and communities. This, he says, will require addressing symbolic aspects of militarization and pursuing compassion and justice. Furthermore, it will also include respect and human rights among cultures and finding ways to eliminate racism and discrimination.[11]

In 1999 the General Assembly of the UN resolved (A/53/243) to initiate a "program of action to build a culture of peace for the world's children."[12] The resolution articulated a goal of seeking not simply negative peace (the absence of overt conflict) but rather a state of positive peace. The program of action designed by the delegates attended to distinct foundations on which a culture of peace could rest, including: education, sustainable development, human rights, gender equality, democratic participation, understanding, tolerance, solidarity, freedom of information, participatory communication, and international peace and security. The UN declared that a culture of peace would include attitudes, values, and behaviors that involve rejecting violence as well as the need to address the root causes of violence in an attempt to prevent conflicts. Moreover, the UN also called for using dialogue and negotiation in problem solving. Since this movement began at the UN, UNESCO's website has documented hundreds of actions taken with the aim of building a culture of peace. Examples include concerts, youth camps, exhibitions, and shows.[13] This development is important even through a traditional security lens. While the absence of overt violent conflict may evidence some temporary, base level of security, overall human security requires the pursuit of a culture of peace.[14]

Methodology

To explore whether and how music might be used to engage young people in peacebuilding, I adopted a two-step approach. First, I completed a literature review on relevant existing sources dealing with intersections between peacebuilding (or politics), youth, and music. This helped me situate my project in the existing field, and provided a strong foundation for the empirical study. I then set about conducting an empirical study of peacebuilding programs that engaged young people in music-making as a central part of their activities. My initial search for appropriate programs to study made clear that, as far as could be ascertained from English-language resources, using music is a relatively new mode for engaging young people in peacebuilding. It appears that few such projects exist. However, I located two groups in two very different cultural contexts, which I discuss in more detail in chapter 3. These sites offered rich opportunities to look at how music can be used in youth peacebuilding work. One group, Third Place, worked locally in Australia to engage young people from diverse cultural backgrounds. The aim was to prevent direct conflict and build more equitable social relations in a community that suffered significant social problems but has not experienced open conflict. The second group, Breaking Barriers, in Northern Ireland aimed to contribute to peacebuilding efforts in an area of the world that had experienced many years of direct conflict and serious civil unrest.

The Chorus (What I Found Worth Repeating)

Music can play an important role in engaging young people in peacebuilding. While youth often do not have access to formal political channels for engaging in peacebuilding, they can be actively involved via informal processes, including through music-making. Music-based peacebuilding programs are a very useful way to enable young people to learn new skills and thus to work toward building a culture of peace. However, a culture of peace must also include gender justice, so gender-sensitive approaches ought to be applied in (re)creating musical peacebuilding programs for youth.

To explore how I came to these conclusions, the remainder of this book is structured as follows: First, I explore the existing ideas and debates around young people, peacebuilding, and music, all the while seeking to illuminate the importance of gender in our understandings. I then explain the two research sites, providing a context for the insights they offer and introducing the youth peacebuilders whose words and experiences are central to this research. In the four chapters that follow, I explore some key concepts that emerged in this exploration of youth peacebuilding: dialogue, identity, space, and gender. In doing so, I propose new ways of understanding that incorporate and value youth perspectives. Sometimes serious, sometimes funny, sometimes frustrated, but always inspiring hope—these young peacebuilders did me the honor of letting me into their world, generously sharing their experience and expertise, and taught me more than I could have imagined. I hope their rhythms will reach across the page, across the world, and inspire a musical curiosity in all those who read this; and I hope that curiosity will lead us all to be more open-minded, creative, and inclusive in the approaches to peace we envision and apply.

1

Youth in Peace and Conflict

Currently, nearly half the total world population is under 24 years old, and about 20 percent of these fall in the adolescent age bracket of 10–19 years. The generation of adolescents alive today is the largest in recorded history, and their proportion of the world population is growing quickly. Thus, numbers alone would lead one to conclude that young people merit attention in almost any field of social inquiry, including studies of peace and conflict.

Despite constituting a substantial proportion of the population, youth often see themselves as minority outsiders.[1] This is not surprising since, compared to older people, youth are less likely to be able to independently access essential services or resources and more likely to be marginalized from political institutions and processes. Most countries restrict access to universal suffrage to those over 18 years of age. Hence, young people are typically characterized as lacking a political voice.

The importance of this situation should not be lost in the peacebuilding field. In post-conflict societies young people are often marginalized from formal political processes even if they helped create these processes. This does not mean young people sit idly by, or that politics exists outside their world. When young people are excluded from mainstream political processes, they often continue to take part in political activities, although these may be violent and confrontational rather than framed by cooperation and dialogue. However, this is not the only way the involvement of young people living in societies experiencing or recovering from conflict can or should be conceptualized.

The UN Convention on the Rights of the Child formally recognizes that young people's involvement in peacebuilding is grounded in their right to active participation.[2] It suggests that across the globe young people are challenging their elders to address the root causes of conflict and engage in the peaceful resolution of differences in pursuing peace. While this indicates the need for better inclusion of young people in formal peace processes, it also suggests that young people may already be engaged in peacebuilding work. If we are to pursue peace, we might do well to follow Lederach's advice that we "[n]ever talk only to politicians and military leaders. Talk to taxi drivers. Talk to construction workers and housewives. Talk to elders, shamans, and for goodness' sake, talk to children."[3] Despite calls like this, what young people think about peace processes and post-conflict reconstruction has been given very little attention in the peacebuilding literature.

Some scholars, however, have recognized that youth participation in peacebuilding is important.[4] For example, McEvoy-Levy argues that the omission of youth from existing peacebuilding literature is problematic.[5] Noting that the limited scholarly research dealing with youth in peace and conflict has tended to focus more on the role of youth in instigating violence than on their peacebuilding activities, she says documenting the role of youth in advocating for human rights and against militarism is needed. Moreover, McEvoy-Levy says this will require reinterpreting understandings of peace activism, by looking not merely for youth peace campaigners, but more broadly to young people who are active in capacity building, social development, and political education for youth. Others agree that this important work needs further attention and argue that excluding youth and ignoring their concerns can impede reconciliation, since it may provoke recurring violent conflict, obscure knowledge regarding war and peace, and sustain exclusionary norms.[6] Moreover, scholarship suggests that youth may be the driving force in creating societies that are more inclusive and open. Hein argues that opportunities exist for youth to potentially affect how diverse groups within a population relate to one another.[7] Still, how such shifts might occur remains undertheorized. Further research about how youth are dealing with and interacting across diversity is crucial, particularly given the continued presence of interethnic conflict even in societies generally considered "peaceful."

Some scholars have referred to young people's work in building cultures of peace, but most of this is brief and anecdotal; it is used to support points about peacebuilding more broadly, rather than offering an in-depth critical engagement of work by and/or for youth. Other scholars have focused on youth peacebuilding but do not provide in-depth considerations that include youth perspectives. Several scholars in the field have suggested that more empirical studies including engagement with youth perspectives in peacebuilding are needed, but much of this crucial work remains to be done.[8]

Some steps have been made in this direction, most notably by Schwartz's work on young people in post-conflict reconstruction in Mozambique, Democratic Republic of the Congo, and Kosovo. Based on these studies, she suggests that the impact of young people in post-conflict scenarios can be either negative or positive, and that this is dependent on the success of programmatic and policy interventions in addressing central issues. Overall, she proposes that success in appropriately integrating youth in the pursuit of peace requires attending to young people's needs for protection, education, reintegration, and empowerment, while accounting for cultural and environmental factors in implementing policies and programs.[9] My work draws on her insights while analyzing music as a tool for use in related programs. Moreover, while she acknowledges that gender was a factor in the cases she presents, Schwartz also notes she has not discussed this factor at any length. Thus, the present work seeks to contribute to further understanding the role of gender in young people's experiences around peace and security.

Ardizzone's analysis of several New York City–based peace education programs for young people also makes an important contribution. She focuses on youth who sought out and joined overtly global, political, and action-oriented organizations, rather than those centered on "recreational" or social activities and examines why youth choose to become involved in such work.[10] Ardizzone argues that incorporating youth voices may assist in transforming societies from cultures of violence to cultures of peace.[11] However, while she engages with youth peacebuilding, she does not discuss issues of gender or any particular methods that might be utilized to engage young people who are not already active. My research aims to bring something different to the field by engaging with young people who came to peacebuilding through "recreational" music-based activities. Moreover, this study lends diversity to the existing literature by broadening perspectives to include voices of young people from other cultures.

Dominant Representations of Youth and Politics

As research considering how young people are understood in peace and conflict is quite limited, it is worth looking more broadly at how young people are constructed in public discourse. Griffin suggests that in modern Western societies, the dominant image of young people is of being prone to trouble and facing disorders based on consumption and transition.[12] Much of the literature noting this trend comes from the United States, where young people are regularly publicly stereotyped and treated as scapegoats by psychologists, politicians, and the media.[13] Youth violence is merely one aspect of the "youth problem" created by the media, but it has captured a great deal of public attention in the United States.[14]

Young people are often demonized in the media and blamed for a wide range of social problems. Media analyses in the United States have found that teens, particularly teens of color, are usually depicted negatively.[15] This is not a new trend, though it is one that can have important policy effects, among other negative outcomes.[16] Given these representations, youth have been assigned a double, contrasting identity as powerful consumers on the one hand and an oppressed, disenfranchised minority on the other.[17] Moreover, Clay says, youth today are a generation who see themselves as a low priority in society, with the worst allocation of public goods from health care to education. It is not surprising then that many youth feel society views them as useless when it comes to performing as citizens, workers, students, and occasionally even as consumers.

While these examples are from the United States, similar representations of young people appear elsewhere, including in Northern Ireland and Australia, where I completed the research for this book. In Northern Ireland, a recent report by the National Youth Agency found that U.K. media depictions of young people tend to be negative. Three of the four most frequent topics when focusing on youth are crime, gangs, and social exclusion.[18] Similarly, there are also negative portrayals of youth in the Australian media, including some media attention to youth violence and depictions that focus on youth being lazy, apathetic, or inactive.[19] Such dominant images can marginalize recognition of the political work youth are doing, such as taking part in peacebuilding initiatives.

Those concerned about youth participation in politics raise the issue of disconnection from formal politics, citing a prevalent worry that youth are not taking part in formal social critique and are thereby losing out on a chance at having a voice in the public sphere.[20] In fact, youth are now scrutinized more than any previous generation for an apparent failure to articulate recognizable political narratives.[21] Young people are not politically inactive, although they are active in ways that differ from the formal political involvement that many adults and political leaders expect or prefer for them. Indeed, there is a growing trend in the United States of youth programs using popular culture to creatively participate in political life.[22] Stewart, for example, looks at music programs and suggests that many offer youth the chance to learn democratic practices, gain leadership skills, and develop political capital.

Harris confirms this trend for youth in Australia and the United Kingdom, proposing that new, less visible kinds of political movement and activism are occurring in locations that sit on the border of the public/private divide, resisting easy categorization.[23] For example, many youth *are* engaging in political action, in forums such as alternative music spheres, underground publications, and other subcultural activities. Harris views this development as an explicit reaction against being prodded to visible participation in public discourse while the traditional public sphere is becoming less accessible. In other words, the repeated expectation that young people *ought* to engage in more traditional political activities may very well be part of the reason many choose not to. However, this engagement tends to be overlooked by most adults who only see more traditional forms of political participation.

How Youth Are (Mis)Understood (or Ignored) in Peace Studies

In the peacebuilding literature young people tend to be viewed in one of two ways, as victims or perpetrators of violence. On one hand, the existing literature tends to categorize youth as innocent children, harmed by the effects of violent conflict while unable to do anything about it. At the same time, the literature has increasingly defined youth as potential perpetrators, likely to use violence when faced with conflict given their own direct experience as victims of violence. These dominant depictions are perpetuated despite the fact that all over the world young people living with conflict are also engaged in working for peace through actions such as conscious objection to conscription, nonviolent political activism, peace education programs, and organizing networks of young peacebuilders.

The tendency to stereotype youth as perpetrators or victims misses an important part of the story, as it obscures other ways young people may participate in conflict and in peace actions, including the role they may play as peace activists. There is thus a need for research that looks at why some young people decide to be peacebuilders as opposed to perpetrators of violence. Del Felice and Wisler argue that throughout their lives young people will often experience violence or conflict, participate in it, but also challenge its existence through peacebuilding work that proposes alternatives. They suggest that when it comes to youth peacebuilders, "[t]heir stories have yet to be told."[24] Realizing this, in this study I aim to look at the circumstances under which young people get involved in peacebuilding and how they understand it, including recording both obvious and less visible work by youth peacebuilders across different cultural and geographic contexts.

Thankfully, there is some evidence that a new international norm of youth participation is developing in peace processes. The UN and many agencies advocating for children's rights have recognized that young people affected by war should be included in peace processes, including in the development of programs and policies for their own education, rehabilitation, and reintegration, and also in community development. Moreover, some aid agencies, most NGOs, and UNICEF have all integrated youth consultation as standard. However, these activities have not yet led to widespread inclusion of youth in peace processes. For instance, while Sierra Leone has been touted as an example of successful UN work in peacebuilding, even there issues affecting youth were not given sufficient attention throughout the peace process; youth remained marginalized in the peacebuilding period.[25] To date, there remain few, if any, instances in which young people have taken part in formal peace processes.

While addressing this exclusion from formal participation in peacebuilding is crucial, youth also deserve be acknowledged for the informal peacebuilding work they already are doing. Around the world young people are taking an active role in seeking political change, and this needs to be looked at in a broader context of peacebuilding in various locales. Yet informal peace education work, often done by or with inner-city youth, receives little notice from academia or the press in comparison to traditional government-run education efforts. Acknowledging the work youth are doing to build cultures of peace is important across a variety of contexts, in places experiencing ongoing intense conflict but also in societies generally seen as peaceful but which include some cultures of violence.

Inclusion of youth, their knowledge, culture, and ideas in peacebuilding is important. Lederach proposes that all people, their knowledge, and their perceptions are crucial resources for peacebuilding that ought to be trusted and validated. His research is then based on identifying and utilizing people's existing knowledge and understanding, even when they may not see it as a resource.[26] This viewpoint gives support for looking not just at how youth are expected to be involved in peacebuilding work, but taking into account how they might be engaged in peacebuilding through skills and interests they already possess. The peacebuilding work youth are doing in local settings may seem limited. However, it can be very important in a global context of conflict, given that young people and their commodities traverse national borders with ease. Moreover, in doing so, they shape and are shaped by a myriad of meanings and structures.

A number of scholars have begun to explore the links between top-down and bottom-up approaches to peacebuilding and the prospects for each in various contexts. For example, Aliyev, in his research in the North Caucasus region, concluded that bottom-up approaches have more potential for successfully addressing conflict and reducing violence, as credible counterparts on the insurgent side are not apparent and available for top-down negotiations.[27] Moreover, he argues, such approaches, when applied with diverse participants, including youth, may be useful in addressing root causes of violence. Civil society cannot bring peace in isolation, but it can play an important and integral role in the complex aim of engaging people for peaceful change using multidimensional strategies.[28] Indeed, focusing solely on international actors or other top-down efforts and failing to incorporate approaches that include civil society can lead to a sense of alienation and the unwanted perpetuation of conflicts,[29] so it is especially crucial to support and learn more about grassroots engagement and change when considering prospects for youth involvement in peacebuilding.

In short, the informal work youth are doing in their communities is a form of political engagement and should be recognized as such. Politics is about power, and by participating in peacebuilding across difference, young people may take part in contesting powerful discourses of violence and segregation in their communities. This work might be considered peripheral when looked at through the lens of formal political involvement in peacebuilding, but continuing to ignore these efforts risks missing out on the chance to support youth who wish to contribute to peaceful change, or even worse, marginalizing

their work as somehow unimportant or far less important than "adult" direct formal engagement. While youth rarely have a seat in such formal initiatives, the so-called informal work they are doing draws on their expertise through experience in youth culture to facilitate cultural change on their own terms.

Young People's Potential Role in Building Peace through Cultural Work

Young people around the world have often used culture in advocating for peace, from Otpor's use of graffiti in Serbia as a tool of nonviolent activism, to the NGO-run youth projects in many locations using music, dance, and drama in their peacebuilding programs. This kind of youth cultural work for peace is important to consider, as youth cultures and youth cultural production can offer a valuable means for getting concepts across in a way that does not require people to learn a whole new way of communicating.[30] By using existing understandings and awareness in addressing conflict, people can see the skills or ideas as simply applying what they already know in a new way rather than having to learn something entirely new and different.[31] At the same time, looking at youth cultural work can be complex and difficult, as speaking about youth culture necessitates engaging with issues of resistance and power.

Thus, it is important not to make sweeping claims, as youth cultures and creativity make up the locations and methods youth use for political critique and engagement, yet these sites are being continually eroded through private-sector attempts at colonization and depoliticization.[32] These efforts to commercialize youth activities can also constitute a barrier to young people taking part in informal political participation. Nonetheless, young people participate in and are shaped by narratives that they also have a role in creating, including songs and other aspects of music culture. Through these narratives they may aid the reproduction of conflict or support peace, so it is important to look at how it may be possible to use young people's knowledge, their potential as peer educators, and their capacity for norm-building as tools for building peace.

Likewise, our understandings of peacebuilding need to be expanded to include alternative methods, such as cultural work, which may be more inclusive of diverse parties to conflict, including young people. For example, Schirch proposes using symbolic actions through ritual, which communicates "a forming or transforming message in a unique social space,"[33] where people learn through doing and may at the same time confirm or transform their identities, views on the world, and connections with others.[34] In her framework, "ritual" can be used to explain both formal and informal acts, including activities like dancing. She thus highlights an area in which young people can contribute, regardless of their access to more "official" channels of involvement. Schirch does not argue that more conventional forms of peacebuilding should be discarded in favor of those that feature ritual, but rather that these can be effective supplements used alongside other tools.

This kind of work is an important addition to the peacebuilding toolbox. Indeed, relying solely on processes that seek to rationalize conflicts is insufficient, since in many cultures the notion of dealing with conflict in rational, analytical ways is problematic.[35] Even in the West, people are both emotional and sensual creatures, so peacebuilding processes should include various ways of learning and knowing. After all, peacebuilding necessitates seeing the world in new ways. Ritual then may be utilized for communication in communities in which different values, beliefs, and worldviews play a role in conflict. This book draws on these theoretical insights in exploring the potential of using music and dance in grassroots peacebuilding work.

It also finds inspiration in work by leading peacebuilding scholar and practitioner John Paul Lederach, who supports the use of art in peacebuilding as a creative means for developing innovative responses to conflict.[36] He explains the need for what he calls the "moral imagination" in peacebuilding, which he says is most clearly expressed through creativity, since creativity goes past the existing and reaches for the novel and unexpected, all the while emerging from and communicating with the everyday. He likens this to the role of artists, as they often live at the edge of communities and in doing so push the boundaries of what we consider achievable and true. This lends support for looking at art, including music, given its presence across cultures. By engaging in such creative processes, he says, great insight can arise unexpectedly.[37]

However, in considering prospects for using creativity in peacebuilding, critical attention is still needed to ensure that these processes are inclusive. Research thus needs to question any exclusion, including gender-based exclusion that may remain or be reified through work using art and culture. Keeping this in mind, this book employs a feminist perspective throughout, analyzing these issues using a gendered lens.

Gender, Youth, and Peace

Most scholarly work focused on responses to violence and conflict, including the peacebuilding literature, pays little or no attention to matters of gender. However, feminist scholars, advocacy groups, and the UN have all formally recognized that gender is a key concept for consideration in peacebuilding, so creating more peaceful societies will require participation by both men and women.[38] Indeed, while gendered aspects of positive peace are rarely mentioned, achieving sexual equality is a necessary facet of positive peace.[39] Pankhurst, for example, points out the ongoing problem of women being stereotyped as peaceful while at the same time being left out of formal peace processes.[40] Given this, she says, women's concerns tend to go unheard and unaddressed during formal peace processes. Likewise, Porter argues that the barriers to women's participation in peacebuilding include these stereotypical attitudes as well as family and work responsibilities, lack of education and training, and the reluctance of men to share power.[41]

Despite these barriers, women actually participate in conflict in various ways, including as agents of peacebuilding. Such work may include actions like publicly protesting violence, campaigning for peaceful responses to conflict, organizing to address inequalities and injustices, and using creativity to advance messages of peace. Porter suggests that women's participation widens the boundaries of peacebuilding beyond conventional methods to include all actions aimed at pursuing peace. She thus calls for acknowledging and supporting this work while also including women in formal peace processes to create significant gender equality as part of peace. De la Rey and McKay also provide important insights with their South African case study report, which found that the women leaders they met reported gender-specific understandings of conflict.[42] Given these understandings, a gender-aware approach requires asking whether policies affect men and women in different ways, and if so, considering ways to redress women's disadvantage.

The existing research on gender and peacebuilding clearly makes an important contribution to the field. However, it mostly does not engage with how gender might impact youth peacebuilding. This is an important omission, because building peace requires not just including men and women, but also boys and girls. Therefore, scholars concerned with youth and peace need to pay more attention to how gender informs young people's identities, experience, and participation, particularly as they relate to issues of peace and conflict. Pankhurst has noted that the experiences of girls, while often terrible and gender-specific, have been given even less attention than those of boys.[43] Additionally, she says that girls who have experienced sexual violence frequently receive less support than women and bear the burden of reporting the violent acts that have been perpetrated against them. These are important points. Gender-sensitive approaches to peacebuilding thus need to include an in-depth engagement of the way girls might be actively involved in peacebuilding.

The UN takes the view that pursuing greater gender equality for youth is especially important, because changes at the onset of puberty generally result in significantly different opportunities for boys and girls due to gender. Furthermore, restrictive gender norms may be particularly impactful and harmful for young women, who may face limitations on their movement, education, personal development, security, and life choices.[44] However, in citing these views, I find it important to point out that gender differences begin long before the onset of puberty, and gender is not only about reproductive roles.

Several feminist scholars of international relations also make an important contribution to this discussion by arguing for the need to deconstruct gender norms in attempts to reduce conflict and build peace. Tickner, for example, suggests that a dichotomy of "masculine" as opposed to "feminine" has been constructed, wherein men are expected to exhibit masculine traits while women should likewise display feminine characteristics. Many attributes are commonly deemed masculine, such as aggressiveness, reason, rationality, and protection; while corresponding feminine-associated attributes include peacefulness, caring, emotion, and vulnerability.[45] Moreover, sites of knowledge production have tended to privilege "masculine" attributes and beliefs over those seen as "feminine." Thus, she argues, it is important to challenge the ways in which these dominant discourses encourage war and violence through a culture of militarism, the construction of which is dependent upon the presence of a devalued femininity. These notions are related to prevailing notions of women as victims requiring protection. In other words, Tickner highlights the dominant assumption that the greatest danger to a man is being like a woman, since women are assumed to be afraid, dependent, irresolute, and weak.

In fact, Tickner proposes that the derogation of feminine ideas and attributes has become a key component of militarizing men and boys. Their willingness to fight, she says, is goaded by casting their sexual identity into question. In basic military training, for example, the harshest insult for a soldier is to be called a girl or a lady. Tickner therefore suggests that the association between masculinity and violence is not dependent upon men's innate aggressiveness, but rather on the creation of a gendered identity that heavily pressures soldiers to "prove themselves as men."[46] Likewise, young men who may not be able to "prove their manhood" on the battlefield are still expected to display their "natural" masculinity through language and actions that meet the same criteria. Different forms of masculinized violence, such as domestic violence and rape, also occur outside of military environments or obvious zones of conflict.

Other feminist authors further explain how the gendered way we speak about conflict can influence our prospects for peace. Cohn, for example, argues that common gendered assumptions about conflict make it exceedingly difficult for both men and women—and I would add boys and girls—to put forth "feminine" ideas or concerns, including peace, and still maintain their legitimacy.[47] In short, if certain ideas are deemed to be feminine and therefore devalued, they can become at once very difficult to speak, hear, or seriously consider, even if someone is brave enough to speak them. Cohn suggests that excluding these ideas impedes our capacities for thinking fully and well. While young women's voices may be silenced, so may the utterances of any young man seeking to talk about peace, since it is often associated with the passivity of women. Thus, challenging gender norms is an integral step toward undermining the world's current war culture, where all members of society have their ways of thinking militarized to some extent.[48] Moreover, Mazali says these presumptions and exclusions are stipulated and delineated by an intensely militarized socialization, which is largely founded upon discourses of a hierarchical gender system that presupposes the superiority of masculinity. This can limit the tactics available for building positive peace. These feminist theoretical insights provide sound justifications for applying a gendered lens when looking at conflict and efforts at peace, and also highlight the need for paying special attention to what gender means for youth experiencing conflict or seeking to build peace.

What About the Girls?

UN Security Council Resolution 1325 calls for gender equality in peace processes. However, girls are often neglected both in UN peace processes as well as in the peacebuilding literature. Scholars and practitioners thus need to ask questions about where girls are in their work and to acknowledge that girls are not merely victims but can also be peacebuilders. Consequently, Anderson counsels that researchers need to be asking urgent questions about how peace movements might propose alternatives for girls, empowering them and listening to them in order to work collaboratively and create a better world for all.

Although Resolution 1325 offers a framework for women's involvement in peacebuilding, girls' participation has remained limited. In large part this is because the implementation strategies have concentrated mostly on older women, who have generally been more engaged in using the Resolution as a device for raising awareness, advocating, and organizing. Despite this, the Canadian Peacebuilding Coordinating Committee (CPCC) counsels that by working cooperatively girls also have the chance for taking some possession of the resolution.[49] The CPCC advocates involvement through gaining knowledge of the ways conflict impacts girls' lives and asking what groups dealing with gender, peace, and security issues are doing to work with girls. In this book I seek to contribute to these goals by paying special attention to gender, including impacts on girls.

Prevailing research assumes that youth, especially girls, are apathetic and apolitical; it focuses on what they do not do.[50] Much attention is thus given to how girls are not participating in various ways, rather than looking at how they are participating. Indeed, for some time girls have been seen as a "problem" in studies of politics because of their perceived detachment from formal political engagement, although this in itself is a contested point among scholars.[51] Instead of accepting these limiting discourses, when doing research that includes girls, scholars ought to seek to learn more about what they are doing, what they can do, and/or how they might be engaged.

Enhancing inclusivity in youth peacebuilding is an important concern, and should include reducing gender-based barriers to participation. While some scholars have acknowledged this in theory, there has been little to no research on how that might be achieved. Thus, more research is needed on what gender inclusiveness would look like in peacebuilding practice. However, Stuart, a peacebuilding practitioner, has examined youth nonviolence workshops in Australia. He explained how, where possible, program leaders could model equality and respect in gender relationships by having a minimum of two facilitators and including leaders of different ages and gender.[52] It is also important to look at whether there are differences in participation or involvement based on the gender of facilitators. Overall, this work exploring gender in youth peacebuilding needs to be carried out with the support of all peacebuilders, regardless of gender, as changes in the gender regime will require support from men and boys.[53]

Conclusion

Young people are a politically significant social group both locally and globally and should be recognized as such and engaged in the peace studies field. One important challenge for the next generation is to incorporate youth peace activists appropriately into the development of peace. Yet this is a regularly neglected area in the discipline, and youth are often viewed negatively. Young people are currently engaged in several means of peacebuilding, including efforts at building a culture of peace, and this needs to be acknowledged and better understood for progress to occur. At the same time, understanding and supporting young people's participation in peacebuilding will also require attention to the impact of gender. Failing to acknowledge explicitly and take into account the impact of gender on youth peacebuilding can hinder prospects for promoting understandings and frameworks that are more inclusive and thus more likely to contribute to lasting positive peace. Therefore, in this study of youth musical peacebuilding efforts I have incorporated a gendered analysis as an essential part of the overall research framework.

2

Music Makes the (Young) People Come Together?

Music plays an important cultural role in several ways, many of which contribute to its political potential. Scholars have described the potential of music to arouse emotions, reinforce social identities, offer hope and meaning, shape consciousness, demonstrate and demarcate belief, act as therapy, communicate information, and organize consciousness.[1] However, although the emotional dimension of music can inspire people and stir nonviolent political action, it can also be used to call people to war.[2] Perhaps because of these wide-ranging possibilities, many have understood music as having political potential, or serving as a possible tool for engaging in politics and political struggle. This is not a new prospect—there are many historical instances of music being used in explicitly political ways. For example, political leaders are well aware that music can play an important role in nation-building—after all, every country has a national anthem.[3]

At the same time, dominant power systems are not the only ones that can adapt and use music for political purposes. Most political movements of resistance and social change have also utilized music.[4] Perhaps this long-term association between music and rallying people against the status quo is why music has often been touted as being inherently progressive and positive. A critical analysis would of course quickly disprove this. Although music has been used to support civil rights struggles, it has also been used to create nationalist narratives of racial superiority, as in the case of Nazi Germany. It is clear that music has immense political potential and implications, and these are not always positive. Music can be used to drive things in directions that feed conflict or promote peace.

Music is an integral part of culture, a way we share ideas about how society is or should be. To this end, artists have sought for centuries to "Critique by creating."[5] In other words, artists—including musicians—may use their art to challenge prevailing political norms. The potency of using music in challenging dominant ideas was well illustrated by one East German communist leader, who said, "'We have planned for everything, we prepared for everything, but not for singing and prayers.'"[6] Based on her research on youth, race, class, and gender, Fine suggests that culture, especially performance and discourse, often grows out of a movement and its members and in turn becomes a resource for them.[7]

For most young people music is a part of culture, discourse, and performance that is particularly important and accessible, and thus may constitute a useful site for engagement and resistance in politics and understandings of peace and conflict. Politics of this sort may be just as vital as traditional formal politics in efforts at altering social structures and power relations.

Part of what makes music so powerful as a potential peacebuilding tool is that it can aid in uniting people in common understanding or common goals. Bell, for example describes how when experiencing a great concert, there is a sense of being at one with others in the room, "We don't know each other, we come from vastly different backgrounds, we disagree on hundreds of issues, but for an evening, we gather around this artist and these songs and we get along."[8] Music has also been posited as a tool to make community organizing more fun, and therefore more effective.[9]

Studying the political use of music can also help us better understand people's political involvement outside mainstream politics.[10] This is particularly relevant for young people who may lack access to formal political participation or see it as irrelevant to their needs and skills. Music can thus offer young people a means to feel they have participated in a meaningful way. As Rycenga explains, "music is life, because it inherently involves motion, perception, reflection, separation/connection, materiality, process, relationality—it is, at root, *involved*."[11] We remember songs because they are experienced through our bodies, and at the same time the metaphysical properties of music can have deep implications for the way we experience our personal realities.[12] Such experiences have important impacts on identities and thus on political experiences, ideas, and participation.

Identity is central to the political potential of music. Frith, for example, argues that music can play an important role in conveying political messages, formulating political consciousness, and mobilizing new modes of subjectivity. The last of these may be particularly important for building political agency that is defensive and transformational, individual and collective. In other words, music may contribute to identity work that is about retaining positive aspects and understandings of self or community while at the same time challenging negative identity constructions, particularly those that rely on "others" in problematic ways. Frith suggests that music may be adapted to use as a political project, providing visions for the marginalized of how things could be. To that end, he says, "by posing the world as it is against the world as the radically subordinated would like it to be, this musical culture supplies a great deal of the courage required to go on living in the present."[13] I have drawn on Frith's contributions in understanding how music can be used politically and can impact identity in important ways. Likewise, his argument that music can provide the subordinated with a sense of strength in current times is particularly relevant in analyses of youth, who are often seen as politically powerless. Overall, he argues that creating novel ways of carrying out meaning-making are an important part of the political possibility of music.

Moreover, Frith says, enjoying music is inherently a practice of identifying with music, and likewise our aesthetic responses are also implicitly ethical agreements. Taking joy in music is never merely feeling; it is at the same time a matter of judging.[14] Keeping this in mind, music should be looked at within the wider contexts of society and institutions in which it is produced, distributed, and received. Being aware of context and specificity is imperative when considering political uses of music, since making, manufacturing, and distributing music can be regarded as political acts.[15]

Munõz and Marín similarly propose that we ought to consider life as art. From this perspective, they articulate the particular need for acknowledging the techniques young people actively use to constitute or create themselves. Considering young people's musical acts of creating or styling the self, they utilize Foucault's ideas of "the exercise a subject does over him/herself and by which he/she attempts to elaborate, transform and accede to a certain way of being." From this framework, Munõz and Marín propose that we ought to be asking about "what processes of self-creation, what alternative forms of existence can arise, and will arise, from cultures and forms of music,"[16] such as the ones they describe in their work on youth music culture in Colombia. Youth cultures, they argue, lead youth forward in creating selves, to producing new subjectivities and searching for the creation of alternatives in the ethical, political, and artistic domains, as well as in knowledge conventions transformed into practice.[17] Thus, they recommend aesthetics as a device well suited for developing new conceptualizations of youth culture.[18] Indeed, Munõz and Marín propose that this aesthetic facet of creating selves, other reference frameworks, novel collective subjectivities, and new art forms enables us to perceive youth cultures, particularly the most creative, as possessing astonishing power in transforming, destroying, and creating alternatives.[19] Although they do not explicitly address issues of peace and conflict, their propositions inspire a curiosity about whether young people might be able to use music in peacebuilding by transforming understandings of conflict and ways to address it, in part by transforming understandings of themselves and others. How, where, and under what circumstances might musical peacebuilding then take place?

Pursuing a Musical Peace

The political possibilities of music are part of what makes it an intriguing phenomenon to study in peacebuilding theory and practice. Lederach has supported such methods for some time, arguing that imagination translated into creative acts is necessary for transcending violence, specifically suggesting that music and dance can be valuable tools in peacebuilding practice.[20] Most recently, Lederach and Lederach have explored issues of music and peacebuilding more deeply, discussing the role of music and sound in peacebuilding in several contexts. In doing so, they argue that music as metaphor can greatly enhance understandings of the need for more complex, holistic approaches to peacebuilding.[21] Such understandings make sense, as music frequently brings together many complex parts to create what may seem like a simpler, and often more pleasant, whole. Music may also contribute to peacebuilding at the individual level, by helping people to heal or recover from trauma related to conflict and violence. Indeed, Boyce-Tillman's research suggests that traditional practitioners of many cultures, music professionals, psychotherapists, and other health professionals have all shown a broad interest in the power of music to heal. Likewise, she says, this widespread belief in the capacity for music to heal makes it a useful tool for reconciliation work across cultures.[22]

While there are limitations, the political potential of music as a vehicle for peacebuilding is evident. We currently live in a world racked with violence and inequality, but change is both possible and necessary. Music may have an important role to play in bringing about change. Continually and uncritically relying on the same political representations and options and expecting them to lead to better outcomes does not make much sense. If we are to change the way politics works in order to create a less violent paradigm, creativity is necessary for envisioning better options. To that end, Bleiker argues that approaches containing aesthetic dimensions are particularly well suited to contributing to this important task, since art can offer unique insights through engaging issues of representation in a self-conscious fashion.[23] Compared to other forms of political communication, such as news or academic sources, artistic approaches may trigger different ways of thinking, since we tend to see them primarily as representations, as opposed to the "facts" reported elsewhere. Yet at the same time these artistic

contributions may challenge not only the way we think about them as representations, but also the way we think about other, more traditional forms of political communication as representations as well.

In addition to its capacity to inspire hope and aid people's realization that things can be different, music can serve a significant function in inspiring a spirit of community and dialogue in public life.[24] Music, Heble argues, can stimulate social engagement and play a powerful role in creating cultural awareness. Likewise, music can play an important role in creating cultures of peace. Making music gives us the tools to register hope, to take risks in relating to others, to cooperate across various differences, cultures, places, and styles, and to find truly novel ways of relating in and with the world.[25]

We often talk about peace in musical terms, noting the need for "harmony." Music may be a tie that binds people together when applied at the right time and place. Indeed music may help by giving people the sense of the good that can come from working well together, trusting and supporting one another in reaching a goal. In the case of peacebuilding, that goal may be the creation of more peaceful and connected communities that can work together across difference. Frost describes this potential well, explaining how, "[w]hen a group of musicians or dancers are performing, every member must play his or her part well, not just individually, but in concert with others." Likewise there is a "profound sense of intimacy felt with teammates when individual contributions . . . create a force greater than the sum of the parts."[26]

Finding new ways of building and understanding community are important in pursuing peace. After all, as Fischlin notes, community is defined less by homogeneity and more by its constructive ability to encounter differences and challenges to homogeneity.[27] The practice of music may then be one means of exploring and understanding that process. This may even happen unintentionally, not just where music is consciously being used for political purposes, but also when it is used as a leisure activity where different groups are involved and interacting. Leisure activities are an integral part of culture, so they may have a role to play in building positive peace. This potential and the relative absence of studies looking at such activities has stoked my interest in looking at music-based leisure activities that may have some role to play in creating and sustaining cultures of peace when occurring in the midst of conflict.

In the existing scholarship dealing with youth and politics there is a tendency to impose a dichotomy between leisure and "serious" activities. This has important impacts on how we look at any potential political role for youth cultures, since they are most often associated with activities such as music that are commonly seen primarily as leisure pursuits. Ardizzone, for example, says what differentiates the young people in her study of youth peace work is that they were looking to take part in political, action-oriented, global groups, as opposed to social or recreational organizations.[28] While probably not intentional, setting up such unnecessary dichotomies can easily reinforce ideas of "serious" youth versus "lazy" youth or "real" politics versus "mere" leisure. Such a framework also constructs the political as separate from recreation and socializing. However, I suggest that these assumptions can and should be subject to critical scrutiny. Rethinking dichotomous categorizations is essential for developing better understandings of the roles youth can and do play in peacebuilding. As suggested earlier, rather than looking at "these youth" who are peacebuilders and "those youth" who are victims or perpetrators, we need to develop a more holistic understanding of young people's experience and understandings of conflict and peace and look at what is relevant to their lives. After all, many young peacebuilders have themselves participated in or been affected by conflict at other times of their lives, and some even had experiences of participating in violence after or during involvement in peacebuilding work. While they may have new ideas to draw on and new understandings of possible selves, these are far from static, and thus require ongoing negotiation and support.

We need to recognize the potential political dimensions of youth leisure activities, including participation in alternative music spheres, as Harris argues these may provide spaces where youth can take part in political critique and civic engagement.[29] Likewise, in studying youth-directed models in the

United States that promote youth leadership, Stewart proposes that youth music programs may contribute to civic education. She also suggests music programs may appeal to a more diverse range of youth than more traditional programs. Nearly all the organizations Stewart examined reported a zero tolerance policy toward sexism, homophobia, and racism; so these organizations may have far-reaching effects as they produce future leaders.[30]

Thus, I am interested in the link between everyday activities and broader political outcomes. For example, Schell-Faucon argues that the balance between how individuals behave at the micro level—including we can assume, their ordinary and leisure activities—and what political and social actions take place at the macro level cannot be severed.[31] Music may thus have some potential for changing both individual views and behavior and larger structural patterns, particularly over the longer term. As individuals adapt their actions and thought patterns, they may influence those around them and mobilize others for change. While this is a slow and incremental process, it is one that can lead to wide-reaching changes over time. Such work could be immensely important in building peace. Thus, I became interested in critically analyzing the use of music in peacebuilding work to learn more about how music might be effectively applied in pursuing positive peace.

To truly foster positive peace, such work must include attention to inclusion and exclusion. While Rees argues that the search for peace would benefit from seeking ideas from all sources, including music, he also points out the need to reflect on how power might be deployed in creative and liberating ways that are both nonviolent and framed by the drive toward equality, thereby contributing to advancing human rights. Throughout this process, attention must be paid to inclusiveness, as failing to do so can render the deployment of music for peace ineffective.[32] Likewise, Phillips notes that in order to facilitate positive peaceful change, musicians must take note of and radically subvert dominant ideologies of power. Otherwise these ideologies might commodify, hinder, or mediate musicians' efforts.[33] While Rees addresses social exclusion based on gender and age, he does not go into any detail about how to mitigate it; and Phillips does not investigate the categories of gender and age at all, so this research project seeks to add something new by investigating these categories in detail.

Music in the Lives of Young People

The active, creative work by youth in producing meanings and alternative ways of being in their own cultures has been neglected in peace studies,[34] and in the social sciences more generally, which have tended to devalue or ignore aesthetic approaches. Scholars focused on politics are especially guilty of ignoring youth cultural production, seeing it as politically insignificant. Addressing this omission is crucial, since young people play important roles in societies in peace and conflict. Thus, the cultural contributions they make may also influence the directions societies take in dealing with political problems. Music is clearly an important aspect in the lives of many youth, making it a relevant interest when looking at how they may engage in peacebuilding.

Over a decade ago, Christenson and Roberts made the argument that a serious consideration of how music fits into the lives of young people is imperative for understanding youth. Music matters to young people, and they invest a great deal "of time, money, and ego" in it.[35] In fact, research has found that for most young people, listening to music is the number one leisure activity.[36] International bodies have also recognized the need for supporting young people's creativity. For example, in 1994 the International Conference on Population and Development formally affirmed the duty to meet the needs of youth, especially girls, with proper respect for their own ability to be creative. Given this acknowledgment along with the importance of music in the lives of young people and the political and peacebuilding potential of music, attention to how musical approaches may be used to engage youth in peacebuilding seems warranted.

Music by and for young people has been generally viewed with suspicion if not outright contempt. Youth music cultures, particularly hip-hop and rap, have been blamed for pessimism, negativity, depression, vulgarity, offensiveness, and aggression among young people. These views have been frequently and publicly espoused by adults, often political leaders or other public figures, who themselves do not listen to hip-hop or rap. These charges are laid on the unfounded assumption that because so many rap songs contain violent or sexually explicit lyrics, all rap music must negatively impact the youth who consume it. Similarly, Hopkins questions the view that political progress can come from youth music, chiding that "[o]nce again, academics may have been overly optimistic in attributing political motives to radical youth cultures. Maybe rock was only ever about making money and having a good time in the process."[37]

Yet, for each older person who believes music is responsible for declining morals among young people, there is a young person who sees music as a positive force remaining in society today.[38] In rejecting the easy argument that music cultures are the cause of youth problems, I agree with Christenson and Roberts that young people's experiences, both positive and negative, are inevitably connected with pop music culture.[39]

There has been little writing on music, youth culture, and peacebuilding. Fischlin says that the research that does exist overwhelmingly shows that youth music can be powerfully aligned with the aims of equality and justice at the global level.[40] For example, in briefly discussing a Sierra Leone–based organization, Peace-Links, Del Felice and Wisler explain that using music and dance has been critical to the organization's success, as it has helped to promote healing for those wounded by war.[41] They note that song lyrics produced in the program promote a culture of peace and dispute a culture of violence, and that using the arts has offered them special power in reaching former child soldiers and other marginalized young people. They also suggest music activities have aided reconciliation in communities, contributed to trust building between participants, and increased confidence of the youth taking part.

Moreover, in the documentary film *Favela Rising*,[42] there is discussion of one organization that has been operating in the Brazilian *favelas* (slums) for over a decade. Vigário Geral, the community where most of the documentary was filmed, had for years been a virtual war zone, with violence reaching endemic levels. Children worked as drug soldiers as the only way of escaping poverty, despite the fact that this usually meant they would not live past their teens. Anderson Sá saw this enduring violence in his community throughout his youth, losing a family member to police violence and experiencing the personal fear of violence that came with working as a drug soldier himself. He thus felt compelled to pursue a different path, one that would provide a different way of making a living and also create opportunities for local youth to foster nonviolent, positive change in their community. He began pursuing this goal despite the continual plague of brutality between warring drug lords as well as from the police, who were often seen as failing at or outright ignoring their official task of protecting and serving. Seeing music and dance as a universal language and thus perceiving that they could have an important cultural role in enacting social change, Sá's response was to form AfroReggae, a community-based activist group that uses music and dance as tools for engaging young people in the community through peaceful means.[43] Given the brevity of this documentary film and the absence of a formal project evaluation, it is difficult to say what obstacles and difficulties may face the group, or what limitations they may have. What is clear from the film is that the organizers and young people involved are thoroughly convinced that music and dance can serve an integral role in bringing peace to their community. These points are intriguing, but they also suggest the need to analyze young people's experiences in these peacebuilding processes, in order to better understand how to engage youth in such work.

There has been a recent emergence of the intentional use of music by organizations working with youth, which makes sense, as music plays a particularly important role in the lives of young people and in youth cultures. Psychiatrists, psychologists, and pharmacologists have agreed that music is a powerful influence and stimulant for young people.[44] Music is central to youth culture, and the development of new technologies boosts opportunity for young people to produce and consume music.[45] At the same time, they say that music can also be significant for skill development and experiences among youth.[46]

Using popular culture for political objectives is particularly relevant for young people today, not least because teens have taken on key roles in creating popular culture and acting as global consumers.[47] Young people's engagement with music can also impact the (re)production of knowledge, even when done without intentional educational objectives.[48] Indeed, it may have even more impact, since most human learning occurs incidentally, outside a formal educational setting.[49] Munõz urges that we need to explore how, through music, young people have constructed "some knowledge of their own about certain political concepts. That is to say, through a process bathed in music. Sonic knowledge—knowledge moulded by sound."[50] Such studies are important because the impacts of these experiences and knowledge shifts can have wide-ranging consequences, as music can cross all sorts of boundaries, inventing different modes of engagement for youth.[51] While young people may be formally politically disenfranchised, music can enable them to participate in democracy and aid in forming political consciousness, which can empower them to contest important issues of inequality, such as racism.[52] This is obviously an important part of achieving a culture of peace.

Addressing issues such as racism and sexism in work with young people may present particular challenges, but these do not appear to be insurmountable. For example, Bulbeck's research on young Australians found that very few respondents showed an awareness of structural inequality based on, for example, race, class, or gender.[53] This implies that education and awareness building may be crucial to challenging racialized and gendered assumptions youth may hold. At the same time, there is certainly potential here, as she also found that youth were more open-minded than their parents on issues of migration and indigenous relations.

The lack of scholarship on how youth may be creatively engaging in peace work is not entirely separable from the negative, patronizing views that dominate public discourse about young people. As a result, a new lens is needed for seeing youth in a way that contrasts with the current way of thinking. The theories, concepts, research methods, and disciplinary lenses through which contemporary thought about young people is framed do not enable us to envision youth as cultural producers and creative social actors.[54] This has to change if the peace studies field is to take the role of young people seriously. What also need shifting are the unbalanced and uninformed perspectives that currently construct young people as deficient, unfinished, "in the process of becoming someone," and which likewise regard youth as inactive receivers of adult mass media and culture who should be objectified and molded in due course into mature adults.[55] In these discourses youth require protection, punishment, and direction from adults. More critical engagement is needed, and it must come from engaging with young people in their own right, on their own terms, on their own turf, if we are to develop more useful, nuanced understandings of the role youth can and do play in conflict and in peacebuilding.

Globalization has made distances smaller, causing change in both social dynamics and global relations. The speed brought about by this has given momentum to dissident practices, such as protest marches, since local expressions can easily lead to global consequences, particularly when shown on television around the world.[56] This might include the proliferation of political activism or dissent. The same could hold true for young people's impact via the production of YouTube videos, DVDs, online radio, and other formats that are easily accessible to a broad global audience. In these ways youth cultures using music may influence and be influenced by others from around the world. After all, music is essential to constructing, merging, and constantly transforming global youth cultures,[57] many of which are based on music.

Gendering a Musical Resistance

Gender norms tend to have a strong impact on musical participation, so a political analysis of youth music work needs to include particular attention to gender as an ordering device. Moreover, young people understand themselves and others as gendered beings, so when looking at how new understandings of identity might be created, taking gender into account is essential. Based on research in Africa, Slachmuijlder extols the benefits of using music, particularly drumming, in peacebuilding. She proposes that music can: promote personal healing, provide a neutral space where groups can build trust, and facilitate the restoration of relationships through allowing expression in a nonthreatening manner. This signifies potential for cultivating positive peace in which everyone, including youth, can participate. However, she also notes remaining challenges, including the cultural and ethical dilemmas that can be implicated in using music-based peacebuilding. For example, she says that taking drums out of their context may negate their cultural importance, and that their association with traditional masculinity may limit their usefulness since women are not allowed to play drums in many African communities.[58]

More broadly, gender has a strong influence on the structure of music, where women have generally been understood as fans, consumers, and supporters as opposed to active makers of music: musicians.[59] This is not a new phenomenon. Historically the music industry has been and remains dominated by males; and women have been consistently marginalized in music production.[60] Gender stereotypes are common in lyrics, but what's more, these stereotypes infiltrate every aspect of the music industry and also limit the access women may have and the possible roles they may play within it.[61] There is also evidence that certain instruments throughout the world are gendered.[62] Dominant gender norms are evident in music videos, the vast majority of which are by male musicians, and research suggests that the visuals usually include women who parade for men's benefit, not vice versa.[63]

These gender differences are not limited to a particular country or region. Even though women's exclusion from music participation often derives from outdated ideas about the roles of women, it is certainly not restricted to traditional cultures.[64] Particular national social values and norms around gender contribute to how music participation becomes ordered along gendered lines.[65] Research on a variety of music genres has established gender as a central issue determining and limiting women's musical participation.[66] Moreover, these authors argue that normative and cultural barriers exist to women's musical participation, making it tricky for women to gain acceptance.[67] These barriers clearly impact girls and young women in their capacity to participate in music-making and be accepted as musicians.

At the same time, music may be used as a critical instrument for challenging existing gender norms that marginalize women and girls. Love argues that music has an important role to play in contesting gender roles and in improving democratic politics. Focusing on women's music, she looks at how music made within social movements for change may contribute to democracy by supplementing aggregative and deliberative politics.[68] She challenges the deliberative ideal, arguing that it accords greatest value to communication methods of males, thereby marginalizing women and other minority groups.[69] Given this critique, investigating the prospect of using music as a source of participation for diverse groups, including girls, appears worthwhile.

Love argues that songs, like language, can communicate and throw into question our deepest ways of thinking. This clearly points to the potential of music in a feminist quest to challenge marginalization based on age and gender. However, such a project may be challenging, since in societies preoccupied with rationalizations, music is readily written off as being an irrational and thus unimportant way of communicating.[70] Music by women, and particularly by girls, might have even larger hurdles to overcome in being heard and respected. Moreover, instead of challenging the marginalization of young women's voices and experiences, music can at times reaffirm "the flux and concreteness of the social world at the same time that, through its categorization and packaging, it denies them."[71] This suggests that music has the power to uphold social boundaries and existing distinctions based on gender and age.

However, there is clearly still an important role here for "flux" and for contesting categorization and packaging. Music may have a powerful role to play in peacebuilding by offering a mechanism for deconstructing gender stereotypes and gender-based discrimination while enhancing participation in democratic societies. For example, the extra-linguistic qualities of music may be useful in challenging gender essentialism, as these qualities make it a powerful means for unsettling subjects.[72] In other words, because music refuses definition through our usual method of using language to categorize things, it may prompt us to reconsider the concreteness of other social understandings, including those around gender. Music may also be politically useful in its capacity to pose resistance to dominant ways of being and understanding. For example, music may offer a method to challenge prevailing standards of gendered identity. In particular, Connell and Gibson note that many women, marginalized on the basis of gender, and lesbians and gay men, marginalized due to their sexuality, have applied music to appropriating space and generating community identity.[73] For example, some women have sought to create safe spaces to meet and collaborate with other women through organizing women's music festivals, such as Lilith Fair in the United States. Likewise, particular music clubs are often designated as a central community social hub for queer communities to gather in a designated safe space where traditional social norms around gender are routinely rejected or resisted. Youth participants in popular music and dance performances can also use performance events and movement practices to negotiate and resist dominant ideologies about gender.

Cultural industry products may strengthen and reinforce existing gender norms, but they can also be used subversively. Likewise, Dibben argues that examining such cultural products is to interrogate the everyday tactics the subordinated use to create resistant meanings from cultural projects that simultaneously bear the interests of prevailing sociopolitical structures. At the same time, she conceptualizes using mass cultural products in a resistant fashion as a practical mode of resisting, empowering, and creating the conditions necessary for creating micro-political and individual change.[74]

But what are the prospects for young women? Young women's resistant use of music has been documented in a variety of genres from Riot Grrrls to Spice Girls to girl-centered hip-hop. For example, emerging in the early 1990s, the Riot Grrrl subculture movement was an openly feminist subcultural movement, whose aims explicitly included deconstructing gender differences.[75] Riot Grrrl began in Washington, D.C., encouraging young women to be not just passive consumers but active participants who engage in a do-it-yourself ethos. They thus encouraged girls to start their own bands and 'zines. While these sound like potentially promising prospects for challenging gender norms, critical reflection is still needed. For example, Wald is cautious about making sweeping statements about the possible positive impact of rock music on girls' lives. She urges female musicians to remain alert to their own privileges and engage in continuous self-reflection. At the same time, Wald argues that independent rock music cultures can offer critical spaces for girls to resist and challenge prevailing notions of girlhood.[76]

This interest in possible feminist deployments of music did not end with the Riot Grrrls. Releasing their debut single in 1996, the Spice Girls emerged as a hugely popular mainstream group, yet one that has also been associated with feminist ideologies for girls. Lemish argues that while they offer contradictory messages, the Spice Girls' popularity provides girls with fertile ground for cultural struggle and that their work challenged and offered alternatives to dominant notions of femininity.[77] However, while the Spice Girls have been exalted for offering a girl power version of feminism, such claims have also been challenged from a feminist viewpoint, charging that they are not sincerely feminist and/or are too commercial.[78]

Girl-centered hip-hop has also received some limited attention in scholarly circles. Weekes, for example, notes the masculinism often evident in hip-hop but at the same time argues that girls can adapt hip-hop music in subversive ways.[79] Over the past decade several writers have explored possible links between hip-hop and feminism. In 1999, Morgan used her own relationships and personal experience as a hip-hop journalist, black feminist, and cultural critic to bring attention to issues of hip-hop feminism through her book, which was released as a mainstream, rather than academic, statement on the issue.[80] She critiques misogyny in rap music and culture while explaining how it is possible to be both deeply engaged in hip-hop culture and also committed to feminism. Pough has also explored issues of gender and hip-hop in her book *Check It While I Wreck*

It, arguing that black feminism could usefully interrogate rap music as a site for social change.[81] While she recognizes the often masculinist leanings of rap and hip-hop culture, Pough also points out the accomplishments and contributions of several successful female rappers. Moreover, she challenges young black women to use rap and hip-hop to their own ends, adapting the appeal, longevity, and historical tradition of activism of the genre to counter sexism and take up public space to present their own views as women.

Answering this challenge, authors from many different backgrounds, professions, and disciplines have since been drawing on examples from around the world to explain how feminist women and men have used hip-hop in their activism. Hip-hop feminism, while drawing on and taking joy in hip-hop music and culture, simultaneously brings forth a critical view highlighting the weaknesses and inadequacies of mainstream hip-hop, particularly in the way it tends to produce "cookie cutter" identities.[82] Female hip-hop artists around the world have been organizing for change, including b-girl (female breakdancer) groups that have been working to create their own crews, events, and safe spaces for women, carving out a place in the often male-dominated world of hip-hop battles, and the many queer women who have been working in creative new ways to engage with their fans and one another.[83]

All of these examples challenge the traditional masculinist assumptions associated with hip-hop and offer concrete examples of how music genres can be adapted to pursuing gender justice. So, perhaps girls can deploy hip-hop or other styles of music for resistant purposes. However, there are also challenges here. Clearly, this sort of work may lose its political impact by going mainstream or may reify certain dominant images of femininity. It may, for example, portray women and girls as sex objects for the viewing pleasure of males, in contrast to feminist aims of reducing gendered restrictions on the ways girls and boys can express themselves and participate. Still, it appears that there is potential for music to be engaged in more political projects that aim to undermine constrictive gender norms, a project central to the pursuit of positive peace.

However, research on feminist hip-hop has focused on all-female groups and their female fan base, so more study is needed to see whether such resistant practice can or will emerge in music programs catering to both girls and boys. What is clear is that the potential for resistant political use of music is not without its hurdles. Indeed, gender resistance in some forms has "relied on and reinscribed hegemonic sexual relations."[84] Likewise, movements falling back on feminine stereotypes can create a catch–22 that hinders their potential to accomplish goals.[85] Political difficulties even arise in looking at a musician's choice of instruments, as women's entrance into rock bands as bass players offers them opportunities and legitimacy in the male-dominated sphere of music production, but can at the same time function in a way that reconstructs divisions of labor based on gender and in doing so recreate dominant gender ideologies.[86] How then might music be deployed in a way that does not merely reflect and reinforce a masculinized view of the world and therefore ascribe this discourse to understandings of politics and peace? What does this mean for scholars, policymakers, and practitioners interested in the use of music as a tool for peacebuilding?

Although in theory it has been acknowledged as important, most research to date has not significantly assessed the impact of age or gender on peacebuilding programs. While gender has not traditionally been included in mainstream studies of security or peacebuilding, the body of work addressing gender in peacebuilding continues to grow. Still, gender has not been given adequate attention in studies focused on youth and peacebuilding. Moreover, there has been almost no consideration of the impact of gender on using music for peacebuilding.

The omission of a gendered analysis in these kinds of peacebuilding work is important. As UN Security Council Resolution 1325 acknowledges, gender equality is a vital part of peace.[87] Yet the active role of girls in peacebuilding has largely been ignored. Girls are usually seen as victims, although it is important to recognize that girls are also active and creative—including in work aimed at building peace.[88] The peacebuilding literature has also tended to ignore or minimize the connection between violence and some practices of masculinity. Thus, in framing this research, I have sought to investigate the possibilities of music as a tool of peacebuilding and to incorporate consciously a gendered analysis of the process.

What It Means for Girls

Another question that scholars and practitioners of peacebuilding need to ask and keep asking is, "What does this mean for girls?" For the most part this has not been done. Reintegration programs for ex-combatants, for example, have typically focused on male youth and failed to target girls who have been active in military groups. Based on research from 20 countries affected by war since the last decade of the 20th century, Sommers points out that girls have been overlooked more regularly than any other demographic group when formulating peace processes and programs. Moreover, he says, the few programs that do exist to work with youth are too frequently dominated by young men, while women's programs tend to be dominated by older women.[89]

Girls deserve better in research and in practice, and they are not receiving appropriate attention in the music field, either. Even in research on hip-hop, which is widely seen as a major part of global youth culture, there is a gender bias. Existing scholarship examining black youth hip-hop culture has mostly focused on young men's experiences, all but ignoring black girls' experiences.[90] Gilman and Fenn's study of rap and ragga music and dance competitions among youth in Malawi confirms the need for considering boys' and girls' differing involvement in performance. They argue that actions that do not conform to expected norms do not inherently demonstrate that a particular social forum is more open; instead, individuals' behaviors may be seen as more acceptable in particular contexts based on their personalities. Yet, they also maintain that individual acts of resistance are important, since pushing boundaries subversively incrementally can over time contribute to social change.[91] This may include the shifting of gender norms.

It is worth noting that there are also gender differences in the way girls and boys listen to and use music. For example, a United States-based study suggested that, at least in adolescence, young women listen to music more often than young men, and that girls tend to use music differently and for different reasons than boys, but these differences need to be understood in the context of gender-role socialization.[92] In other words, girls' social and cultural training demonstrate that the expectations of their behavior is quite different to that of boys. Moreover, gender differences in musical preferences appeared to be particularly distinct with young people in high school and junior high, although they did note that gender differences did not show up in punk rock, classic rock, or rap.

But what do these broad generalizations mean when applied to concrete applications of music in youth peacebuilding programs? What kind of questions do they suggest need to be asked? For one thing, it is worth questioning whether particular genres of music might carry more possibility in terms of their potential for gender inclusiveness. This will be relevant for any peacebuilding program utilizing music participation. Rap music is particularly interesting, since research on middle-class populations shows that it is popular with girls as well as boys in the U.S. population.

Research suggests rap is generally represented as masculine and misogynist, thus implying that girls would not be attracted to it (and may even be harmed by it). However, Christenson and Roberts suggest that since dancing is so important for girls, it may be that the high dance potential of mainstream rap offsets the potential threat posed by the lyrics. Saldanha likewise argues that young women exhibit a different subcultural creativity than young men, and that compared to boys, girls appear to have more interest in dancing and the cultural influence offered by dance.[93] It would be helpful then to see more research on projects that use dance as one aspect of a music-making program to consider any gendered differences. One cannot safely assume that girls can and will be included merely because a program incorporates dancing, so in research looking at youth music programs involving dance, a gender-sensitive evaluation still needs to be applied. In fact, as I explore later in this book, the program I studied that involved dance was heavily male-dominated.

While he did not critically engage with it, Allsup, in his work on school music programs, did briefly mention the potential importance of considering gender by reporting one young woman's feeling that group composing was a male domain like rock music and garage bands. For her this meant that to work with the boys she had to adapt to fit in with them, while the boys themselves made few if any concessions to gender, since they did not even recognize this as an area needing consideration.[94] Based on this finding, it appears that making boys more aware of gender issues may be an important and necessary aspect of including girls in music programs.

This is particularly needed since research on youth participation in community-based music programs in Australia, Germany, the United Kingdom, and the United States has found a lack of girls in a great number of the programs studied. In fact, Baker and Cohen reported that in all the places they researched, boys dominated most of the supposedly coeducational music activities for youth. While the programs were in theory accessible to all young people, over time the activities had been appropriated as male. When they asked facilitators why they thought more girls were not taking part or how this could be addressed, some believed male domination of such spaces is inevitable and thus gender-segregated groups are necessary, while others believed some activities, like break dancing, are simply better suited to boys.[95] At least one facilitator they interviewed also described girls' lack of ability or interest. It seems plain that attitudes around gender on the part of facilitators can influence the process. For this reason, successful programs need skilled female facilitators. While they may be difficult to find currently, the prospects should be increasing, since as more girls are trained in music practices like rapping and break dancing, there will be more girls available to become trainers in these activities.[96] While limitations of funding might impact here, hiring and supporting female music facilitators is a sound investment. Patience may be required, as programs may take time to fill, and sufficient publicity is needed to draw girls to participate. Research including programs with female leaders needs to be conducted to learn more about what may occur, so I have sought out female leaders where I could find them in the programs I studied.

Gendered behaviors and norms based on stereotypes are difficult to change, as girls still experience music activities inside a wider "context of gendered roles and experiences,"[97] which have important implications in considering how to be inclusive for girls. Single-sex programs are not the only or best way for creating music-making programs that will attract girls; rather, research suggests that girls may need girls-only groups when starting an activity, but often want the choice of coeducational groups once they have gained sufficient confidence and experience.[98]

Most community organizations have not been regularly working with girls in interrogating gendered attitudes, but interventions with girls may not be what is needed. Instead, maybe what needs critiquing is the general assumption of community organizations that create "girls as problem." What may also be needed is work with boys to investigate and challenge their attitudes on inclusion and their views around girls' participation in music-making. Likewise, better practice needs to be developed and adopted in order to support girls and boys in interrogating ideas and experiences around gender roles in music-making in a way that fosters greater gender inclusion, so research on how and why that might be framed is needed. In that aim, I have explicitly asked the young people in this study questions to learn more about their views on gender and how it relates to music and peacebuilding.

Throughout the process of seeking to include girls, it is important to take care to avoid essentializing them as victims or losers. According to Harris, girls are "reflective, critical agents" who are not conforming to the narrow, essentialist expectations society has of them as "can-do or at-risk, consumer or loser."[99] Girls are regularly using creative means such as art, music, and performance. Often this creativity by girls is aimed at engaging with other young people and expressing their views. Girls also use their creations to spawn activism around issues they recognize as significant for themselves and other youth. It seems likely then that many young women would be interested in participating in music and peace work, and they may already be involved. Yet when it comes to community youth music programs, girls are often conspicuously absent. Keeping in mind existing explanations of why that may be and the discourses through which exclusion takes place, I hope to contribute some useful ideas in this book of means by which peace projects using music to engage youth might move forward in a way that is more gender-sensitive.

Boys, Masculinity, and Prospects for Peace

Little research has been done on whether or how boys and girls may experience or understand conflict differently. This omission is not just important for girls. Like girls, boys too may be exploring the meaning of their gender, so looking at what this means for their involvement in peacebuilding is also important. It is clear that boys and girls experience violence in very different ways.[100] As one assistant principal at a coeducational school explained, he works in a culture "informed by the belief that 'boys will be boys,'" but there is now greater awareness of the need for changing boys' violent behavior in order to create better schools for boys and girls.[101] However, these issues appear to be far from resolved. As Renew argues, the liberal discourse on violence focuses on a male person with male needs, defining violence as rational and understandable. This leads to the expectation that allowances will be made for violent behavior by boys. Likewise, she says, girls are taught to cast aside the experiences they have with male violence, supporting and accommodating acts "as random, individual, aberrant, male behavior."[102] These norms are often a constituent parts of local gender regimes. As such, change is frequently resisted.[103]

Feminists demanding that education policy address boys' violence have met with discourses by the public and government that have constructed "boys as the new victims of schooling," through saying they have fallen behind academically.[104] The debate continues in Australia, where men and boys have tended to be the perpetrators of violence, which has often been taken up against "women and girls and those men and boys constructed as 'other'." Mills thus puts forth a critique of these discourses that do not attempt to problematize the behavior of boys, as they can limit possibilities for challenging gendered violence. In fact, he says, safe schools cannot be created without deconstructing dominant notions of masculinity.[105] Hedemann likewise argues that all members of the community have a responsibility to evaluate critically the narrow representations of masculinity that are built on power, strength, and aggression. Moreover, she says, both boys and girls who behave outside "acceptable" behavior for their gender in school are often subjected to gendered violence.[106]

At the same time, much of the discussion concerning boys and violence has universalized boys' behavior and ignored alternative ways of understanding young men's behavior in schools. Imms argues that some boys take part in seeking out more inclusive and egalitarian understandings of masculinity and notes that in his experience this has been particularly highlighted in art education programs.[107] This provides further justification for looking at projects involving art when exploring ways of furthering inclusion in a gender-just framework. However, because his research was conducted in a boys-only school, questions remain about how boys' behavior may differ when girls are included or whether co-educational projects may lead to outcomes of greater gender awareness or sensitivity for boys.

These contributions are helpful in furthering understandings of young men and violence. However, schools are not the only sites for education, much less conflict. Because of this, broader understandings that take into account extracurricular activities are also needed. Some limited research has been conducted dealing with young men, masculinity, and conflict in wider cultures of violence. For example, an Australian survey of 5,000 youth found that boys were more likely "to agree with statements condoning violence" and more likely to see abusive behaviors as normal conflict rather than domestic violence.[108] Indeed, gender-based violence is grounded in pervasive gender inequalities and prevailing social norms.[109] Likewise, research from the United States suggests that boys are four times as likely to be involved in fights as girls.[110] Similarly, in Sub-Saharan Africa, fighters in all wars are most often male youth;[111] and homicide rates for young men are higher than for young women across the globe.[112] Such statistics have led to the youth bulge thesis, which posits that male youth are inherently violent and thus where they exist in high concentrations, massive violence is inevitable.[113] However, such sweeping statements ignore the fact that most African cities, which are home to large concentrations of young males, are not experiencing major conflict. Of course these same areas may still have high levels of domestic violence and sexual assault, which are important to address in challenging obstacles to positive peace, even if they are not typically recognized as direct conflict.

In any case, an essentialist position that paints boys as violent actors detracts from recognizing that boys can be victims as well as perpetrators. After all, many of the boys who participate in violence have themselves been victimized or witnessed violence. Since young men tend to spend more time outside their homes than girls in most cultures, boys are more likely to witness or experience physical violence. In this context more research is needed to improve our understanding of the process through which young men are recruited to violence, including how they become combatants.[114] In doing so, we also need to ask questions about how they might become something else in their pursuit of masculinity.

In looking at issues of violence and conflict, applying a gendered perspective makes visible the construction of masculine identities and the links with manifestations of violence and "becoming a man."[115] As Barker explores in the context of Sub-Saharan Africa, conflicts in the region are related to how masculinities are constructed socially.[116] Looking at how gender identities are constructed is thus important. After all, fixed understandings of gender hierarchies and manhood produce vulnerabilities for boys and girls, as well as for men and women.

Researchers studying boys' participation in violent conflict suggest that particular patterns of masculinity can dominate and be consolidated through socialization in settings such as schools.[117] However, most reports considering boys in conflict do not investigate the "underlying factors that lead young men to use or participate in this violence."[118] There are some exceptions. In Barker's writing on young men's involvement in violent *comando* groups in Brazil, he reports another study's finding that participation was tied to looking for connection or belonging they did not have at home, searching for identity, and attraction to the model of masculinity that came with being a *comando*.[119] This kind of work is an excellent model, but a significant research gap still exists in understanding how notions of masculinity impact boys' participation in violent conflict.

To improve prospects and move toward a more peaceful world for boys and girls, spaces need to be created where alternative models of masculinity can be questioned and rehearsed in seeking to activate cultural change around dominant gender ideologies by dealing with issues such as identity, self-esteem, violence, transforming conflict, and new forms of masculinity.[120] Research in the United States and Brazil supports this, as boys who did *not* participate in gangs were able to explain this in terms of being able to achieve a sense of self or access alternative identities that held positive value in their social settings, especially with their group of male peers.[121] Some examples include doing well as an athlete, student, worker, or musician. Other options also included involvement in a non-gang male peer group that could provide positive reinforcement for alternative masculine identities. Grassroots community organizations working with young men through leisure activities may thus have a big impact if they teach gender-equitable nonviolent behaviors to boys participating in their programs.

After all, young men have an important role to play in reducing violence in their communities, including violence against women and girls. While most prevention strategies to address intimate partner violence have been directed at girls and women, an increasing focus has emerged on engaging men and boys.[122] As Connell explains, gender is not inherent; it is something that occurs and thus must be made to occur through particular performances. For boys and girls the dominant messages they receive from society are based on a "gender order" that teaches girls to be desirable and boys to be hard, dominant, competitive, and tough. At the same time, gender can also "be unmade, altered, made less important."[123] This is work in which both boys and girls can take part, contesting the norms of hegemonic masculinity to create something better, or as Connell puts it, "democratising gender relations."[124]

While more research is needed on how this might occur in practice, Barker's research in Brazil suggests that there are certain key factors there that correlated to more gender-equitable understandings in young men. They included: the presence of family or other role models presenting alternative understandings of gender equity, personally experiencing negative impacts from some traditional expressions of masculinity, and locating a group of peers or a social space in which alternative notions of masculinity were presented.[125] Furthermore, in their work on Africa, Barker and Ricardo have called for explicitly discussing masculinities and gender norms in programs and seeking to change social environments in this regard.[126] This needs particular attention when considering young men, who so often participate in conflict. While noting that young men frequently take part in violence, it is important to note that they are also impacted by it and have an important role to play in transforming conflict. Thus, looking at the role of masculinity and identity is a key aspect of considering boys' potential role in peacebuilding. Therefore, organizations working with boys in peacebuilding efforts need to take this into account seriously in their planning, implementation, and evaluation.

Conclusion

Music is an important part of the lives of young people and is often central to youth cultures. At the same time, it is being used in very specific ways in youth-focused programs. It is important, then, to make visible the various kinds of work young people seeking to build peace are doing with music cultures. However, given space and time constraints, I have chosen to limit my scope to examining the use of music in ongoing organized peacebuilding programs run for and/or by youth. It appears that music can be usefully deployed in building positive peace with young people, but it is also clear that doing so requires constant reflection and an awareness of processes of inclusion and exclusion to avoid merely reproducing dominant cultural norms that operate hierarchically to exclude particular ideas and identities. This is particularly relevant with regard to the role young women can play in musical work. More understanding is needed of how gender norms impact young people's participation in peace processes and in turn prospects for long-term, sustainable peace. What is clear is that building positive peace requires democratizing gender, and men and boys have important roles to play in that process. This is not to suggest that young men and women cannot or should not adopt musical work together as a strategy of pursuing peace. Quite the contrary: by doing so, they may choose to challenge discourses of gendered differences that have impeded prospects for peace.

3

The Beat on the Ground

Introducing the Case Studies

For purposes of comparison, I decided to study two groups in diverse cultural contexts with different experiences of violence and peacebuilding. Northern Ireland is considered a post-conflict society, while Australia is seen as a country at peace, though violence does exist there. The search for suitable groups suggested that using music is a relatively new mode for community-level programs aimed at engaging young people in peacebuilding. This provided yet another reason for studying projects that are breaking this creative ground, to provide insights into what they do, how they do it, and the challenges they may face. The different applications of music to youth peacebuilding examined here can help to illuminate how differences in programs may influence outcomes. Additionally, looking at two significantly different cultures of conflict makes it possible to examine how music may be adapted to local needs in building a culture of peace. Furthermore, it is interesting to consider two case studies in which one (Third Space in Australia) is youth-run while the other (Breaking Barriers in Northern Ireland) is delivered as a program to young people, rather than *by* and *with* them. Throughout this project, I have sought to learn from and share information on the experiences of youth peacebuilders, paying particular attention to how they deploy their own contextually relevant skills and knowledge in creatively pursuing peace.

From the beginning, I want to make clear that I have not attempted to provide a formal evaluation of the groups/programs chosen. Rather, the intent has been to gather information on whether music-based activities generally indicate potential for effective peacebuilding among young people. While this does appear to be the case, the success of these programs does not imply that all organizations attempting to use music for youth peacebuilding will do so in a positive or effective manner. Instead, the work that these organizations are doing suggests that such outcomes are possible. I have thus sought to critically engage with their work to learn more about why and how they have been successful and what challenges and limitations exist.

A Methodological Overview

In both of the youth peacebuilding groups selected for these case studies I engaged in participant observation. To do so, I worked with young women and young men who produce and perform music. I was particularly concerned to record observations about the nature of the group and group interactions, the style of leadership, the ideas about peace and peacebuilding that dominated in the groups, the impact of the music-making, any visible gendered behavior, contestations of gender norms, group and interpersonal conflict, failures and successes. These observations were then used to facilitate later analysis of interview data.

At both research sites I also conducted semi-structured interviews. In the interviews I sought to investigate the impact of group activities on the young people involved. This included the effects on identity construction (including gender identity) and on perceptions about the ability to engage as peacebuilders. I was interested, therefore, in the meanings the young people assigned to their activities in the group (as these also reflected broader processes of social construction, including in relation to gender). Thus, the epistemological position, or what counts as knowledge and meaningful data here is people's motives and perspectives, the actor's point of view, and intentions and meanings in context. Relevant sources of data therefore include personal statements, actions or behavior, and broader understandings of culture.[1]

Before conducting each interview, I undertook steps to obtain informed consent from the young people asked to participate as interviewees. In each case, I described my project to the potential interviewee and explained that participation would be on a voluntary basis and that s/he did not have to consent to take part in the interviewing. After obtaining permission to conduct the interview, I then asked the permission of the interviewee to record the interview digitally in order to preserve the conversation in better detail and avoid possible confusion. All of the interviews reported in this study were conducted with young people who verbally agreed to being interviewed and recorded.

Some general topics for questions included whether the youth felt music had been particularly enabling for their involvement in peacebuilding activities, how they thought their participation might make a difference, whether they felt this experience will facilitate their formal involvement in peacebuilding in the future, how they would suggest such programs be modified, and what role, if any, they thought gender played in their involvement.

While I developed an interview schedule, my approach was flexible rather than rigidly structured, as I could not anticipate all the relevant questions beforehand and some became apparent during the interviews. However, to make sure all relevant issues were covered, I developed a basic list of topics and themes prior to the interviews; this did not exclude the possibility of other issues arising during the interviews. I also used open-ended questions to introduce the various topics without suggesting a particular response.

At the end of each interview, I concluded by checking whether I had understood any unclear responses and asking if the interviewee had anything further to add that could aid my understanding. Next, I transcribed the interview to prepare it for analysis and reporting. In order to establish confidentiality and protect the privacy of youth participants, I have changed or omitted their names in all material published or otherwise made public. To further ensure the young people's anonymity, especially since I have used some identifying characteristics to aid in understanding their responses, I have also used pseudonyms for the organizations participating in the study.

It was impossible to interview all of the participants in both organizations, so I had to select a sample, and this was necessarily limited to those young people and organizers/leaders who were willing to undertake an interview. Similarly, for participant observation, I was able to observe only a selection of the activities during musical practices, group meetings, and performances.

The combination of participant observation and semi-structured interviewing allowed me to gain a broader picture of the young people's experiences than could be gained from either method alone. Interviewing was useful in encouraging the youth to articulate their motives and perspectives, and participant observation helped me to observe how the interviewees interacted and engaged with each other. Moreover, certain events, such as concerts and practice sessions, were more amenable to observation than interviewing. In both case studies I used purposive sampling to select interviewees and observation site(s). This helped ensure that my interviewees included both youth and adult leaders of the groups.

Throughout the case studies I have considered what impact, if any, gender has on the process of music-making for youth, especially as related to building peace, because I firmly believe that democratizing gender roles and challenging gender norms is a vital part of peacebuilding and achieving positive peace. In this project, I have followed the advice of Letherby, who counsels that feminist researchers ought continuously to attend "to the significance of gender as an aspect of all social life and within research."[2] To that end, feminist scholars have contended that by failing to investigate "how their personal, professional, and structural positions frame social scientific investigations, researchers inevitably reproduce dominant gender, race, and class biases."[3] With this in mind, I have sought to address this issue to the best of my ability during the research practice by adopting a framework that is reflexive, prompting ongoing ethical reflection throughout my research, writing, and analysis.[4] The extra work is worthwhile, since important issues are often ignored in traditional interview practice, in which "[i]nterviewees are relevant to the research as sources of data, not as analysts of their own experience."[5] I have therefore sought to avoid such a situation by using reflexive strategies to better involve the young people who participate in the study. For example, I asked them follow-up questions to check whether the assumptions I had made about their behavior or remarks reflected their own understandings.

As questions of gender and the contestation of gender norms are an important component of this research, I selected programs that included boys and girls in the same programs at the same time. However, there were also times when participants would self-segregate by gender prior to, during, or after the programs. I was therefore also able to see, for example, girls interacting with other girls only and girls' interaction with a mix of boys and girls. This enabled me to examine the differences between how youth might behave or feel within groups of their own gender as compared to mixed-gender groups. I wanted to know how, if at all, their perceptions and capacities are affected by the gender make-up of the groups in which they participate. For example, I was curious to know whether girls would perceive or experience different opportunities or restrictions on their participation when boys were present, and vice versa.

Case Study 1: Australia and Third Place

Before discussing the program itself, it is worth considering the broader context of conflict and peacebuilding in which Third Place operates. Australia is home to descendants of arguably "the oldest indigenous peoples in the world,"[6] who now account for 2.5 percent of the population. Due to migration Australia is also a multicultural nation. Demographic diversity is evident, with 25 percent of current residents born overseas. Despite this, while an international war has never occurred on Australian soil, conflict has been endemic since European settlement, which displaced or exterminated much of the Aboriginal population. While the government officially, "recognises, accepts and respects cultural diversity,"[7] structural and direct violence based on racism is visible today. Race-based violence particularly impacts people from indigenous, migrant, and refugee backgrounds. El-Leissy suggests that race relations in Australia have noticeably shifted in the last 10 years. Previously, he says, violent racist attacks tended to be more isolated incidents by individuals or small groups, whereas recently there have been much more widespread expressions of racism involving large numbers of people, such as the widely publicized racially motivated riots that occurred in December 2005 in Cronulla.[8] More recently, attacks on Indian students have prompted an ongoing public debate about whether the government was doing enough to protect Indian students from racist violence.[9] Despite politicians maintaining that underlying racism does not exist in Australia, young people from diverse linguistic and cultural backgrounds have regularly reported experiencing racism and a lack of harmony in their communities.[10] Gender-based violence, including sexual assault and domestic violence, also occurs. The United Nations Population Fund (UNFPA) reports that for young Australian women domestic violence is the biggest health risk, which results in around 6.3 billion dollars per year in economic losses.[11] Much of this conflict is underpinned by dominant discourses that applaud aggressive expressions of "Australian" masculinity.[12] It is in this context that Third Place operates and the youth participants live.

Originally aimed at addressing violent conflict between youth from Aboriginal and Pacific Islander communities, Third Place's peace program has broadened its goals to include youth from other communities. In particular, its work aims to contribute to peacebuilding by challenging racism through building understanding between youth from many different cultural communities. Its work also seeks to build peace by providing a safe space for young people from refugee backgrounds to recover from violence experienced in their countries of origin. The organization does not have a permanent funding source and thus must rely on external donors for its continuing operation. However, it has been very successful at securing several short-term and longer-term grants over the past several years, so it appears likely that the Third Place program will remain financially stable. Funders include the Australian government, the state government, city councils, and other local and national funding bodies supporting arts, youth, and/or multicultural development. Based in a major Australian city, Third Place has many years of experience offering youth arts programs in the local area, where the organization works with young people from diverse cultures including, but not limited to, youth from migrant and refugee communities as well as Aboriginal and Torres Strait Islander and Pacific Islander backgrounds. All of the work by this organization is guided by the principles of social justice and peacebuilding practices. Their programming is designed with these principles in mind, to be sustainable, consistent, and to employ capacity-building strategies to support a diverse group of youth and artists in being dynamic agents of change in their communities.

Third Place uses hip-hop workshops including singing, break dancing, MCing, and crump dancing as part of a peacebuilding initiative. Break dancing, developed in New York in the 1970s, is a typically fast-paced, acrobatic solo dance style. MCing refers to the art of rapping—speaking or chanting lyrical rhymes normally accompanied by rhythms. Crumping, originating in South Central Los Angeles in the 1990s, is an urban dance style using fast-paced moves that often appear to be aggressive. "Crumpers" often participate in nonviolent skills competitions termed "dance battles." The use of hip-hop activities makes the project appear particularly relevant in the local context, given that reports from Queensland, New South Wales, and South Australia all confirm that popular music is important to both the lives and livelihoods of young people living in Australia,[13] and research suggests that Australian hip-hop has played a major role in culture since the 1990s.[14]

The application of hip-hop in this diverse context, including among youth born outside Australia, is interesting given that hip-hop is often understood as an international phenomenon. Hip-hop, Lock argues, records the experiences and concerns of urban youth, crossing the globe in a way that promotes youth culture as a different lifestyle to the current cultures that mostly neglect youth.[15] Emerging from African American and Afro-Caribbean youth in New York City in the mid 1970s, hip-hop culture includes rapping, its own style of dress, break dancing, graffiti, MCing, and DJing. From its origins hip-hop was built on principles of nonviolence, making it a likely candidate for application in the peacebuilding field. Historically, hip-hop has been strongly linked to social and political struggles, with many hip-hop artists taking part in what could be seen as a resistance movement. However, some scholars argue that over time the movement has degraded into a search for profit and in doing so has lost its effective voice while falling prey to violence and sexism.[16] Indeed, even artists who are politically involved and socially aware in their local contexts risk sidelining these issues when they enter the global commercial music field.[17]

Nonetheless, many continue to see hip-hop "as a cultural protest system, an alternative identity affirmation,"[18] so potential exists for resistant uses or transformation of the genre as a tool for peace. This is particularly relevant for youth who, based on their cultural knowledge, can generally decipher hip-hop with greater ease, and use it as a framework of expression that does not require training or expensive equipment. Munõz and Marín suggest that by demanding that participants produce a style of their own, hip-hop lays a foundation for young people around the world to develop indigenous forms of expression; to construct selves using images, rhythm, sound, and movement; and to build up knowledge that more accurately reflects their lived realities.[19]

Looking at hip-hop dance styles as I have done here helps in understanding music practice, since music permits and sometimes compels direct participation through activities such as dancing, clapping, and singing.[20] Dancing then can be understood as a nonlinguistic interpretation of music, through which the dancer may create and recreate abilities, cultural cognition, relations, and patterns.[21] In short, if looking at music politically, Brabazon contends that dancing ought to be understood "as an act of social change, a politics absorbed through the feet."[22] I was thus very intrigued to see whether or how this might occur at the research sites.

The Third Place project was held in two stages, in late 2007 and early 2008. Work originally began in October 2007, with the project managers intending to run a 10-week program that would end with a final performance in December. However, due to unforeseeable circumstances, the company halted operations in November 2007 and postponed the project until February 2008. From then, the project began again and ran a full 10 weeks to accommodate new arrivals as well as returning participants. The project culminated with a film screening and public performance held in the city center as part of National Youth Week activities.

Music and dance workshops were conducted for two hours each, one day per week at a local scout hall. The suburb where the program was run is home to a diverse population, with 41.8 percent of residents born overseas, substantially more than the national average of 22.2 percent. The area reports an unemployment rate of 7.8 percent, compared to the national average of 5.2 percent, and also has a lower than average median weekly household income: $942 per week as compared to $1,027 nationally. At the same time, the area experiences higher than average rental costs, with median weekly rent at $240, as compared to $190 Australia-wide. Child poverty statistics for this specific area were not available. However, according to UNICEF, 11.6 percent of all Australian children live in relative poverty, which is defined as living in a household with income less than 50 percent of the median income for the country.[23]

All of the young people reported attending high school in the local area, predominantly at the two closest state high schools. The diversity of the local area was heavily reflected in the demographic makeup of participants in the project, with young people attending from a wide range of cultures, including immigrants from Samoan, Maori, Tongan, Sudanese, Liberian, Fijian, and Slovenian backgrounds, among others, as well as young people whose families have lived in Australia for several generations. None of the youth I interviewed identified themselves as Aboriginal. There was one Aboriginal facilitator present in the first part of the program, but because she left before the program finished I was unable to interview her. Both young men and women attended, although a male majority was present throughout the program. Participants came from an assortment of socioeconomic backgrounds, with parental occupations ranging from factory worker to resort owner. Most youth attending were in their mid-teens, with 14 being the most common age, but overall participants ranged from 13 to 21 years of age.

One of the advantages of conducting research with Third Place was that several long-term participants were attending, and some of the facilitators had been long-term participants themselves, so it was possible to learn more about young people's views and experiences over time with the project. This is important because debates continue regarding whether peacebuilding workshops generate lasting or temporary change, and analysis needs to be undertaken on the long-term value of informal activities that are at times used in such workshops.

Participant Observation

I attended almost all workshops scheduled for the program. Third Place's facilitators and administrators offered me open access to attend all staff meetings held before each workshop and the reflection sessions held after each one. I also observed the group operating in a different location during the video film shoot, which was held across town at an arts space. Finally, I attended and observed the final performance for the project, which was held in a public space in the city center.

Outside of the times I was immersed in observing, in order to become more familiar to facilitators and participants and build rapport, I became part of the project in whatever way I could. Program facilitators often asked for my opinion or input during their pre-workshop meetings and post-workshop reflection sessions, and I contributed where possible. I often assisted in the kitchen with preparing food for youth participants; I helped in setting up and taking down chairs when the group came together in a circle for games or discussions; and, I regularly did whatever was needed to assist in clean-up after the workshops had concluded. Other times I helped out by driving crew members to pick up extra food that was needed or dropping people off at the train station after the meetings ended.

I also participated in whole-group activities with the participants, such as the icebreaker game sessions that were run at the beginning of each workshop and the reflection circle held before leaving most nights.

While these activities took some time, I was able to spend a significant amount of time directly observing participants' interactions: outside the hall before each workshop; inside at meetings, whole-group discussions and activities, and break-out sessions for specific music/dance practices; and inside and outside after each workshop. During the "break-out" sessions in which participants were divided up to focus on their particular art form (i.e., rapping, singing, crumping, or break dancing), which constituted the vast majority of time participants spent in the workshops, I would shift from group to group to observe their participation and interactions. The two dance groups, crumpers and break-dancers, were both located in the large, open-space front room of the hall, while the singers and MCs shared a much smaller closed room down the corridor. In both spaces I would sit somewhere that would facilitate easy hearing and viewing without being in the way or disturbing participants' creative process. When possible I recorded observations as I noted them, although at times this was not feasible (i.e., when participating in games and activities), so in those cases I wrote up observations shortly afterward or after leaving the workshop for the evening.

Based on my research question—"Can music play an important role in engaging youth in peacebuilding?"—I focused on various aspects of the use of music, including participation in a range of activities, in this case performance via singing, dancing, and otherwise appropriating existing music to forge new musical creations. In the workshops I observed the learning and practice of musical expression, but was also able to learn more about the context in which this took place by seeing the ways youth participated and interacted in the space when not directly engaged in music-making. While remaining open to simply being present to observe whatever appeared significant, I did have several specific ideas about what I might be on the lookout to see and explore. All of these observations helped me to structure my interviews.

Semi-Structured Interviews

When requesting interviews with participants I attempted to select those who had been in regular attendance, as I assumed they were most likely to have more in-depth knowledge and experience of the program. I began the first week with a boy and girl who had both spoken with me quite a bit during the workshops. Interviewing them first allowed me to feel more comfortable talking to the others at a later stage. I had no problem getting other participants to interview; most of the youth I asked were eager and willing to talk about the project with me. In drawing out participants for interviews I was able to select young people from diverse demographic backgrounds, based on their genders, ages, art forms, and socioeconomic classes. In all, I interviewed 10 youth participants. A descriptive list of demographic characteristics (including cultural/racial background, gender, age, art form, and parental occupation) of respondents is provided in Appendix 1.

All interviews were conducted during normal workshop times at a covered picnic table in a park located adjacent to the hall where the workshops were held. After conducting two initial interviews, I then made some slight revisions to the wording of questions so I could provoke more in-depth responses. The revised interview schedule is presented in appendix 2.

I returned to interviewing the following week and over the course of the next month of the workshops I reached my goal of interviewing 10 participants. Interview duration ranged from 10 to 45 minutes, depending on how much each respondent was willing or able to talk. The last interviews with participants were conducted during the farewell barbecue during the week following the final performance for the program. For each of the interviews I brought along the interview schedule I had prepared and asked most of the questions on it, adding and adjusting my inquiries and comments based on the respondents' individual interests, replies, language abilities, and level of engagement.

Because the Third Place project is run for youth by youth, with facilitators ranging from 18–25 years of age, I also wanted to interview some or all of the facilitators who ran the program.

However, due to the limited funding for the program, all of the facilitators were only employed on a part-time or casual basis, so most of them were busy with outside jobs and/or training. While it may have been preferable to interview all six young people in facilitator roles, after several scheduling issues it became clear that conducting interviews with half of them would be a more feasible goal. For demographic data on facilitators, see appendix 3. These interviews were intended to open up opportunities for gaining further insights on issues raised by the youth participants and to learn more about notions of leadership in music- and dance-focused youth peacebuilding programs. In the end, I was able to schedule a day that would accommodate three of the six facilitators. For their convenience, I agreed to meet them at their office. Interview times ranged from 40 minutes to one hour and 40 minutes. Most of the questions from the participant interview schedule were retained for the facilitator interviews although there were some minor revisions and additions. The interview schedule used for facilitator interviews is available in Appendix 4.

In addition to making an important contribution to my research on its own accord, the fieldwork conducted in this case study served as a sound training ground, as the experience helped in developing skills and knowledge that were useful when approaching the second case study.

Case Study 2: Northern Ireland and Breaking Barriers

Although young people in both of my studies have experienced and/or been involved in conflict, the types of conflict in the two locales need to be understood contextually. With divisions dating back over several centuries, Northern Ireland has been experiencing ongoing ethnoreligious political conflict for over three decades. The more intense period of direct violence prior to 1998 is known as "The Troubles." Community relations activities and interethnic dialogue have been in place for some time, but this work is hindered by ongoing violence and ethnopolitical tension, such as the March 2009 sectarian shootings of two soldiers and a police officer. In 2008 news reports cited the threat of violence from dissidents to be the highest in six years. Indeed, the peace process there is "one of the longest-running processes," both in reaching and implementing the agreement.[24]

While an official peace accord was reached in 1998, Northern Ireland's young people are still living in an environment that is decidedly segregated and heavily militarized.[25] During my stay there, "peace walls," which physically separate Protestant neighborhoods from Catholic ones, were going up, not coming down. Indeed half of the population live in districts "that are 90% Catholic or Protestant," and these divisions are further reified through the education system, which is legally segregated. In fact, schools that are predominantly Protestant or Catholic account for more than 90 percent of all schools. Despite being officially part of the United Kingdom, which is considered one of the richest nations in the world, there are estimated to be 100,000 children in Northern Ireland who are living below the official poverty line. According to 2004 data, 8 percent of children there live in severe poverty while another 42 percent live in poverty that is nonsevere.[26] In the context of the ongoing global financial crisis, unemployment in Northern Ireland has been rising, but at present the unemployment rate is less than EU and U.K. averages.

In addition to sectarian violence, immigration to Northern Ireland has increased after many years of very low levels prior to the cease-fire, and racism has emerged as an additional challenge to building a culture of peace. In fact, reports in 2000 stated that racism had become twice as prevalent as sectarianism.[27] By late 2004, news reports cited community leaders' concerns about the increasing number of attacks on immigrant families and suggested that racism is threatening to overtake terrorism as the major face of violence.[28]

Peacebuilding strategies need to take into account the broad culture of violence while aiming for socially and culturally appropriate ways to meet the needs of young people, since youth are taught the predominant attitudes held by their ethnopolitical communities in this context.[29] This process starts from an early age. In Northern Ireland research suggests that by the time children are three years old, they can identify people as

Catholic or Protestant and assign negative or positive meanings to these identities.[30] However, research also suggests that young people actively "shape and negotiate these attitudes and their identities, that they play with and adjust sectarian stereotypes."[31] So this process may be open to peacebuilding efforts. In particular, the engagement of young people in Northern Ireland in youth cultures or sub-cultures may be significant in disrupting the prevailing cultural bipolarism.[32] For this reason, peacebuilding programs that engage with youth culture may be particularly important.

Yet at the time of my visit to Northern Ireland, many organizations reported that they were struggling financially as funds were depleted from Peace II, a European Union Structural Funds Programme developed to reinforce progress toward peace and reconciliation,[33] and Peace III, the last of the installments for peace program funding, had not yet arrived. Moreover, Peace III was scheduled to be the smallest and the last of such payments, meaning that many community organizations may have to cut programs or staff, leaving youth without these supports despite continuing violence. The impact of the global financial crisis was also mentioned as a key concern for many community organizations with unstable funding.

Programs that engage with cultural practices such as music may play an important role in working for a culture of peace in Northern Ireland. Historically, however, music has been used divisively in the conflict. Even particular instruments, such as drums, are identified with political positions. The bodhrán is seen as symbolizing the nationalist (Catholic) community, while the lambeg automatically brings to mind marching bands and the Orange (Protestant) tradition. Marching season is a time of traditional parades, and issues around marching define "the Northern Ireland problem in microcosm."[34] Often resulting in violence, the parades are primarily organized by Protestant groups termed Loyal Orange lodges, and while most of them are not contentious, a few inflame conflict as they travel through Catholic neighborhoods playing sectarian songs. One program facilitator, a Protestant, told me of his former girlfriend, a Catholic, who lived on one of the marching parade routes and thus would be stuck in her house for days each marching season as she was too scared and intimidated by the militants blocking the street to leave. There are also Catholic/nationalist/Republican parades, but these are much less common. In short, as one community worker said during my interview with him,

> Culture was used as a weapon by marching bands. . . . It was a way of delivering your side of the conflict to the other side. . . . It's whether you want to use culture positively or negatively. It's about how you deliver it. If you want to use it as a weapon you can, but if you want to use it to bring people together and build trust you can choose to do that.

The problem is that music styles and instruments have already been categorized politically and repeatedly adapted to tools of conflict rather than tools of peace. As one program facilitator stated,

> When you start to get creative, people say you know . . . so there's no way you can like this type of music, cuz you're Catholic. . . . Some people say well you shouldn't like it, you should be liking this you know.

Despite this, he and many others I met in Northern Ireland explained that music can be and very clearly has been a uniting force across sectarian and other differences. As the community worker quoted previously says,

> The commonality is already there—people are much more into music than difference. Music is the great leveller. It still applies today. Music is the kind of conduit to get to someone that you don't know.

Breaking Barriers began in 2004 when its founder first saw *1 Giant Leap,* a film in which two musicians travel the world to engage with global issues through recording music and meeting locals. After watching the film, the founder of Breaking Barriers felt inspired to show it in Belfast. His request to do this was rejected in several places because he was not affiliated with an official organization. Within one month he started the charity Breaking Barriers, which enabled him to start showing the film around the area. Since then he has been continually working on and expanding the project, which is now more focused around his passion for working with youth and bringing together people from different backgrounds to play music. He says this has been an organic process, with the organization following the sort of "no plan" ethos the musicians featured in *1 Giant Leap* used, that is "going along with things as they happen" in the project. Breaking Barriers has never had guaranteed public funding for all necessary program expenses, but it has consistently received sufficient funds to pay overheads, wages, and office accommodation, so it appears that it is very well placed to continue growing.

The program has its primary office in Belfast but conducts programs in most of the large towns across Northern Ireland. I conducted my field research by traveling around Northern Ireland with the organization. In addition to Belfast, I visited Newtownards, Armagh, East Belfast, Omagh, Glengormley, Ballymena, Portadown, Bangor, Portaferry, and (London)Derry. During these travels I was able to meet and have discussions with many community leaders who work in peacebuilding programs, community arts projects, youth organizations, and good relations councils. All of these discussions helped broaden my understanding of the topic in the local context. I also conducted participant observation at the various locations where the projects were run and used semi-structured interviews with youth participants and program facilitators.

The key objectives of Breaking Barriers include: addressing sectarianism and racism in the local area by using multicultural art programs; promoting positive views of a multicultural society; supporting multicultural arts to benefit Northern Irish people; promoting harmonious race relations through arts; supporting the maintenance of peace in Northern Ireland; increasing cross-cultural awareness within Northern Ireland; increasing ties between different cultural communities; and presenting, promoting, organizing, managing, and producing shows of cultural and educational value. In addition to hosting an online multicultural radio station, Breaking Barriers runs several music-focused projects around Northern Ireland with a diverse range of participants—those from Northern Ireland as well as immigrants, Catholic and Protestant, musicians and laypeople, male and female, youth and adults. People in Northern Ireland tend to distinguish themselves in broad categories of working class or middle class, and participants included young people who reflected this diversity in socioeconomic backgrounds.

Many of the initiatives, taking place in schools and youth centers, are provided specifically for youth, and these were the main focus for my research with Breaking Barriers. Young people are involved in Breaking Barriers in many ways, including participating in the programs called Youth Movement (YM), Musical Exchange of Culture (MEC), and Project Movement.

YM, held in various locations, often in youth clubs, brings together youth from different communities in Northern Ireland to produce original music with the help of professional musicians from other countries. The project aims to utilize music in encouraging better cultural relations. This process often includes a series of workshops and culminates in the production of a CD of the music made in the workshops.

MEC, which is delivered in schools, was piloted in 2007 and was fully launched in 2008. The project was conceived as an enjoyable, interactive way to increase diversity awareness and provide education on global issues for young people. The program generally consists of two half-day workshops that include: presentations by international musicians and a facilitator who specializes in peace education; viewing a section of the *1 Giant Leap* video, which uses music to explore global issues relating to fair trade; and multiple interactive music-making and discussion sessions in which the youth participate.

Finally, Project Movement is mostly composed of older musicians, with one teenager taking part as a drummer, but young people often attend and participate in the activities they run. Project Movement is a Northern Ireland-based multicultural music collective that includes musicians from a number of countries; the group travels to all six counties of Northern

Ireland to provide interactive music experiences, as well as performances and other programs. This work is often done at community celebrations and in schools. The aim of Project Movement is to counter racism and sectarianism by demonstrating that working together can lead to good outcomes. In doing so, the project offers youth the chance to meet people from different cultures, to learn about other cultures, and to play, hear, and learn about music from around the globe.

Participant Observation

Throughout my fieldwork I had full access to Breaking Barriers' meetings and resources and spent considerable time speaking with people in their office and attending events with them to gain more understanding of the background and immerse myself in the organizational culture. In addition, I conducted participant observation at all of the three programs previously described, such as with the YM program held at a youth club housed in a high school after-hours. While the youth club itself was for both boys and girls, attendance in this specific program was only open to the boys, who were all aged 14 and students at the high school. The youth club was located in a Protestant, working-class area, which also included one of the largest public housing estates in Europe and featured an intersection between Protestant and Catholic areas. There is currently ongoing conflict in this area between young people from these two sides of the sectarian divide.

I also investigated the MEC programs through participant observation at an all-girls Catholic school in (London)Derry. There was one boy present during the first half of the first day, as he took music lessons with the music teacher. Participants were mostly 12 and 13 years old. An impressive array of extracurricular activities was on offer at this school. The program was held over two half-day sessions in the mornings.

Finally, I engaged in participant observation with Project Movement through one-time interactive music experiences at: (1) a community festival in Portadown, a majority Protestant town, which garnered participation by all ages; (2) an International Peace Day concert held at a public venue in Belfast city center, which is considered neutral ground in the Protestant/Catholic divide and was attended by various ages and sexes, but with a majority of young women in their late teens or early 20s; and (3) the International Kid's Day program, which was attended by young people from four different elementary schools, including girls and boys, and was held in a large convocation center in Ballymena, a predominantly Protestant area, which band members described as "deprived" and the "heroin capital of Northern Ireland."

Given the highly interactive nature of the programs, it was easy to take part by playing along on the djembe, maracas, or bodhrán, for example, so I spent a good deal of my time in the workshops doing so. This allowed me to fit in easily and thus made observation less obtrusive. At other times I would assist facilitators in whatever way was most useful. This often included photographing the participants and activities, encouraging anyone not participating to join in, and loading and unloading musical equipment. With the YM program, we often arrived early to set up and the boys participating would already be there and remain afterward, so I was also able to observe them outside the project. By contrast, in (London)Derry at the girls' school they all came from and had to go straight back to class, so I only saw participants at the project. The situation with Project Movement would often be more fluid, with a large number of people coming and going throughout the program, making it impossible to note what was occurring at all times.

As with my first case study, I sought to be open to whatever might materialize, but kept in mind specific issues that would merit particular attention. Moreover, after identifying certain key themes in my first case study, I was especially curious to see whether these would also be reflected in Breaking Barriers' musical peacebuilding work with young people. To explore these questions, I consistently observed, listened, and engaged participants and facilitators in discussion when possible.

One important difference between Breaking Barriers and the Australian case study was that in Northern Ireland two of my major observation sites were much more homogeneous, with most participants being the same gender, age, class, and religion. One difference this made was that I had to rely solely on interviewees' own statements of their views of or interactions with "others," since I was unable to see firsthand how they interacted across difference in many cases. Although the events I observed with Project Movement were more diverse, they were also very large and thus more difficult to observe and document. Nonetheless, I observed what I could there and also looked for other important aspects of peacebuilding that might come into play. As with my Australian case study, I looked to see if there were any visible representations of the use of music as a tool for peacebuilding. Moreover, I attempted to remain alert for any signs relating to levels of inclusiveness in the space. This required being especially attentive to whether social exclusions based on age, gender, race, or other characteristics were being upheld, challenged, or reified in this space. Once again, my observations were helpful in formulating appropriate questions for the interviews.

Semi-Structured Interviews

In the end, I had to employ a wide-ranging strategy to complete my interviews with young people who had participated in the programs. I was able to interview all of the young participants at the YM program I had observed for three weeks by going in the week after the program finished to interview them one-on-one. Through my attendance at many of the Project Movement shows I was also able to meet the young drummer, and his father agreed to let me interview him during a visit as a dinner guest at their home. The project manager also knew the father of one young man who had participated in a previous YM workshop, so he was able to call him and get him to bring his son to the Breaking Barriers studio one afternoon so I could interview him in a spare office.

By spending time at the office, I got to know one young woman who had participated in and helped facilitate some of the YM programs and now serves on the board of the organization, so I was also able to interview her. Finally, the project manager and another staff member knew the music teacher at a school where they had done the MEC program the previous year, so they were able to schedule to take me there during a break time to interview four of the young people who had participated. Because I had not met them before and they were shy, they were happier with me interviewing them as pairs rather than individually. This meant the respondents would at times just nod along with each other or say "same" rather than articulating their own views, but it also presented the opportunity for recording their interactions and exchanges.

With nearly all of the young people in Breaking Barriers' programs, I obtained less in-depth responses than I had from my previous case study, most likely because I was not able to develop the same kind of long-term relationships with them as I had with the youth participants in Australia. However, the information that I gained was helpful and relevant, as reported in the following chapters. Scheduling interviews with facilitators was unproblematic, so I spoke with four of them. A demographic description of interviewees and general question schedules can be found in appendices 5–8.

In most of my youth interviews I was able to use the same question schedule. However, for the YM project, which I had observed, I slightly altered the questions on gender issues based on my observations, as noted in the appendices. For consistency, I also asked the former participants from the MEC program from the previous year about their feelings regarding the gender makeup of programs.

Reprise: Bringing It Back to the Beat

Observing and interviewing such a substantial number of participants in two countries and from a wide variety of backgrounds yielded a large data log. This included over 200 pages of interview transcripts. Some key themes stood out as prominent in the interview responses. Identifying these key themes was the beginning of the process of data analysis and formulation of findings. Here I discuss two key findings before outlining the concepts that are considered in more depth in the following chapters.

The first key finding here was that in both programs in Northern Ireland and Australia, when asked, "Do you think music/dance has been a useful tool for your involvement in peacebuilding?" all of the young people interviewed said it had. For example, some of them responded:

> Hell yeah, for sure.
> Well like it's been good for me . . . and for others.
> Yeah, it has.
> Uh, yeah definitely, definitely.
> Um yeah uh I think so, yeah.
> Yeah, yes.
> Yeah, definitely.

With these responses the youth participants themselves established and confirmed that they saw music as a valuable tool for youth participation in peace work.

The second key finding here was that most of the youth participants in my case studies would not have attended a peacebuilding workshop that did not involve music or dance; it was the draw card for their involvement. They were not interested in nor did they see the point of attending something passive or irrelevant to their lives. When asked whether he would have attended a peacebuilding program without music or dance, one young man illustrated this point by saying he would be uninterested in attending a program where youth would be expected to

> like sit down in a room and like, talk about peace, like you know you go to church on a Sunday.

Instead he wanted something different and interactive, and for him and most of the young people involved, music was what made the program relevant to their lives. Another young man shared similar sentiments, saying:

> It would just be . . . like talking and that . . . I like to mix stuff together, so I probably wouldn't. I'd probably go for just like the first session and like that's it.

Even one young woman who had been involved in other non-music–based peace initiatives in the past felt music was now the best way she could take part:

> No, it would have to involve music. Because being a guitarist now, I absolutely love it. Anything to do with music is just bring it on!

Most young people attended the program primarily because they were interested in the music participation rather than peacebuilding. However, for most of them, their experience at the program led to several outcomes that imply successful paths to peacebuilding. So these first key findings establish my main argument that music can be a useful way to engage young people in peacebuilding. In the following chapters I explore *how* and *why* music can be a useful tool for engaging youth in peacebuilding. Here the main point is that while many participants initially came solely to seek leisure activities, in the end—through engaging with other young people from different cultures, genders, and backgrounds—most participants developed an awareness of and commitment to building peace in their communities. Music was simply the vehicle needed to take them there.

4

Building Peace Through a Musical Dialogue

In recent years, many scholars of peace studies have agreed that dialogue is crucial to building peace and responding to global problems.[1] However, important questions remain about the meanings and parameters of dialogue and how it might take place. Etymologically, the term is of Greek origin, deriving from *dia* ("through") and *logos* ("the word" or "meaning").[2] Bohm argues that this conjunction of terms brings to mind "a stream of meaning flowing among and through two or more, out of which will emerge some new understanding, something creative." While this could lend itself to many interpretations in peacebuilding, dialogue is most often associated with a verbal process,[3] including conversation and negotiation. Nonetheless, it is likely that other ways of conducting dialogue exist and that these can also be mobilized for peacebuilding purposes.

Indeed, our understandings of dialogue in the peace studies field need broadening to be more inclusive of those, including youth, who might be more willing or able to participate in peacebuilding through alternative modes of dialogue. In this chapter I explore the possibilities of music as an alternative method for youth to engage in a dialogue for peace. Given its appeal and accessibility to young people, music may offer an appropriate way to engage youth in creating new dialogues for peace and thus encouraging the formation of a culture of peace. To be clear, I am not suggesting that music is some instant fix to alleviate all the issues associated with spoken dialogue. Rather, its addition to the repertoire of dialogue for peacebuilding may aid in opening up more spaces for participation by offering alternative frameworks for expressing, sharing, and creating meaning.

In the peacebuilding context, the term "dialogue" tends to be used to connote formal political negotiations taking place in the international arena. This frequently involves two or more parties talking to each other to communicate their issues and directly address their differences through workshops, diplomacy, and/or conferences. The process is usually framed as a kind of debate or contest of ideas, which may certainly have a role to play in peacebuilding.

At the same time, some scholars suggest that dialogue can be conducted in a less antagonistic framework that encourages other ways of talking. Scholars supporting narrative approaches to reconciliation see the oral "telling" and "retelling" of stories as vital to rebuilding society after conflict.[4] For example, according to Senehi and Byrne's research, storytelling connects people across the peace process in divided societies such as Northern Ireland.[5] The stories of each participant are accorded value, rather than seeking to have one viewpoint eventually triumph over another. Participants are encouraged to construct new narratives or stories together in order to transform their conflict. Narrative approaches are thus based on a different view of dialogue, yet they also remain focused on speech.

Oral dialogue can be valuable, but several challenges exist. For example, frameworks that envision dialogue as a tool for "resolving" conflict by creating shared meaning may leave no room for ongoing contradiction in the views of parties to a conflict.[6] Parties may find some issues impossible to agree on. In short, frameworks that seek to use verbal dialogue to create a shared story may offer little utility in some aspects of conflict.[7] Likewise, engaging authentically in dialogue requires acknowledging that conflict will remain. So, instead of being solely about pursuing mutual agreement, dialogue can also be envisioned as way of building understanding and seeking ways of living with difference that do not hinge on resolving all issues.

Given the limits of language, conceptualizing dialogue as only comprised of verbal processes also raises serious issues of inclusivity. For one thing, verbal dialogue places significantly different expectations on the participants. Parties from marginalized cultural and language groups may find their experiences and views inexpressible in the dominant language. They may remain silent, especially when the dialogue is conducted on such terms.[8] When it comes to verbal discussions, some modes of communication tend to be privileged over others, reflecting existing power arrangements, which may be unjust. For example, certain discourses are accorded privilege, and the use of related "legitimate language" is seen as requisite for engaging in discussion.[9] But legitimacy is frequently based on what is dominant, so some people experience unfair difficulties in getting meanings across in situations where "legitimate" discourses are expected yet remain inaccessible to them. In short, if one is unable to "talk the talk" of the privileged class, s/he may be marginalized entirely from the conversation.

Hostility is also expressed nonverbally,[10] so nonverbal communications clearly deserve recognition when aiming to address conflict. After all, people can use conversation to engage in meaningful exchange of thoughts and feelings, but actions and attitudes are also important.[11] Moreover, since language does not constitute the borders of cognition, certain sorts of meaning are beyond the reaches of language.[12]

Likewise, I suggest that to encompass more inclusive mechanisms for sharing meaning(s), a definition of dialogue ought to include nonverbal methods of communication, such as music. Thus I use the concept of dialogue broadly, to refer to any situation where two or more people use nonviolent methods to express and exchange meanings. This includes dialogues that involve both music and verbal processes, such as those that were apparent in my case studies.

Many scholars, practitioners, and policymakers have suggested that arts and music can foster and encourage dialogue, promoting positive social change.[13] If some people, based on social hierarchies and language abilities, are unable to participate in a spoken dialogue in a way that is fair and inclusive, perhaps in at least some cases music may offer them another method for contributing. Indeed, some scholars have suggested that music may have an important role to play in communicating across difference, since it requires no translation.[14]

The notation for reading and writing music is internationally recognized, so it is no surprise that music is often said to be a language that crosses borders. For this reason, music may indeed provide a more inviting tool for reconciliation. Music frequently includes lyrics sung in particular spoken languages, but the meaning of the music itself also influences how this is understood. Likewise, people may be able to "understand" or enjoy the same music even when they do not speak the same language.

Using music is one way of applying common understanding and knowledge as tools for peacebuilding. This is particularly applicable and important to young people's participation in a dialogue for peace. Many young people may not feel comfortable in addressing conflict through more traditional forms of dialogue, but youth have often seen music as a way to express themselves, get involved, and at times just to have something to do. However, music can be much more than this. Youth have used hip-hop music, for example, to communicate with one another in a way that is relevant and interesting, and this has been central to political organizing around conflict mediation and other issues.[15] Indeed, hip-hop's expressive practices have spawned the saying "fight with creativity and not with weapons."[16] The potential of hip-hop thus provokes curiosity about the role music may play in addressing conflict among youth by serving as an alternative form of nonviolent dialogue. While most writing on youth, music, and politics focuses on hip-hop, other types of music enjoyed by youth in a setting may have similar potential.

Music can be understood as located in the borderlands between verbal and nonverbal communication. After all, music frequently incorporates elements of both, and the meaning music conveys is often a complex melding of the two. Music may thus be uniquely placed to provide new insights, offering an alternative and a supplement to exclusively verbal linguistic understandings of dialogue. Dialogue is most often thought of in terms of conversation and debate, but the concept can be pulled apart and expanded to better address the needs of peacebuilders in diverse contexts. Doing so may aid in developing peacebuilding practices that are more inclusive and accessible to a diverse range of participants, especially youth.

Music-Making as an Alternative Form of Dialogue

In both case studies youth participants and facilitators reported seeing music and dance as creative, accessible ways to engage in dialogue across difference. These differences may be based on race, gender, or religion, for example. In any case, interviewees often noted the importance of music in drawing people together when they would otherwise remain unwilling or unable to engage in dialogue. This understanding of dialogue contrasts with more traditional, limited definitions of dialogue as speech or purely linguistic exchanges. Examining these experiences makes the case for developing a broader understanding of what may be understood as musical dialogue, where youth exchange meaning through music.

While people living with conflict may be reluctant to come together to engage in formal dialogue (especially if they have failed in the past), they may be more willing or open to take part in a kind of musical dialogue. This was apparent in Breaking Barriers' work in the Northern Ireland context, where a variety of world music styles and instruments were used in interactive music-making sessions in the youth peacebuilding programs. Music in these cases is a form of dialogue—participants are *sharing* their meanings through the music rather than, for example, playing or listening to music alone in their bedrooms. This capacity of music to draw people together to communicate may at times make it a more accessible form of dialogue than more traditional verbal forms of dialogue.

Engaging through music enables the young people to "explain" themselves with confidence, as this is a mode of dialogue that is not predicated on notions of intelligence that value years of education or "wisdom" over their daily lived experience. There is, then, a deemphasizing of rational, academic modes of intelligence and a shift to the kind of knowledge that the youth participants in these programs feel they possess and can deploy well without the need for extensive formal training or previous experience. This is not to say that words are never included in the music-making or performance process; rather that they need not always be seen as primary or be delivered in a conventional fashion. While the youth participants may often feel they do not have the words to say what they mean, they are able to creatively convey their message through these alternative means in a way that is effective and equally, if not more, descriptive. As one participant and one facilitator reported in the Australian program:

> Through your music you express a story . . . as well through dances you can express it and they pick up the story and understand what you're telling them. (Samoan/Maori female, 13)

> It's better . . . than talking. . . . You feel . . . more comfortable. . . . It's a different way of creating dialogue. . . . [L]ike . . . I've had this fear of . . . public speaking. . . . I sing . . . it's much . . . easier and you can just embrace the music and just be in that moment and . . . just express yourself freely . . . (Samoan/German female from New Zealand, 25)

Many of the peacebuilders I met in Northern Ireland also saw music as a different way to get a message across, to engage in dialogue. According to many of the people with whom I spoke, music is a particularly effective mechanism for pursuing peace through dialogue, as it is a mode of expression that is more inclusive than many other ways of conveying a message. As some of the youth participants I interviewed explained:

> Music's one language. . . . In any language it all means the same thing. Through music [you] can say so much

> cuz the different moods and textures and sounds that come with it and all the different sounds from different cultures can be combined . . . like [Project Movement] from [Breaking Barriers] actually shows all the music can be combined . . . to make you know one language . . . that everyone can listen to. Everyone understands. (White Northern Irish Protestant female, 17)

> It's just a good medium because everybody, no matter where they're from or what religion or race . . . can all like relate to music . . . (White Northern Irish Protestant male, 16)

Furthermore, while programs focusing on traditional modes of dialogue may leave people who are more quiet or shy feeling they have not fully participated, the interactive use of music in these projects is more likely to leave participants feeling they have taken part in the dialogue. It seems clear that the interactive nature of the music programs make them a useful means of engaging young people in peacebuilding through dialogue. As two of the facilitators said:

> It isn't being done in a classroom, you're not being told . . . not to do it . . . it's not boring. It's something that they can come away and think . . . I played an instrument . . . from like a Chinese background . . . and we all sat in the same room and we played instruments . . . they can come away . . . saying, "You know we're able to sit in a room and do that, and why are we not outside?" (White Northern Irish Protestant female, 21)

> [Y]ou have to do something interactive . . . they're . . . having a sort of feeling that they are contributing all together to one piece of music or one piece of dance. . . . For dance, for example . . . if you're going to choreograph it, everybody has their role but you have to create a sense of collective thinking in those groups. (Mexican female, 31)

Music and dance can also be used to bring together previously segregated communities. Many of the young people in both the Australian and Northern Irish programs joined the peacebuilding programs because they wanted to take part in music and dance workshops, and through doing so, they came to interact with and know young people from groups many had previously seen in a negative light and thus avoided. In this way, music, which plays a key role in youth culture in the areas, helped bring these young people together. The workshop activities may thus be understood as opportunities for dialogue based on respect for difference as well as an alternative way of looking for commonality. While engaging with youth from different backgrounds did not occur on the same scale at Breaking Barriers in Northern Ireland, young people there did interact with or receive instruction from adults from different cultural origins, which could have some influence on the way they understand communicating across cultural difference.

In both case studies participants and facilitators saw music as an inclusive mechanism for communicating across difference and therefore engaging in a peacebuilding dialogue. However, I wanted to learn what limits might exist to this. In the Northern Ireland context, when I asked the facilitators if they thought any youth who were different in some way (for example, gay, disabled, or from another cultural group) would have trouble fitting into the project, all of them mentioned thinking of music as a useful way to engage in a more inclusive dialogue:

> [E]veryone can understand music and enjoy music. So . . . as a facilitator we have to include them as well. I have to recognize these kinds of situations and try . . . (Colombian female, 31)

> I think obviously at the start no matter what . . . everyone's gonna be quite . . . aware of everyone else around them . . . that's wherever you go . . . once people relax and see everyone else having fun, and . . . not caring about anything else, they surely start unwinding and

> doing it as well. (White Northern Irish Protestant female, 21)

A couple of the youth participants in Northern Ireland offered more caveats, giving possible reasons, including lack of confidence or disability, why other youth might feel left out of a musical dialogue for peace. Likewise, in the Australian project, two interviewees noted that people who are nervous might have trouble at first. So, rather than saying these young people might feel excluded based on being different, the issue was seen in terms of people who had problems with shyness or lack of confidence, not any exclusion in the space or the practice. However, more research needs to be undertaken with young people who have left such programs or decided against attending them to find out what barriers to inclusion might exist to engaging youth in peacebuilding through a musical dialogue.

Music as a Nonviolent Form of Dialogue for Dealing with Conflict

Verbal dialogue has traditionally been seen as a way to get a message across during a conflict without resorting to violence. Music can also meet this criterion for dialogue. Youth participants in both case studies learned nonviolent skills they could use for dealing with conflict. While it may be unconventional, using music as dialogue during conflict may in some circumstances be both gratifying and productive. After all, conflict often evokes intense physical feelings, and music may offer a chance to express and adapt feelings such as anger through physical musical expressions rather than by taking part in direct violence. This may be especially important for young people such as those attending Third Place (Australia), who live in some of the most violent communities in their region. For example, one young woman pointed out how dance and music could both provide alternatives to getting into a physical altercation:

> For dance you can just express your anger in your body and for singing you can express your anger in writing a

> song or writing a rap. (Black African Sudanese female, 15)

Some of the young people involved in the crumping program expressed how their participation in this dance style in particular had equipped them with alternative ways of responding to conflict:

> When they get in my face, I like crump . . . until they like, the relationship is of respect, respect you and not fight or something. (Black African Liberian male, 16)

> . . . [I]t's been good for me . . . and for others cuz . . . crumping's like replacing fight, so yeah, that's why I like it cuz it just replaces the bad stuff. (Samoan/Maori male, 14)

This makes sense, as crumping, also known as krumping, originated in South Central Los Angeles as an alternative to involvement in gang violence.[17] One young woman who had worked as a crumping instructor echoed these sentiments, saying:

> [T]he crumping does help. . . . Cuz . . . I remember once the boys just saying yeah that they used to fight, but now they just solve their problems by crumping. . . . Battle each other. . . . But you don't actually have to fight. (Samoan/Chinese female from New Zealand, 18)

Her comment points to the need for considerations of gender that require serious attention in the field of youth peacebuilding. It seems that while hegemonic norms of masculinity as violent may be "proven" through skill in battle, young men involved in the crumping project have decided to enter a new battle arena, one where their skills are demonstrated through dance-offs rather than through fighting. While in other arenas boys may gain respect through being the best fighter, here they do so by being dancers with amazing command of technical skills, which facilitates building better relationships based on this respect. In short, crumping may be used as an alternative, nonviolent means for dealing with conflict.

This is particularly interesting, because rather than the role accorded to physical strength in fighting, respect in crumping may be attainable through means that can include others, such as girls and smaller boys. However, it should be noted that while this is a possibility, no girls took part in the crumping stream of the Third Space workshops in Australia. Interviews revealed that several girls were interested in participating in crumping, but did not feel the group was open to them as young women. This kind of exclusion clearly must be addressed if such projects are to be truly inclusive and pursue positive peace that includes gender justice.

While dancing was not a part of the work of Breaking Barriers in Northern Ireland, the physicality of music work also came up as a way of dealing with conflict without perpetrating violence against others. As one girl explained,

> If there's a drum and they'd hit the drum . . . with music like if I'm angry I would just go listen to some music and it would calm me down and. . . . I just think it would help you through. (Northern Irish Catholic female, 13)

Moreover, among the major things many youth participants specifically learned were skills that could be used in responding to conflict without violence. At Third Place when I asked participants if they had learned any skills that could help them in this way, all but one answered in the affirmative. All the facilitators interviewed in this project also felt that they had learned or taught some skills that could be used nonviolently in situations of conflict.

Similar results appeared at Breaking Barriers, as nine out of 13 young people and all four facilitators interviewed had a positive response when asked, "What skills, if any, have you learned/taught in this project that can help you address future conflict nonviolently?" All but one of the young people interviewed said they would use the skills they had gained through the workshops to make peace. Examples they gave included telling others what they had learned or teaching others. Facilitators also said they had gained skills and knowledge they would use to continue to make peace. When asked what they had learned or taught, they said:

> The capacity to be flexible. . . . I think that everyone has the capacity to do music. (Colombian female, 31)

> . . . I think having an understanding and the confidence to just . . . explain to people. People sort of know . . . but that's just one side of the story you know . . . (White Northern Irish Protestant male, 31)

> A lot of people use violence . . . and to kind of explain to kids, yeah a lot of people use violence to communicate, but that's not the way. (White Northern Irish Protestant female, 21)

> [P]eople will learn that . . . you can talk about [how] to manage your emotions. . . . [Y]ou can channelize that through dance or music. . . . [S]ometimes, some teenagers they're just passing through a difficult stage, and you have a choice . . . just wandering on the streets or maybe . . . learn to play the drums or learn to play an instrument or dance. . . . [Y]ou are giving them . . . options and let them know they have options in life . . . and you don't have to conform with . . . everybody. . . . [T]he important part is showing people that they have a choice. (Mexican female, 31)

While four participants in the Breaking Barriers program, all young Protestant men, could not name any skills they had gained for dealing with conflict nonviolently, each of them responded in the affirmative when asked whether they thought the program can help reduce or has already reduced the violence in their local community. Two of these four did preface their answer by saying a reduction in violence could only occur if more people got involved and if this occurred across (both Protestant and Catholic) communities.

In summary, there is evidence that these programs in Australia and Northern Ireland have contributed in different and important ways to promoting a nonviolent dialogue through music. They have taught young people nonviolent skills they can deploy when faced with conflict, and they have also provided an alternative activity to taking part in fighting.

Returning to Talk-Based Dialogue

By participating in the alternative dialogue of the music-based peacebuilding programs, the youth were also able to gain trust and build verbal skills that could then be used in more traditional forms of dialogue. While I propose widening conceptions of dialogue to include music, I am not suggesting that dialogue as talk should be rejected as a tool. The peacebuilding programs in these case studies, whether they intend to or not, appear to provide a training ground where young people can develop their verbal linguistic skills and abilities. Although they acknowledged the importance of music and dance as alternative modes of expression, the participants and facilitators also expressed their belief in the importance of more traditional modes of dialogue for peacebuilding. Several young people indicated that participation in the project had helped them develop trust and enhance their verbal skills and ability to engage in spoken dialogue. One participant mentioned benefits from the opportunity in the workshops to practice English, which was a second language for many participants in the program. Two arts workers also reported learning about "talking things out" before resorting to violence.

When asked, "Do you feel being involved in this project will make it easier for you to be formally involved in peacebuilding in the future?" all interviewees responded that it would. In response to queries of how the project would facilitate involvement, some pointed directly to the skills they had learned that would enable them to talk more easily to others:

> Yeah it's helped me a lot cuz I've been able to talk to people and to dance together . . . (White Australian male, 14)

> Yeah, it's helped me, helped me with group work . . . and socially, talking to other people. (White Australian male, 16)

> [I]t helps me to have more confidence to be able to talk to others and get along with others and understand . . . how people think so I don't have to be so uncomfortable around other people and same with them around me. (White Australian male, 17)

Interestingly, when asked how the workshops may have prepared them for future involvement in peacebuilding, the only participants at Third Place who mentioned improved talking abilities were young white males born in Australia. While I cannot conclusively explain this, it does suggest the need for further study on young people's understandings of what peacebuilding is or should be and how this relates to race and gender.

In the Northern Ireland program, three of the 13 participants interviewed said they had learned improved communication skills, with two boys specifically mentioning talking, and one girl listing communication in her response. Also, when asked about why music might be a useful tool for young people wanting to engage in building peace, one young man said:

> Yeah . . . Cuz you can have something comfortable for talking to people. (White Northern Irish Protestant male, 14)

In other words, he suggests that music helps put people at ease talking to one another when they might otherwise feel unable to do so. Finally, when asked whether and how they might use the skills they had gained through the project to continue to make peace, some of the young people mentioned talking about what they had learned:

> Just having the confidence to talk to people about like what they're about and who they are and . . . just like especially learning about people, about like where they

> come from and how they grew up and what their life was like before they came here. (White Northern Irish Protestant male, 16)

> Just talk to them. (White Northern Irish Catholic male, 13)

> And tell them, learn stuff. (White Northern Irish Catholic female, 13)

Part of this ability to engage in more traditional dialogue is clearly based on confidence built through participation in music-making. In her answer to another question, one young woman pointed out how the confidence participants had built left them better able to engage in traditional modes of dialogue:

> Like if we were to . . . go on stage . . . and play in front of friends and family it takes confidence no matter what the kids are doing, be it slapping the drums, you know, with their friends, they're creating confidence . . . even with their communication with other kids, life skills. (White Northern Irish Protestant female, 17)

While music was seen as a useful way to engage in alternative modes of dialogue, many long-term community workers in Northern Ireland acknowledged that talking is also important. Some specifically noted that their work in music had helped ease their way into discussions. One such community worker told me about how being part of a music community as a young man enabled him to meet people across the political divide and talk about issues. He saw similar opportunities being created through the work of Breaking Barriers with local young people.

Likewise, the assistant project manager at Breaking Barriers mentioned that:

> Music and dance can be . . . something you can get involved in and can be united with other people. It's a

> common ground where you start talking. . . . Music is something that even with a stranger it's a kind of common ground between you, so you can talk about music. You can talk about dance. . . . Even if you're not talking about serious issues, you're still interacting. (White Northern Irish Protestant female, 21)

Perhaps this type of interaction is a means to pave the way for talking about more "serious" or contentious issues. Trust is an essential element to be developed in transforming conflict. These findings suggest that music workshops may be used to build trust that can facilitate more traditional engagement in dialogue. As one community worker put it:

> Music recognizes no cultural boundaries or barriers. It was that commonality that was a vehicle for trust and eventually friendship. . . . Music and art are the means of bringing people together in a common aim where suspicion is diminished and trust building is a feature.

Moreover, one Breaking Barriers facilitator, who has lived and worked in several conflict areas around the world, noted how music can be a way of engaging people to build trust, saying:

> [I]n working with communities . . . there are many . . . sensitive issues that sometimes you have to discuss with different communities and it's very, very difficult to make them come personally. . . . But if we start preparing the line, as we say in Colombia, and we engage with people first and then we sit down . . . they can be engaged with music. (Colombian female, 31)

In the MEC programs in particular, young people were encouraged to discuss issues of global development and inequality. In the workshop series I observed, after watching a musical documentary film excerpt about money, the youth participants were separated into groups to discuss their initial reactions and write down key words, which a leader from each small group then shared with the wider group. Many of them talked about feeling sad, angry, sorry, or guilty about the issues discussed in the film, which included, among other things, child labor and sweatshops. They were also asked to come up with ways they would address the issues. Their suggested actions included protesting, boycotting, contacting government leaders, and making different consumer choices. In this way, they were participating by using traditional communication while still in the music workshop.

In summary, participants and facilitators in both case studies agreed that while different modes of engaging are important and should be accepted and supported, talk-based dialogue is important, too. What is particularly intriguing here is that according to the youth and facilitators interviewed, these alternative forms of engagement can actually serve as a means for participants to build trust that is necessary for taking part in more traditional formats and for developing skills and confidence that allow them to improve their participation in such discussions.

Outcomes: Expanding Dialogue for Peace

Findings from these studies suggest that music can also be a useful way of engaging and encouraging members of the wider community to take part in dialogue for peacebuilding. The fact that many youth felt these musical peacebuilding programs gave them an opportunity to engage in dialogue is important on its own merits. However, the potential for expanding upon what these programs have started is also significant. When asked whether they would continue to use the skills they had gained at the workshops to make peace, the youth involved offered several responses indicating that they would share the artistic skills they had gained, use their improved speech abilities to talk about what they had learned, promote the growth of the project by inviting others along, and use the knowledge of peace practice they had gained to try to spread peace in a wider context. In short, music and dance in this case were seen as a draw card to engage effectively in a new and creative form of dialogue for peace, and as a relevant way to encourage other people to take part in peacebuilding.

Interviewees suggested that music and dance were modes of communication that could be expressed and understood even across languages, cultures, and religions. From these understandings, several young people and facilitators at Third Place explained how they see music and dance as a mode of cross-cultural dialogue that provides the kind of meaningful engagement required to build more peaceful societies. For example:

> [D]ancing and singing is the best way to show to the world what's your message. . . . It's easier to do than if you talk with somebody. If you talk with somebody that doesn't . . . respect you or something, he won't listen, but if you [get] crazy and start dancing and singing he will start listening. . . . Music and dance just got something inside it that like bring you there. . . . It's . . . trying to get [the] message across . . . It doesn't matter what religion. . . . No matter what you are, how you do, whatever, you can do dance and singing . . . (White Slovenian female, 18)

At both programs I observed several instances in which people unfamiliar with the project happened by or intentionally came to a performance and ended up speaking to participants or facilitators or getting involved in some way. I asked facilitators at both programs, "Is there anything you think is unique to music and dance that can be particularly useful in engaging people outside the program?" They all agreed that there is:

> . . . I think music's the easiest; it's accessible you know . . . if you wanna engage it's a very easy tool . . . (White Northern Irish Protestant male, 31)

> I find that it's easy because people love music . . . if you kind of measure that with just running a peacebuilding

> workshop without music, I'm not sure if the general public would be actually interested in . . . like if you're gonna create a ten-page document . . . more likely to be drawn to the music. (Samoan/German female from New Zealand, 25)

Interviewees at both programs also suggested that talk-based dialogue has an important role to play in engaging others in building cultures of peace. When asked whether and how they would use the skills they had learned to continue to make peace in their communities, participants in Australia and Northern Ireland said they would do so by talking to other youth about the work they had done to get them involved. Some of them had the following to say:

> . . . Yeah. I'll tell them. I wanna spread the word about this [Third Place] because it can . . . help you . . . if you feel like you don't fit in. . . . It can help you change your life and become confident. . . . I've told gobs of people! . . . They wanna come next year. I know a lot of my friends are coming cuz I've told them about it. (Maori female, 13)

> Yeah I think . . . like giving people music and . . . talk to them. Because people who are like violent have no real reason to be violent. . . . If it comes out of them, they just might be . . . nicer people. . . . I told . . . A class and C class. (Northern Irish Catholic female, 13)

> Yeah . . . we could even get . . . everyone together and like tell them about it and then ask if they wanted to do it . . . (White Northern Irish Protestant male, 14)

In summary, based on their participation in musical peacebuilding, youth in these programs became inspired to share their ideas and experience with other young people. This form of peer education can play an integral role in recruiting more youth to work for peacebuilding. These young peacebuilders may also use their musical expression and related skills to communicate with adults and the wider community in seeking to create a dialogue about peace.

Acknowledging the Limitations

Of course, not all uses of music will constitute an act of dialogue. Sometimes people may merely be listening for enjoyment, not really paying attention, or even engaging in a leisure activity in the same location as others with whom they have conflict without interacting with them. The activities for engaging young people in building positive peace vary across the programs I researched, with some seeming to be undeniably promoting dialogue, while others might not. For example, the young people who came to Third Place and sat at their own at tables drawing while others sang and danced together would probably not feel they had taken part in a dialogue; whereas youth who collaborated with others from different cultural backgrounds in creating a song or dance would probably feel they had experienced dialogue through music. However, even activities that do not promote a peace dialogue may at times aid in building skills that can better enable the youth participants to engage in dialogue in the future should they choose to do so.

It is important to make clear that the claims made here are, for the most part, based on what interviewees said, and sometimes what people say is different from what they do. Moreover, as it provides no comparison with youth programs using other methods to engage in peacebuilding, this research design does not allow me to claim that the particular changes would only have occurred in a music-based program. Indeed, I do not suggest that music is the only way such changes may take place, nor do I argue that it will always be the best medium for engaging young people in peacebuilding. Music is not inherently peaceful and therefore can be used to confirm exclusive or xenophobic identities. Thus, in at least some instances, it may be necessary to combine musical participation with other activities that critically engage more directly with issues of injustice.

The evidence of the effect of these musical peacebuilding projects remains limited. However, there is some evidence to suggest that these programs have facilitated long-term continuation of dialogue across difference in the lives of some youth. For example, in interviewing long-term and former participants at Third Place, I found evidence that many had continued participating in this dialogue for peace, as they had made and maintained friendships across cultural difference, whereas prior to the program they had not engaged in relationships with people outside their own cultures. Finally, it bears repeating that the focus of this research is not on evaluating the impact of these individual programs, but rather on looking at what they are doing, what they are hoping, what they are saying, and seeking to gain whatever limited evidence is available about the possible impacts.

Conclusion

Scholars in international relations and peace studies have pointed to the prime importance of dialogue in building peace. Still, going further to interrogate our assumptions about this concept is necessary. "Dialogue" is frequently discussed in highly theoretical terms without an in-depth consideration of practical challenges. Responses from the young people interviewed in this project suggest that our scholarly conceptualizations of dialogue need to be understood much more broadly than current scholarship allows, particularly (but not only) in order to improve the inclusion of young people in peacebuilding processes. Moreover, while most youth may not have the training or interest required for engaging in more formal, conventional modes of political peacebuilding, many have years of experience in music-making, so employing such resources is useful in acknowledging and building on the skills young people already have that can be applied to their work as peace-makers.

In the two case studies presented here, youth participants and facilitators, through their words and actions, demonstrated several ways that music can serve as an important form of dialogue for pursuing peace. First, the young people interviewed for this research suggested that music can be important in providing alternative modes of expression and dialogue, which can play a vital role in dealing with conflict and facilitating communication across difference. Moreover, many youth participants expressed the feeling that they could use music or skills they had learned through music-making when faced with conflict instead of resorting to violence.

While acknowledging the potential of music to support alternative forms of dialogue, interviewees also recognized the relevance of and need for more traditional modes of dialogue. Many explained that participating in music-based activities offered them a chance to practice and improve their skills in traditional dialogue. These musical peacebuilding programs are important for the youth directly involved, but they can also have a broader impact, as music is particularly useful for conveying the young people's message in a way that encourages the development of a culture of peace by engaging people "in the outside world" in a dialogue for peace. Furthermore, many participants said they had or would tell others about their musical activities to try to get more people involved in work promoting a culture of peace through music. Not all music activities will constitute an act or dialogue, nor will they all promote peace, but these findings suggest that musical activities can be a relevant and effective way to engage youth in a dialogue for peace.

5

Shifting Identities, Performing Peace

The chance to challenge conflict identities is another important outcome that may emerge from, or alongside, the musical dialogue just discussed. This is important because identity is a key issue in resolving or transforming conflicts. Many have posited that issues of identity often fuel conflict and that greater understanding of the "other" (and/or a deconstruction of the self/other divide) is essential for building peaceful societies. Given its strong association with identity, music may have a powerful role to play in altering notions of identity at the individual and collective level. Participation in music and dance activities offers opportunities for (re)producing and revising identities, both of individuals and groups, and of self and others. While music is not inherently geared toward creating more peaceful identities, it may have a role to play in strategies aiming to build peace through identity work. By offering the chance to perform alternative understandings of identity for self and engaging with others, music may help parties to envision different understandings of themselves and others. If these identities differ from previous conceptions associated with conflict, this work could facilitate peacebuilding.

Moreover, given the central role of music in young people's understandings of their identities as well as those of others, it appears especially likely to offer a relevant framework for engaging youth in identity-based peacebuilding work. Participation in music and dance activities can offer opportunities for young people to work on their identities in ways conducive to the construction of sustainable positive peace through (re) producing and revising identities, allowing them to see individuals and groups differently. For example, they may see themselves as more confident, peaceful, open, or engaged, and, at the same time, may see others in a new light that contrasts with previously held negative stereotypes.

Identity in Peace and Conflict

Identity has been seen as central both to the generation and continuation of conflict.[1] For example, Baily argues that cultural identity issues will likely be among the serious problems humans will have to address in the 21st century.[2] Other scholars have proposed that identity has been a cause of many recent wars.[3] In particular, several scholars and popular commentators have focused attention on the potential for differences in ethnic identity to lead to conflict.[4] These scholars who focus on "ethnic conflict" often understand ethnic difference as essential to the conflict(s) in question and tend to assume this difference is either the cause or, at minimum, one cause of the conflict. In international relations scholarship concerning conflict, this view is often linked with the "ancient ethnic hatreds" approach, which suggests that little can be done to alleviate conflict in areas where different group identities are assumed to be the cause of the conflict.

Such a reading is too simplistic, not taking into account the complex role that identity plays in conflict dynamics. For one thing, definitions of ethnic difference are difficult to formulate and continue to inspire ongoing debate. Ethnic identity can be based on a wide variety of characteristics, with a combination of indicators such as religion, language, location, skin color, or history. Moreover, identity in and of itself is clearly not the causal factor in conflict—rather, particular understandings and expressions of identity may certainly fuel conflicts. Mueller argues that the very concept of "ethnic conflict" could be terribly mistaken, as it implies a conflict by all members of an ethnic group against enemies who include everyone in another ethnic group. He conducted a careful examination of conflicts in Yugoslavia and Rwanda, which have both been frequently characterized as ethnic conflicts resulting from possible ancient ethnic hatreds. However, based on the evidence uncovered in his research, Mueller proposes that both cases could be more accurately conceptualized as wars led by small groups, often criminals, claiming to be fighting in the name of a larger body, even though their views were not representative. These conflicts were not inevitable and were not necessarily based on ethnic difference; instead ethnicity was the trait perpetrators used to recruit and organize themselves. Other scholars contradict claims that differences in identity cause conflict. Berdal, for example, investigated Yugoslavia and its common classification as an identity conflict. In doing so he pointed out that adversarial cooperation still took place there during the conflict, often in well-organized ways and over long periods of time.[5]

I am not suggesting that identity is not important in conflicts; it most certainly is. At the same time, I agree with Mueller's claim that identity factors such as ethnicity can be better understood "as an ordering device than as an impelling force."[6] In other words, identity itself does not cause conflicts. However, people are often called to participation in conflict by appealing to their sense of identity and/or suggesting that the "enemy" seeks to challenge or obliterate it. In this sense, it is not the presence of difference in itself that leads to violent conflict; rather, conflict is fueled by the dangerous insertion of such difference into particular political allegiances "and the politicization of ethnic identities."[7] Political leaders may thus use ethnic difference to mobilize people to participate in violent conflict. These differences may then be drawn upon in the continuation of conflict, as asserting group identity may become attractive to people when they are experiencing insecurity, since doing so may enable them to make sense out of what is occurring. Violent conflict may also coincide with a suspension of thinking, particularly self-critical thought, as members of a group may identify themselves with a larger effort in conflict and reject the selfhood of others they identify as enemies.[8] In fact, studies of war across cultures suggest that there is a common tendency to seek to build greater unity within a group while dehumanizing members of other groups who are seen as enemies.[9] The development of such a heightened and exclusionary sense of group identity can make conflict more difficult to address.[10]

Negotiating identity often remains a challenge in post-conflict scenarios. After all, conflict transforms perceptions of self and others, and prejudice is also connected to notions of self and others.[11] Indeed, negative stereotyping can become pervasive in extremely tense situations,[12] such as war or ongoing conflicts. This kind of stereotyping can be used to delegitimize an opposing group and thereby justify violence. Dehumanization through stereotyping does not end merely because direct violence ceases; if former enemies are not able to see others as real people, reconciliation can be obstructed.[13] This can lead to a vicious cycle, as the parties remain segregated, which can further fuel conflict. Cultural isolation can likewise breed stereotypes and encourage exaggeration of the perceived negative characteristics of the "other."[14]

While identity can be an important aspect of conflict, it is also central to the production of peace.[15] Thus, more attention is needed to uncover prospects for developing nonviolent frameworks for interacting across difference. Here I am referring especially to differences associated with identity, such as race, religion, and nationality that have been used to define and differentiate groups and individuals in a way that supports conflict. Seeking to build peace, however, need not be about erasing differences in identity; instead it can involve working to build nonviolent identities or at least challenging the violent or exclusionary aspects of existing identities. Peacebuilding projects must therefore seek to create relationships through enabling adversaries to come together and to challenge existing identities built on prejudice and/or violence. Through such work participants may be able to challenge the engrained identities they associate with the "other."

Musical Responses to Conflict

Music and culture may make important contributions to rethinking the role of identity in peacebuilding. I am looking at social identities here as constructed through a process of cultural work or performance in which we are constantly becoming or "doing."[16] Through this lens, performance can offer a space of transformation in which participants "can imagine themselves in new ways, where they can be 'other' and can engage with the different dimensions of themselves."[17]

Acknowledging the potential for such shifts in understanding of self and others is crucial, since creating sustainable cultures of peace requires not just a cessation of direct violence, but changes in attitude toward the other. These attitudinal shifts may begin at an individual level but must also spread to the broader community. A rehumanization of the enemy is required in order to dispel stereotypes and thus reduce the risk of future violence. This need not be about resolving all differences but instead making room for an acceptance or even celebration of what Halpern and Weinstein call "dissonant conjunctions" of identity.[18] This means that people can hold different ideas, understandings, and experiences of who they are but nevertheless share some commonalities with one another as humans. In this way, we might be able to appreciate different identities *in* their difference, rather than seeking to adapt the other into the identities or views we hold ourselves. This concerns something more than mere tolerance of difference; it is about moving toward accepting and valuing difference.

Of course, I am not suggesting that contact between groups or individuals will always, in and of itself, lead to conditions of sustainable positive peace. However, contact is frequently a prerequisite for social change. Indeed, contact is required for communication and likewise for developing, administering, and upholding peace agreements. At the same time, by actively engaging with one another across difference, parties to conflict may have the chance to live and internalize their common ground.[19]

Identity can be developed within and between groups, so the chance to work together on something can be particularly useful for transforming understandings that are competitive or antagonistic. This may be more difficult for some individuals and groups than others. Males, for example, tend to place more importance on identifying through competition and differentiation.[20]

Scholars seeking constructive ways of addressing conflict have proposed that we must learn to "live in harmony."[21] It seems no wonder then that music-based practice could be a useful tool for peacebuilding. A dialogue across difference, after all, is premised on negotiating identity and being able to deal with challenges to particular types of fixed subjectivity.[22] Some have argued that this is about escaping, however briefly, certain ideas about ourselves in order to share with others and communicate across boundaries of difference. However, framing this as a renegotiation of identity is more useful, since we can never escape our identities entirely.

Music may be particularly useful in this regard, because as Frith suggests, identity can be experienced and arguably "most vividly grasped as music."[23] Drawing on Slobin's work, he sees music as providing a sense of self and others and suggests that it can even stimulate "the simultaneous projecting and dissolving of the self in performance."[24] If this is the case, a person engaged in music-based performance may encounter experiences that compel a rethinking of the boundaries between self and others.

Music is integral in the processes through which both personal and collective identities are imagined, formed, represented, confirmed, challenged, deconstructed, and reconstructed, both to audiences and to selves.[25] To that end, DeNora argues that music can be a resource for being, doing, and naming features of social realities, including that of the self.[26] In particular, her research suggests that individuals regularly use music in their ongoing self-creation.

Music can also clearly play an important role in constructing social groups. For one thing, music can influence how people feel about others. It may lead them to feel especially associated with or disconnected from others based on similarities or differences in musical preferences. Moreover, through music, members of social groups identify with others through shared experience and therefore come to know themselves as groups through cultural activity. By making music, the groups do not merely express ideas; they live them.[27] Music-making may also ritualize the reality within the group, thus producing the group and its cultural values.[28] This is a broad claim that cannot be empirically tested, but it seems clear that identity work involves the performance and negotiation of such ideals, and that such work can occur, at least in some instances, through participation in musical activities. While providing opportunities for this, music produces our sense of identity and allows us to experience or "make real" imagined cultural narratives.[29] In the case studies reported on here, for example, individuals from diverse races, ethnicities, and genders do not merely express a need or desire for people to interact across difference—they actually do it, at least in some limited ways.

Youth, Identity, and Music

It is important to consider here what might impact young people's identities in ways that could help in reducing and preventing violence by and against youth. For one thing, levels of self-esteem clearly impact identity (re)creations, including for youth, and therefore affect prospects for conflict or peace. Researchers in the United Kingdom and the United States cite low self-esteem as a predictor of violence or aggression in young people.[30] Some researchers have found this propensity to participation in violence particularly relevant with regards to girls with low self-esteem.[31] At the same time, high levels of exposure to violence in young people have been correlated with lower self-esteem.[32] These results are also noted in adult case studies, with research suggesting that women who experience domestic violence are more likely to develop decreased self-esteem; similarly, adults who have experienced dating violence exhibit lower self-esteem.[33] Lack of self-confidence has also been found to be a risk factor for a young person's becoming a victim of bullying.[34] In summary, the links between violence and self-confidence are complex, but it appears that lack of self-esteem is related to higher rates of both participation in violence and victimization. Young people who develop adequate levels of self-esteem may then be less likely to engage in or fall victim to violence, as they may be more likely to (re) develop identities that are not based on or prone to participation in violent conflict.

Building self-confidence and self-esteem are also important factors for helping young people recover after violent trauma.[35] Research has suggested that creative arts can play a useful role in developing self-acceptance and providing coping skills for girls who have experienced trauma.[36] Some scholars have even posited that increasing personal self-confidence can aid in preventing and controlling violence.[37]

However, a critical analysis would suggest that having a positive self-view is not always conducive to the development of peace. For example, if one's self-esteem is based on being part of a group that is perceived as "better" than others in the social hierarchy, then violence and discrimination may follow. In such cases, work challenging the premises on which that particular aspect of self-worth is based may be needed. Therefore, peacebuilders working with some groups, such as young "white" males, who may exhibit high self-esteem based on their dominance in a social hierarchy, might do well to engage them in questioning the relative value of their whiteness and maleness while supporting the value of other identities. So, the goal of fostering peace might also require some destabilization of confidence in particular situations.

Where does music come in here then? Music is an important part of identity for many young people and is central to many youth cultures. We all start with rhythm, as it characterizes an infant's environment before birth,[38] since the first sound we hear is our mother's heartbeat. From there, children learn the music of their culture as they grow, and the style offers an important link between the young person and his or her culture.[39] Like adults, youth construct their identities through contact with others,[40] and music is often a particularly important part of that contact. In fact, young people often use music to define themselves, their peers, and their wider affiliations.[41] Through music and culture, young people produce representations of their selves and community.[42] For instance, hip-hop culture may enable young people to situate their experience, enabling both identity and community.[43] Youth who take part in hip-hop may use its style in many ways to express themselves, create themselves, and link themselves with other hip-hop lovers. Such work need not be limited to hip-hop alone, although much of the research on music and youth has been conducted in this area because of hip-hop's widespread popularity. Incorporating music into peacebuilding projects may thus provide a relevant and fun framework for young people to engage in identity work for building a culture of peace.

Imagining, Performing, Experiencing New Identities

The empirical evidence collected in my two case studies suggests that participation in music and dance activities can offer opportunities for young people to work on their identities in ways conducive to creating a culture of peace. Youth from both the Australian and Northern Irish programs reported seeing themselves differently in ways that could promote peace. For example, several youth reported they had developed new understandings of themselves as more peaceful or confident. Some of the youth also expressed a desire to be seen differently, and reported that seeing a difference in the way they were viewed by others had a large impact on their self-identities. In both cases the young people's participation led to identity work that could clearly contribute to peacebuilding.

When I asked participants at Third Place in Australia, "How, if at all, has being part of [the project] changed the way you see yourself?" nearly all respondents indicated that participation had changed the way they saw themselves. While responses were varied, several key sub-themes emerged, with young people reporting they felt more peaceful, confident, and in one case, healed. Two youth participants and one arts worker were exceptions, not noting any changes. However, in most cases it appears that participation in music and dance challenged these young people's preconceived identities and broadened their understandings to expose them to new identities.

At Third Place some interviewees said they could see themselves as more peaceful and less prone to violence as a result of taking part in the project. For example, two young male participants in the crumping stream explained that their work in the program had led to such changes:

> It's changed a lot. . . . I used to be sort of like I'm not saying mental . . . but more like [aggressive]. . . . But now I'm more like just calmed down a bit. (Samoan/Maori male, 14)

> Yeah man. . . . Cuz . . . I used to get into a lot of trouble and then I be like chasing that person. . . . And I always come here and I now not do anything, just be friends with them. Like at school crumping and that. (Black African Liberian male, 16)

Other young people in this program also reported changes in sense of identity as linked to feelings of increased self-confidence.

> Yeah. . . . I see myself as like a better person today and more confident in what I'm doing. (Maori female, 13)

> I've got more confidence and . . . things are better now, like I'm not so shamed. Like if you'd've talked to me before this [Third Place] I wouldn't've been talking. Like I'd be too scared. (Samoan/Maori female, 13)

> I guess it just all comes down to self, self-confidence and that. . . . Back then I . . . didn't really have that much confidence. I just had more of a confidence as in like going up to the stage, doing my thing, and if someone doesn't like it say what's up after you know what I mean. [Suggesting he would fight/challenge them] . . . But now you know just it's kinda like self-confidence . . . you know, it's just like kinda like a thing for self help, make yourself beyond that. (Fijian Indian male, 20)

> It's made me aware that I'm able to do more than I thought I could actually to start off with. At first I didn't know half the people here and now I get along with almost everyone here. And when I started here I barely could do a thing, and now I'm doing things I haven't done before. (White Australian male, 17)

Finally, one young woman shared her particularly touching and inspiring story of how participation at Third Place had led her to a journey of personal healing through music and dance. Her identity previously had been based on an understanding of herself as having little value, and thus deserving violence. While she previously lacked self-respect, which led her to self-harm, by participating in the break dance group she had gained a sense of worth, seen herself anew, and stopped cutting herself. In her statement she directly links her identity work of healing to gains in self-confidence and self-respect.

> I respect myself more. . . . I used to not respect myself . . . actually I'm ashamed of this . . . but like it's true and why I should hide the truth if it's true? I used to cut myself. Cuz I wasn't respect[ing] myself. I used to . . . close myself in and never talk with nobody, that was probably the problem. . . . But now . . . I think it was stupid. . . . Now I just respect myself and others . . . Every single day when I'm here actually I'm getting . . . new confidence, every single day. (White Slovenian female, 18)

At Breaking Barriers in Northern Ireland the responses drew on similar themes. Most of the respondents agreed that their engagement in the programs had changed how they see themselves. In particular, respondents in Northern Ireland shared the increased sense of self-confidence reported by Third Place participants. Indeed, at Breaking Barriers, confidence emerged as an even stronger theme, coming up more frequently in responses. For example, when asked if participating in the program had changed anything about the way they see themselves, and if so, how, participants responded as follows.

> [I]t's definitely given me more confidence, as like performing and like being on stage and interacting with people. . . . just having the confidence to talk to people about like what they're about and who they are and . . . learning about people, about . . . where they come from and how they grew up and what their life was like

> before they came here . . . (White Northern Irish Protestant male, 16)
>
> Confidence. Self-confidence. I always had trouble, when I was a kid, standing up in front of a class and even just reading a sentence. I couldn't do it. I would like break down and cry. Where now I've been on the radio, I can stand up in front of my school and give a speech, which I have done. . . . I think Breaking Barriers's just really given me a boot up the ass if you know what I mean. . . . It's just like "you can do it, get out there." (White Northern Irish Protestant female, 17)
>
> Well it's built my confidence up a bit. . . . Can talk to people. (White Northern Irish Protestant male, 14)
>
> I learned I've got more confidence than what I thought I had. (White Northern Irish Protestant male, 14)
>
> That I know I could do it. And just see it. . . . Know I can do it if I put my head to it. (White Northern Irish Protestant male, 14)
>
> Yeah, like I never knew I would've been able to do half the stuff in front of people. But I didn't really mind cuz well yous like encouraged us. (White Northern Irish Protestant male, 14)
>
> . . . I didn't really consider myself as like someone who could do raps or anything before and now I . . . know that I can do that. (White Northern Irish Protestant male, 12)

These are important findings, because, as noted earlier, research suggests that young people with healthy levels of self-confidence are less likely to participate in or be victimized by violence.

At Breaking Barriers however, none of the interviewees reported feeling more peaceful as a result of their participation in the program. I suspect this is because none of the programs run by Breaking Barriers directly addressed physical violence and alternative options for young people. This could also be because the programs were not explicitly discussing their aim of building peace, as Third Place does.

While participants at Breaking Barriers tended to make general statements about increased confidence, they did not expand as much on their ideas as the participants at Third Place had. This may have been because the young people in the Australian program were more familiar with me and thus more willing to discuss their ideas in depth. Also, the Australian group participated in their program for months as opposed to hours in some of the Northern Ireland programs, so they had more time to develop their understandings.

In Australia some interviewees also noted that their self-images were greatly impacted by the views of others. For one thing, many were aware that young people are often viewed negatively by society, and they wished to change this impression. Others provided narratives of how their self-confidence levels had increased through having people believe in them; and from there, they expressed a sense of pride in changing the ways others viewed them. For example, some interviewees at Third Place in Australia had a sense of teenagers being belittled in society. However, they rejected this identity and sought to counter these views through their actions in this peacebuilding project. Through their peacebuilding work, they wanted to redefine the stereotypes they felt had been universally applied to their age group by adults. They rejected the views of older people focusing on what is "purportedly wrong" with youth. Moreover, they refused to accept the expectation that the supposedly obvious problems of youth ought to be addressed by disciplining them to fit into accepted adult patterns of behavior. Indeed, these young people saw their existing modes of engagement in creating peace as relevant, valuable, and effective.

> [F]or me it was like an opportunity to get out there and show them what I had. And what I wanna become. And show them that it's not just crime that kids do, kids can also be good you know, like sometimes they're just always saying "ah teenagers are just like, just bad," but there's other sides to us. (Maori female, 13)

> If people can see that teenagers can start off as complete strangers and in the end become good mates I guess it can show that if teenagers can do it, why can't adults? (White Australian male, 17)

These statements suggest that while adults may ascribe violent or passive identities to youth, many young people are displaying alternative youth identities and playing active roles in promoting peace. In some instances youth peacebuilders may even influence and educate adults about peace. By doing so, these youth identify themselves as peacebuilders and work to create a broader view of peacebuilding that includes contributions from youth.

Interviewees at the Australian program also reported gaining inspiration through the confidence of others. This may be related to the fact that leaders in the program are peers working collaboratively rather than older adults asserting a hierarchical position of dominance. The Third Space program emphasized that it was for youth by youth, which gives the young people a degree of ownership of the project. This is an innovative and significant contribution to peacebuilding, as youth play a role in educating other young people about involvement in building cultures of peace. In doing so they may model peaceful identities to their peers, proposing alternatives to violent images often assigned to youth. They may also support a new, more inclusive mode of peacebuilding that values and encourages collaborative work by young people. For example, two interviewees commented on the peer support:

> It allows people to get along, to be able to help each other. . . . It does bring people closer together because they can basically show each other and impress each other on what they can do. (White Australian male, 17)

> Before I perform . . . there's always someone that I talk to . . . you know somebody at [the program] . . . will be like "What do you mean, brother? Go up and kill it!" [i.e., he was nervous about performance and his peers encouraged him to be confident] . . . Then I'm like "Oh yeah," you know I just get all amped up and shit

> like you know . . . like I just have this reassurance. . . . And now I'm just kinda trying to give that to myself . . . you have self-confidence but also you need someone to amp you up . . . (Fijian/Indian male, 20)

Several interviewees also reported a sense of pride in successfully changing the negative images other people held of them, indicating that the identity changes they had experienced had been noticed and valued by those around them.

> [T]hey look at me like a different person. Because I guess before I had like a chip on my shoulder type thing. . . . I was an asshole back then. But then I was just like changed a lot and I . . . tell people about that and I'm like man I'm changed. . . . But I've just changed so much when I came here and I think people noticed that a lot. They're like, "Whoa, you've changed man! Like coming here done changed your ego." . . . (Fijian/Indian male, 20)

> Yeah . . . it will help me by showing other people that I have the courage to take care of the group and stuff like that. (Black African Sudanese female, 15)

> Yeah . . . taught me not to be so ashamed, like to be more out there now . . . I'm doing that now and everyone's saying like, "Oh you're different, you're better now. . . . You're not so hiding, you're not hiding anymore." (Samoan/Maori female, 13)

In all of these ways, youth experienced changes in understandings of the self that could make complex but significant contributions to building peace.

Seeing Others in a Different Light

In both case studies participants also reported changes in their perceptions of the identities of others. At Third Place in Australia, interviewees reported that interacting with people from different cultural backgrounds had changed their views about others in a variety of ways. Through their work in music and dance, participants had come to question previously held stereotypes and xenophobic understandings and thus to transform their own cultural prejudices. For example, when asked if their views of others had changed, some participants reported:

> Yeah it changed heaps! . . . Cuz I've never had like say African friends or like white friends . . . for me it's like you gotta keep with your own background. But coming here it's like you can just be whoever you wanna be. Like you can be friends with this person. . . . It doesn't matter what other people say . . . (Maori female, 13)

> [B]efore I had stereotypes, that's all gone, and I just look at everyone else just like how I look at myself. So you know just like [a] normal person, no one's higher than, no one's above no one . . . (Fijian/Indian male, 20)

> Definitely. Like Africans they're just people now, they're normal. I'm not scared of them anymore . . . They're just other people. (Samoan/Maori female, 13)

There were some participants who reported that their involvement had not changed the way they saw others. For example, three white males reported no change in their views. However, they were all involved in the break dancing group, which was made up entirely of "white" young people and included only one girl, so they did not regularly interact with "other" young people in the program. It is also interesting that some participants, including girls and young people of color, told me how they had realized they had negative stereotypes and changed their views. Yet all three "white" males denied any experience of having stereotypes or changed views based on interacting across difference. This is not a broad enough study to extrapolate a broad argument from this, but it does draw attention to the need to look at understandings across racial and cultural differences when researching youth peacebuilding.

This is interesting in light of the work at Breaking Barriers, where all participants were "white" Northern Irish youth. Their responses to my questions about seeing others differently were much more hesitant, and interviewees appeared eager to avoid painting themselves as people who would hold racial stereotypes or racial prejudices. Again, the data is too limited to extrapolate on a broader scale, but the responses in these two case studies suggest that it may be more difficult for "white" youth to acknowledge or understand that their views and experiences are situated in a racialized context, especially in an all-white environment. Perhaps their experience as "white" people in a society that privileges whiteness has led to them feel that race does not apply to them. However, if this is the case, these views will require challenging if positive peace is to be achieved, since racism cannot be overcome by denying its existence. Further study is needed in this area, as recognizing racism and prejudice is an essential part of building positive peace.

In the Northern Ireland context, when I asked the young people questions about interactions across difference and whether this had impacted their views, several of them reported that the new selves they had created were able to create new visions of others and engage with them as such, at least to a limited extent. When asked, "Has it changed the way you see others?" five interviewees reported no change, but, the majority had a positive response. For example, one girl said:

> . . . [I]t, just made me realize how . . . sad it can be and how like that they [people from poorer countries] need help and all and sometimes we get everything and they just have to live with nothing. (Northern Irish Catholic female, 13)

Moreover, many interviewees had similar responses when asked whether interacting with people from different backgrounds had changed any views they had before:

> Definitely. . . . Like I don't know their accents and stuff, like I'd thought they'd be completely different than what they were. (Northern Irish Catholic female, 13)

> [Y]eah . . . before even I would never have like had any preconceived ideas of like anyone because of their, their skin color . . . or their gender or anything like that, but it's just good to, to like know about that . . . cuz I'm more aware and like how people are. . . . From different cultures. . . . Like actually talking to them face to face and it's really good . . . like not being worried about like asking them questions about what their background or what they're about . . . I don't think it's changed that much . . . it's definitely had a better effect, like a positive effect, but I wouldn't say it's that drastic because . . . I never had really any . . . like I would've never thought like badly about any of that already . . . (Northern Irish Protestant male, 16)

> Uh huh . . . I just felt . . . understanding each other . . . (Northern Irish Protestant male, 14)

As in the Australian case study, although to a lesser extent, the participants in Northern Ireland reported seeing others in new ways, ways that contrasted with their previously held negative stereotypes. For instance, Katie, a community relations worker who assisted the project manager accessing several of the area schools, said she has spoken to many youth who remembered participating in Project Movement. She said they told her they really enjoyed participating in the program and that as a result they saw foreign facilitators in a different light as musicians instead of viewing them through the lens of racial stereotypes as they had previously. While young people did not report this to me directly, it seems likely that they may have been more open with Katie, whom they do not see as an outsider and could thus more easily admit to stereotyping in the past.

Even in a program like Youth Movement that was quite homogeneous in terms of participants (all white, Northern Irish Protestant boys), about half the boys involved reported feeling a greater sense of inclusion in their own peer groups based on their participation, so this seems to imply that music-making can aid in building community. While the boys may be from quite similar backgrounds, exclusions still occurred for particular individuals, and the music program had helped in addressing this. Programs more explicitly aimed at addressing racism had deeper results on changed views of "others." For example, at Breaking Barriers' MEC program, which was specifically aimed at using music to build cultural diversity awareness, two youth participants mentioned changed views about immigrants.

> It changed like what I thought of people from different countries and stuff. You know like thinking more of them and to understand them more sort of. (Northern Irish Catholic female, 13)

> And like we're all the same, yeah. (Northern Irish Catholic male, 13)

While participants at Breaking Barriers were unlikely to confess to any personal prejudices or stereotypes, a couple of facilitators did report changes in such views.

> What I learned is that . . . everyone has the capacity to do music. And I had my own prejudices and I have changed a lot. (Colombian female, 31)

> . . . I've always had this stereotype that you can't communicate with people . . . who are from a different language, but you know everyone has humor. . . . I think there still is that stereotype that you can't communicate with someone who doesn't speak your language but you can in different ways . . . (Northern Irish Protestant female, 21)

This led me to wonder whether more direct antiracist programming might benefit participants by bringing these challenging issues to the table more openly. I suggest there appears to be a solid case for mixing methods, as these findings imply that providing some direct talk or education with the young people on issues of inclusion and exclusion may be helpful in building on the connectivity or openness that has been initiated through their music participation. It is also interesting to note that female facilitators made both of the comments acknowledging previous prejudices, so again the issue of gender comes up in willingness to address these issues. When considering gender, as was the case with race, members of the less dominant group in the social hierarchy were more open to expressing and challenging their own stereotypes and exclusive attitudes.

Conclusion

Identity is undoubtedly a key issue in conflict and therefore must be a key consideration in attempts at peacebuilding. It seems clear from this study that music can play a major role in encouraging identity work that may offer alternative understandings of identity for young people, both of themselves and of others. While limited, the evidence discussed here shows that music may be used in developing more peaceful understandings of the self, developing greater self-esteem, and aiding in healing. At the same time, this musical work across difference enabled youth to develop different concepts of the identities of others, challenge stereotypes, and experience working together collaboratively. These outcomes differed across the two programs, but they were evident to some degree in both. I suggest that the less extensive outcomes at Breaking Barriers are at least in part a result of the shorter duration, which offered less time for shifts in understanding, as there was less time for performing and rehearsing new narratives. Based on the case studies and literature review, I suspect that the level or likelihood of these shifts occurring is strongly related to the duration of the program and the level of ownership young people have. Nonetheless, even in short-term projects some level of change occurred in youth participants' understanding of identities of themselves and others.

To be clear, my intent here is not to suggest that issues of violence, stereotypes, or confidence, among others, have been somehow permanently addressed or resolved by these programs. Rather, this evidence suggests that music can be adapted to youth peacebuilding work in a way that gives participants the opportunity to imagine and experience alternative, more peaceful identities for themselves and others. While this process requires continual attention, for many participants this was their introduction to peacebuilding and thus provided them with a lived experience of identities that they may draw on in future identity constructions. On the whole, these findings suggest that music is a potentially powerful resource for unsettling identities in ways that may offer alternative nonviolent responses to conflict and difference.

6

Making Space, Creating Common Ground

Efforts at building peace by (re)constructing identities require paying attention to space. Indeed, music may alter spaces in ways that create opportunities for contesting identities that support conflict. In particular, music-based peacebuilding programs can play a role in constructing spaces that support and encourage nonviolent interaction across difference, and they may even contribute to changing perceptions of a local area more broadly, which can aid in building wider cultures of peace.

Space has been conceptualized in many different ways. Space can refer to both "real" material physical sites and to virtual sites[1] such as the internet. Space can also be understood as what might be termed relational space, a location where it is possible to share opinions and ideas. Lefebvre dealt with this complexity by arguing that there are multiple levels of space, ranging from "natural" or "absolute" spaces to "social space," which is more complex.[2] Soja then adapted and built on this concept to account for what he called "thirdspace."[3] The concept of "thirdspace" includes space that is at once real and imagined. It includes social space, which is in addition to and indeed created by the binary of imagined versus real. Research suggests that imagination, representation, individual experience, and social interaction all come together in constituting our notions of space, so the process is inevitably colored by power relations.[4] Space can thus be seen as both socially constructed and political. After all, space is inevitably tied to power, since it is essential to (re)producing social difference.[5]

The (re)production of space is linked with the (re)production of identities. The links are complex, but it appears that music can be used, both in its production and consumption, to create a sense of both space and identity.[6] Foucault explains one aspect of this relationship of space and identity through his discussion of counter-sites called "heterotopias."[7] He defines these heterotopias as material locations where incompatible spaces could be juxtaposed, such as theater. Heterotopias are real sites in which "all the other real sites that can be found within the culture are simultaneously represented, contested, and inverted."[8] In these spaces, Foucault suggests, people have the chance to view themselves from another angle and adapt this in reconstituting themselves. Such spaces then, either existing or newly created, may facilitate identity work.

Though it may seem mundane, the way space is negotiated and shared on a day-to-day basis can have important impacts on individual and group identity. For example, certain spaces may be (re)created in ways that are more inclusive and/or which stimulate challenges to existing identities that are integral to conflict. In other words, particular places that are not seen as "owned" by one party to a conflict may be developed and understood in ways that facilitate communication and interaction across difference, which are integral aspects of peacebuilding.

Music, as a mechanism for transforming space,[9] can alter the way people experience or understand particular places by leading them to view the space as familiar, calm, dangerous, or exciting, depending on the particular type of music being deployed. The presence of music within social spaces can suggest certain modes of being, feeling, acting, and moving.[10] For example, familiar music associated with childhood memories might lead one to feel at home in a space where that music is playing; or, playing music with a beat that listeners regard as fun may inspire dancing. So, it is worth considering how music may be used in peacebuilding to alter environments in a way that allows people to feel at ease in interacting with one another.

Music can constitute space in a way that encourages certain activities more than others, and this can be used for positive purposes.[11] However, just as it can be used to build bridges, music may be used in particular local contexts to erect and justify boundaries. For example, consider the use of music by some sectarian drumming bands in Northern Ireland using music to "take over" the space in which they march, singing divisive lyrics, and intimidating local residents from other backgrounds with their dominance in the space. When used in this way, music is clearly counterproductive to peacebuilding efforts. However, there are other possibilities. Programs aimed at building peace through music then ought to take into account local needs and preferences to ensure that the work is relevant and worthwhile. At the same time, they also need to take care to avoid (re)creating space in a way that supports or further inflames conflict.

Peacebuilding and Space

Questions of how and where space is shared are important to building peace.[12] As Brewer explains, "Peace asks a lot of you. . . . It asks you to share space, territory, specific concrete places. . . . And all this you are asked to do with and in the presence of your enemy."[13] So, the way we understand ourselves, our cultures, and our histories is strongly tied to the spaces in which we live or have lived our lives. Greater understanding is likewise needed of relational spaces in particular geographies.[14] Lederach says peacebuilders need to think strategically about local social spaces within areas of conflict where people from diverse groups meet and interact in ways that often go unnoticed. For youth this may mean places such as schools, street corners, or sports clubs.

However, when conflict has occurred, space is often understood in terms of divided, dangerous, or contested territory. For example, during the period of conflict in Northern

Ireland known as the Troubles, particular neighborhoods or areas were often seen to be "owned" by certain groups, and any incursion by those labeled as outsiders would tend to provoke violent responses. In such situations space may become so divided that there are few, if any, places where people associated with opposing sides interact. Thus, peacebuilding requires thinking not only in terms of spaces where interaction may already be occurring, but also about creating spaces where none currently exist. Physical locations influence how people see conflict, themselves, and others,[15] as they may understand their identities and others as tied to the places they live and may define others as enemies or allies on this basis. At the same time, since space is socially constructed, people may influence understandings of the space they inhabit. In other words, individuals and groups may play a role in (re)creating spaces, just as space may play a role in (re)creating those who inhabit it.

One key to reconciliation is finding novel ways of creating "relational spaces" within populations where people affected by conflict can meet to deal with the past and future.[16] Moreover, for positive peace to be pursued, these spaces need to encompass change processes that are nonviolent and sustained.[17] So attention should be paid to how such transformations may be initiated in particular physical spaces.

While finding or creating neutral spaces is imperative for constructively dealing with conflict,[18] it can be a difficult task, since it requires finding a material place outside where the conflict tends to occur and which is not owned by any of the parties to the conflict.[19] Schirch suggests that peacebuilders, "through constructing a ritual environment that is set aside or separated from everyday time and space," can create "safe spaces," where peacebuilding can occur.[20] However, it is worth noting that since peacebuilding requires attention to learning about and exploring difference, it may not always feel safe. In fact, peacebuilding may need to occur in ways that participants experience as somewhat *un*safe, since the work of troubling identities associated with conflict is necessary but also very difficult. Therefore, to be clear, when I use the term "safe" here, I intend it to signify a secure space, free from violence rather than one in which comfort is privileged in a way that makes challenging conflict identities unlikely.

Youth and Space

Acknowledging, encouraging, and supporting youth participation in peacebuilding clearly requires the creation or adaptation of spaces in which young people can participate. This is no small task, given that the public space young people are allowed to occupy has narrowed in recent years. In Australia, for example, laws have been passed over the last two decades that make it a crime for youth to be present, at given times, in public spaces, such as parks or to meet in groups of three or more in these public places. Such laws may be intended to create safe spaces where gang activity has occurred. Still, it is important to note that the law does not differentiate between young people occupying public space to engage in gang activity and youth occupying public space to engage in cultural activities, including those aimed at building peace.

Scholars such as Schell-Faucon argue that youth, particularly those living in violent areas, require safe spaces that may serve as a sanctuary from pressures such as gangs and drugs, where they can build youth cultures of positive peace.[21] Still, many questions remain about how such a safe and meaningful space may be created in both the literal and metaphorical sense. It is also worth asking whether youth coming to a space outside their normal spheres and learning to interact differently there could have a significant impact outside that space for those youth or others.

Finding safe, accessible spaces for youth to engage in peacebuilding can also be made difficult by a lack of resources and/or a lack of trust by adults in charge of spaces. As Harris points out, the ability of young people to hold power, be visible in, and occupy public space is in many cases dependent on participation in consumerism. However, this relies on having the ability and access to engage in such activities, so many youth are excluded. At the same time, many centers and programs have been introduced to lure youth to sites approved by adults, where "proper" supervision can be conducted. In short, young people's access to public spaces has decreased while regulation and surveillance have increased.[22]

In response, many young people, particularly girls, are utilizing spaces on the margins of society, such as alternative music communities, to develop strategies and engage with their peers away from the adult gaze. For example, youth may use their musical productions to express the diversity of their personal experiences that have not been acknowledged in mainstream public discourses. While youth cultures associated with hip-hop and rap have been seen as particularly dangerous and thus often singled out for additional surveillance,[23] these cultures can also be seen as ways young people in particular contexts have been able to "to construct spaces of their own," and "transmit a strong sense of place."[24] Forman, for example, argues that young people have used hip-hop and rap as key tools for articulating their feelings about space and participating in "social debate on the contemporary convergences of youth, race, space, and place."[25] In youth cultures where rap is particularly popular, performances and shows have offered a tangible place where youth of different racial backgrounds can and do "hang out," as opposed to shows featuring rock or R&B, whose audiences tended to be more homogeneous.[26] It is thus important to ask questions about what kind of music might usefully draw youth together while supporting an inclusive atmosphere and how and where this may occur most effectively.

Gender, Music, and Space

Creating inclusive spaces for musical peacebuilding practice will also require attention to gender. Many of the tangible places associated with music activity are differentiated along gender lines.[27] Moreover, music, because it is tied to identity, can play a part in creating spaces as gendered and sexualized.[28] When this occurs, some groups may be excluded from participation in music-making, and it is often the girls who are left out.

Indeed, girls tend to have more restrictions placed on the space they can reasonably take up.[29] While the numbers of young women in cities is increasing, gender inequalities persist when it comes to occupying public space.[30] Girls may face exclusion, lack of acceptance in these public spaces, risk losing respect for frequenting them, or be prohibited by parents from doing so based on such fears. Moreover, when girls do appear on the street they are typically constrained by subordination, which they are taught early in their lives.[31] Based on this social training and a desire for respectability, girls often "self-censor" by limiting their access to space.[32]

These issues of gendered space are particularly relevant in the context of music. Rock ideology, for example, has masculinist links to a gendered production of space, where male musicians take up public spaces which women are expected to avoid.[33] Likewise, music-making spaces bring with them certain ideas about how women and men should behave.[34] This can be especially restrictive for girls. The ideology of popular music paints the street as a sphere for young males, while young women are expected to hang out in private spaces, often at home in their bedrooms.[35] Girls desiring to be musicians are often faced with particular issues of access to space.[36] Youth participation in music production may have gendered limitations when it occurs in places where males can go freely and without concern yet that are potentially problematic for young women's reputations.[37] For example, in her consideration of the music scene in Liverpool, U.K., Cohen found that spaces were configured in ways that suggested women were present largely for sexual reasons.[38] Such assumptions have influenced parents in their concerns for their daughters' involvement in music scenes,[39] making them more likely to limit their ability to frequent such places.

This can narrow girls' choices, as well as their ability to participate in many activities. However, Saldanha proposes that girls have contested these gendered requirements through their dancing. While limited in time and space, she says girls' dancing works to resist the norm of puritan patriarchy, which holds that girls and their bodies should be seen and understood as private and passive, rather than active and public.[40] Brabazon likewise argues that pop can offer women space, politics, and a voice. Female pop stars, she says, set themselves up to be politically and sexually subversive. They do so by taking up space while performing the opposition between the public and the popular. This occurs through female pop stars "being and doing" things that are either not allowed or not expected outside the pop realm.[41] Of course, the same argument could be made (and contested) for other musical genres, including rock and hip-hop.

Keepin' it Real: Material Space

In the case studies conducted in Australia and Northern Ireland space appeared as an important aspect to consider when pursuing peacebuilding with youth. For one thing, music and dance projects always require a physical place that allows room for bodily movement and, more importantly, the freedom to produce noise that would not be allowed in many public spaces. However, locating spaces for young people to meet where they will also want to go is not an easy task. Nevertheless, when such space can be secured, the location may offer participants a center they can return to, and from which they can reach out to others. One of the facilitators at Third Place [Australia] recalled her time as a participant, expressing how important it was for young people to have the space to be among other young people and share. She stated:

> [A]s a participant . . . I was drawn to this space because . . . just as a teenager . . . you go through firsts and pressure and all that kind of stuff and you just wanna kinda find a space where you can kind of vent out . . . and . . . I came to realize that it's . . . just a space where you can . . . share your stories . . . do what you want. (Samoan/German female from New Zealand, 25)

In other words, the space is important for performing and sharing their identities. By providing a space to engage in peaceful musical activities, program sites may also serve as a physical refuge for young people living in violence-ridden communities. As one young facilitator and former participant explained:

> [Third Place] is held where . . . there tends to be . . . a lot of violence around in that community, so you just, having that safe space within that community for kids to come and hang out and just do whatever . . . they can . . . go out into the community and not be afraid . . . (Samoan/Chinese female from New Zealand, 18)

Unlike many community programs, the Third Place program was fortunate enough to secure grants-based funding to hire a hall for its workshops over ten weeks. Still, certain characteristics of the space could be restrictive, as funding for community-based organizations does not necessarily give them the flexibility to maintain permanent spaces with the ideal set-ups for such programs.

While these issues were significant in the Australian case study, even more difficult issues can arise with the contested nature of local geographies in areas experiencing more widespread conflict. Indeed, throughout my time working with Breaking Barriers in Northern Ireland, it was clear that building sustainable peace would require significant attention to space. In Belfast, space is a constant source of confrontation, given the divided nature of the local geography. When I drove through Belfast with program leaders, they pointed out hot spots for violence, generally located at "interface" areas between Catholic and Protestant communities. These communities are often rigidly physically divided by enormous "peace walls." Seeing these imposing structures as an outsider can leave one feeling shocked or intimidated, but beyond that they make it difficult to travel easily from one area to another. Moreover, as schools are overwhelmingly segregated, finding a space in which young people can interact across difference in Northern Ireland is challenging, requiring attention to space and the ingrained local understandings about ownership and identities of particular spaces.

These limitations often mean that programs are held in schools or youth centers with young people who are either Protestant or Catholic, rather than a mixture of the two. Also the focus in those workshops is on multicultural interaction with facilitators of different racial backgrounds, often immigrants who now live in Belfast. This work is of course important, but it is notable that issues of space and identity are working against the possibility of peacebuilding between the two main religious groups, generally seen as the "sides" of the Northern Ireland conflict, and against peaceful interactions between young people.

Even when suitable places can be found for holding more integrated projects, questions can arise about the music activities that can take place, given the political identities associated with particular musical instruments. Breaking Barriers leaders became aware of these issues after making the decision, without considering any possible political repercussions, to use the bodhrán, an Irish drum, in their programs. Program leaders explained to me that they had had some trouble taking the bodhráns into schools, because it is seen as a Catholic instrument. Some local councils berated them, saying they had to bring "Protestant drums" (lambegs), too. This is particularly interesting, given that the two men relaying these experiences were themselves Protestants; so it was unacceptable even for Protestants to play a "Catholic drum." The reason they chose bodhráns was merely because they are small and easily portable, while the lambeg is much bigger and thus difficult to transport for use in large groups. Despite the councils' complaints about using bodhráns and not lambegs, program leaders did not change or add any instruments to their programs. However, they did come to realize how small details such as instrument choice can be political.

The site of the program office can even be problematic. The office for the Breaking Barriers program was at the time located in East Belfast, which is known to be a Protestant area. In Northern Ireland, one common way to tell which "side" someone is on is to ask where s/he lives; a program that is housed in East Belfast would immediately be labeled as Protestant.

Because of this, the facilitators decided to name their project there Belfast East rather than East Belfast to try to diminish the initial reaction and encourage more people to come.

Such political divisions across space are not just the domain of adults, school administrators, and community leaders. I heard numerous accounts from community workers, young people, and other locals of how young people fight at particular interface areas that separate Protestant and Catholic neighborhoods. Nevertheless, in my observation I noted that providing youth with a free space where they could spend time as an alternative to fighting may aid in reducing direct violence. This is far from the end goal of building a culture of peace, but it is at least a starting point. Because music is relevant and important in these young people's lives, they may be drawn to the alternative of participating in a space designated for music rather than heading to one where conflict is expected. I observed an example of this occurring one night while attending a YM workshop, which was attended by several working-class Protestant young men.

On that particular evening, once we arrived and brought in the workshop equipment, the boys kept entering the room early, as they were eager to begin. Then, just as we were starting the workshop one boy received a phone call and said "The taigs [a derogatory term for Catholics] are over at Queen's Park. One of them bashed James." The call was from his sister and another youth. They wanted him and others to come fight. He said he could not because he was at the youth club, but he told the others and a discussion ensued. One boy, the self-appointed leader of the group, said, "We have to go; our country calls us!" This was considered by the group, but after a brief back-and-forth discussion the boys all decided they wanted to stay and do the workshop, as they were excited by the chance to make a hip-hop CD. This seems a clear example of how the project aided in promoting peace by giving these boys an alternative space and activities they would choose to do over going out to engage in sectarian fighting. If the workshop had not been held, they would likely have been out in the park rioting alongside the many other young people involved. While this is only a beginning, such projects when taken further to include meaningful engagement between cultures can also be important in expanding inclusiveness through space.

Territory is constantly being contested in this land with a history of disputed ownership, so finding places that will be perceived as neutral to host projects can be a difficult task in itself. In Belfast this would mainly be limited to the city center and western area near the university. These areas are associated with more well-to-do residents, and much of the violence occurs in the working class neighborhoods. Where trust has been built up through contact with community workers and goodwill, Breaking Barriers has also included some programs that have been integrated by bussing youth from one area to participate at another. Arranging more programs of this nature may play an important role in the work these music programs can provide.

However, a more promising, though also more difficult, route would involve (re)creating particular spaces as neutral for purposes of these programs. This may involve using a tool such as music that appeals to people on all sides of a conflict, making them feel welcome through their identification with the music. Youth might have the opportunity to engage in spaces like this that can be understood as "heterotopias," where they can see themselves from another angle and adapt this in reconstituting themselves. This can take place through music performance, which allows them to simultaneously see and be seen, to act as audience and performer. Through this sort of work, youth may create the space to explore issues and identities in a non-threatening context unconstrained by constant adult direction and expectations.

Directing this work toward peacebuilding may also require adopting and publicizing policies of nonviolence and inclusiveness in the program space. Such innovations would require a spirit of creativity and inclusivity, as well as patience, given the obstacles. Nonetheless, my research suggests that most youth participating in these projects would not have come to a peace project that had not involved music or dance, so these art forms may be key to enticing youth to participate in (re)creating spaces in a way that is relevant to them, engages them across difference, and paves the way for building a culture of peace.

Relational Space: Providing Space to Come Together

Securing an adequate material place in which young people can participate in these music-based programs is the first step toward creating possibilities for what is to take place: the gathering together of people across difference. As one young man participating in the Third Place program indicated:

> [A]fter school all of my friends are going home and . . . I'm coming to [Third Place] and they [will be] walking and I [will be] saying [I'm going] for [Third Place] and they [will say] like "Why you going there?" They don't really know what happen here, they think I'm just coming to crump at this. But it's not what's happening you know. (Liberian male, 16)

He clearly thought something more was occurring. Indeed, the importance of the site goes far beyond merely serving as a place to perform music and dance.

The creation of a "third space," means not only that young people can hang out (as they normally would), they can also interact with youth from other cultural backgrounds in ways that would be more difficult in other venues, based on the norms in their cultures, families, and friendship circles. This is important for peacebuilding, as the aim of positive peace is not just the cessation of direct violence, but rather being able to come together and share spaces through peaceful interaction. In one facilitator's description of peace, her first key point was that peace is "people coming together and getting along . . . in one space." Over time her understanding had expanded to see the potential for building peace as the key purpose of the Third Place programs and the space in which they were located:

> It's not just about hip-hop, and it's not just about . . . getting on stage and showcasing . . . these young people's talents. Actually, behind it all, it's actually about the Third Place policy, it's about giving them that space to come together and create something . . . beautiful. (Samoan/German female from New Zealand, 25)

She thought the program's location served as an important site for peacebuilding by providing youth with a space to meet in which different cultures could interact in a way that is constructive rather than destructive. Several respondents expressed similar understandings, explaining how the site was a different kind of space for young people to use, not just physically sharing the space, but having significant interaction with one another. For example, two young men explained how interaction with people from different backgrounds was not just possible in the space but was supported and even expected.

> Coz you can't just like talk to people from the same country like you gotta know someone else here you know? . . . Talk to them, know them, really befriend them. That's how we make friends and peace here. (Liberian male, 16)

> [I]t's not like other places where you just go and you don't really know anybody there like the kids and everyone. (Samoan/Maori male, 14)

The physical space served as a place for youth to meet across difference, which makes it an important site for considering identity issues. Indeed, it is clear that space has a complex interrelationship with both dialogue and identity. Many young people in the Third Place program reported feeling that the site for the project had become a different kind of space, one in which they could understand themselves in different ways. This allowed more interactions across difference and in contrast to identities that they have previously felt obligated to uphold. For example:

> . . . I couldn't believe you could see that back in the day, it was all just like different groups. . . . But now I just like came here and am like holy fuck, they're all friends? I've never seen that in my life. (Fijian/Indian male, 20)

> [C]oming here . . . you can just be whoever you wanna be . . . you can be friends with this person . . . It's just, we're just a family and that's what matters the most. (Maori female, 13)

Creating these spaces where young people can gather and interact with youth from other backgrounds can make room for the shifts in identity necessary for building peace, one young person at a time. While many of these youth participants would not previously have engaged in conversation or music-making with young people outside their social or cultural groups, they were drawn to Third Place by the music participation on offer.

The importance of creating space in which people can gather through music also appeared in my Northern Ireland case study. For example, a community relations officer for a local council near Belfast told me he had observed the Breaking Barriers programs in various locations. He said the music gives the youth participants a safe space to experience and interact with different cultures, so they could hopefully become more open-minded. Many of the areas where the projects are held, he said, have no people of color, so it is a new and unique opportunity for some of the students involved. Overall, he said, the program had been very popular and successful, and he was very impressed with the program's work. Similarly, one program facilitator said that music could play an important role in bringing people together for meaningful interaction, rather than merely drawing them to the same physical location. As she noted:

> [I]f you want to bring them together you have to do something interactive. Otherwise you end up maybe in a single room with two different groups separate. . . . So it's not the real point, so you have to like create a program that they will be with each other instead of all spread out. (Mexican female, 31)

Several youth participants also supported the claim that music can be an important way of getting people to come together across difference. When asked, "Do you think music/dance has been a useful tool for your involvement in peacebuilding? How?," they answered:

> Yeah, . . . Cuz music, it brings everyone together. (White Northern Irish Protestant male, 14)

> Yeah. . . . Um well it just kind of really brings people together. And like in [Youth Movement] we have a lot of people from different countries and we all got together and played music. (White Northern Irish Protestant male, 12)

> I think it's . . . just a good medium because everybody, no matter where they're from or what religion or race, they're, can all like relate to music and from all the different cultures there's different music and when it comes together it's just, like it's really good. It's a great thing. (White Northern Irish Protestant male, 16)

> Yeah. . . . Definitely . . . I don't know cuz you can hang out with . . . different types of music and stuff and then you know different cultures. And then those people can just join in. (White Northern Irish Catholic female, 13)

In summary, it appears that the use of music in these projects drew young people to come to a space and participate with others from different backgrounds when they would not otherwise have done so. Facilitators and participants frequently reported that the use of music was the draw card for youth involvement. Thus, while many young people would not necessarily go out of their way to gather in spaces with people from different backgrounds—some may even go out of their way not to do so—music united them and paved the way for a coming together across difference. In at least some cases, this led to participants building greater understanding and lasting friendships.

(Re)creating Spaces, Reducing Violence

The evidence from the two case studies also suggests that music may play a role in transforming what was once a violent or hostile space into a more inclusive, open, and nonviolent one. The process must be ongoing, constantly (re)creating the place as a space where youth can engage in a free, safe, and nonviolent way. One facilitator and former participant at Third Place explained how her experiences had led her to this view:

> When I first came to the workshops I thought it was just about music, but . . . when I . . . mingled with . . . a lot of the diverse cultures that were there . . . I started building . . . an understanding of why I was there at the space and . . . why the coordinator was . . . putting on a project like this and why people were telling us stories and . . . I came to realize that . . . us coming to the space was about . . . finding a safe space . . . where we can safely meet and just create positive change through music. (Samoan/German female from New Zealand, 25)

Music may play an important role in helping people engage in situations where they might not feel totally "safe" or "comfortable," like when their self-identities are being challenged. Indeed, one facilitator working with Breaking Barriers explained how music could be used to put people at ease in various locations. Despite being the only facilitator who was not a musician herself, she shared her view that music can be an effective means for getting people to connect in places where they otherwise might not have:

> [I]f . . . we engage with people first and then we sit down . . . they can be engaged with music at any place and time. So for me, music is the transport; music is the way. (Colombian female, 31)

This may be a crucial aspect in developing the dialogue necessary for peacebuilding. Likewise, another facilitator at Breaking Barriers expressed how the project has actually changed her view of the space around her home:

> For me I couldn't wait to get away from Belfast, I saw only the bad and horrible side. . . . But coming back to Belfast and getting this job it's changed my perception of the place. . . . You know it's like oh this is my home. Like there is good people doing good stuff. It's . . . changed my view on everything. (White Northern Irish Protestant female, 21)

These statements suggest that young people and facilitators may come to experience the sites where workshops are held as spaces where different identities can meet and interact peacefully.

I was also interested in exploring whether participants and leaders felt these programs could make changes to the wider communities associated with conflict, rather than impacting only the participants. To investigate this, I asked young people and facilitators at both projects, "Do you think [the program] can help reduce or prevent, or has already helped reduce or prevent, violence in the local communities where it is held?" For those who responded in the affirmative, I normally followed with questions about how they thought this was accomplished. In the Australian program, all the interviewees indicated a belief that the program could help in reducing and preventing violence in the local area. Two girls said it does so by providing a space where young people can hang out and engage in alternatives to violence:

> [I]f they can have a [Third Place workshop] in my community I think it will help the young kids and they'll learn what's right and what's wrong. (Sudanese female, 15)

> I reckon . . . if they teach them stuff, [Third Place] . . . Like all the kids that are bored out here and they go and look for something to do and then if trouble's the first thing they see, they'll do it cuz they're so bored

> and like going here can stop that. (Samoan/Maori female, 13)

Moreover, some of the participants indicated a belief that the program had already made such changes.

> Yeah I reckon it has. I reckon they've done it to our school. (Samoan/Maori male, 14)

> Yeah it has . . . I know one of my friends used to come here and they were real, real bad. . . . And since that, they've made friends like, true friends, they've changed totally. Like they haven't done anything bad, like they've been going to school every day and that's what like makes me really happy about this is it can change your life. . . . And make you see it different. . . . It made me happy knowing that my friend has changed into something better. (Maori female, 13)

> Yeah because a lot of people are like, more friendly with each other because they all dance together . . . (White Australian male, 14)

These responses in the Australian program indicate a belief that the program could help make community spaces safer and less violent. These responses also show how the way people feel and interact in spaces is linked to the way they perceive those spaces.

Similar results were found in Northern Ireland. Many respondents suggested the program provided space where youth could engage in nonviolent alternatives. As two of them explained:

> [I]t keeps a lot of people off the streets and doing . . . musical work . . . whereas if they're all on the streets there's bound to be some fights between people. . . . But if they're all in there it's okay. (White Northern Irish Protestant male, 12)

> [M]aking music can just like calm people down sort of. (White Northern Irish Catholic male, 13)

However, there were some participants who were more hesitant about whether the programs could help with reducing or preventing violence in their communities. For example, some of them said:

> Depends if people get involved like when they're doing it, if they're interested in that. . . . If they were interested in it, yeah. (White Northern Irish Protestant male, 14)

> I don't know . . . (Northern Irish Catholic female, 13)

> Uh if it was like mixed between, a mixture of people. [Implying the need to get Protestants and Catholics together, as the program he participated in was all Protestants] (Northern Irish white Protestant male, 14)

> Not too sure. (White Northern Irish Protestant male, 14)

It is worth noting that all of these doubtful respondents participated in programs at segregated schools, so perhaps working with the adult multicultural artists was worthwhile, but not seen as likely to reduce the main violence between youth or more generally between Protestant- and Catholic-identified political groups. However, the majority of participants in Breaking Barriers projects did think the project could aid in reducing or preventing violence in their communities.

Finally, one longtime participant, while taking care to avoid any sweeping claims about the overall political conflict, indicated a belief that by helping people learn about other cultures, the program could at least help in dealing with the racist violence against immigrants that has become commonplace in Northern Ireland.

> Yes . . . well it's a good attempt. But it'd be hard, especially here. . . . I know it's not nearly as bad as it was 20,

> 30 years ago, but . . . it's really good . . . just to make people aware of . . . like there's not a lot of . . . immigration . . . not a lot of . . . mix of different cultures in Northern Ireland, but . . . it would definitely be good to let people from here know about . . . other people's culture. (White Northern Irish Protestant male, 16)

Project facilitators overwhelmingly believed that their work could help in preventing and reducing violence, thereby creating safer communities and working toward building peace. As Breaking Barriers' director explained:

> Definitely it has, absolutely . . . that's why we're doing what we're doing you know . . . it's hard to measure, but there's definitely lots of them come out of there and think . . . So we have to ensure that we're doing something right you know in everything we do. (White Northern Irish Protestant male, 31)

Hittin' the Streets, Sharin' the Beats: Making Space for Peace by Recruiting Peers

While the space for these programs is currently limited to certain geographic and temporal sites, young people in both Australia and Northern Ireland reported a strong belief that these can and should be extended into their communities to create more places that enable the sorts of changes needed for building peace. Responses indicated that many of these young people believe the workshops can play a role, not just by impacting their own lives, but by creating lasting, widespread change. To that end, many reported a desire to increase the number of workshops and participants or take them out to other locations in the wider community. As two participants at Third Place explained:

> I would really like . . . more people . . . just like maybe advertise it somehow in some way and not just like one type of school. You know if they branch out and just get all schools together . . . that would be way better

> . . . I mean if there was more people . . . I'm pretty sure everyone . . . would feel like this, no matter where they are, which community they're in. And even if they're in their own community they'd feel like it's a lot better. . . . They can even make like their own community type of thing you know? (Fijian/Indian male, 20)

> If we get more and more people in . . . I think this group is kinda actually small. . . . But if they put us as . . . not leaders, but just like try to put us to be, to get more people . . . to get into it. I think that really if each of us would try at least to tell 10 people, two of them will go in . . . 100 percent. And like if, if there is like 10 people and two of them, that's already 20 people. And those 20 people, plus us, we, like we learn about it, like I don't know, half of [the] year, and then again we go out, us 30 people go out. . . . We can always get again and again and get more people . . . (White Slovenian female, 18)

Young people participating in Breaking Barriers' work also reported a desire to boost numbers of participants in the programs where they are currently held or to introduce them to new locations in the wider area. When asked whether they would continue to use skills they had gained from the program to continue to build peace in their communities, many suggested they would do so by attempting to create opportunities for more people to get involved in similar music peace work.

> Yeah. . . . Trying to arrange something. . . . For another group. (White Northern Irish Protestant male, 14)

> [J]ust get more people in it. . . . Get more people involved. (White Northern Irish Protestant male, 12)

> [I]t would be good to get like so many more people and . . . get them like more involved. . . . And like meet up more often . . . (White Northern Irish Protestant male, 16)

In summary, in both programs, many of the participants appreciated the space they had experienced and both believed and hoped that this could be expanded to other people and places.

Challenges and Limitations

While participants reported feeling positive about the programs, there were also a number of unresolved challenges and limitations related to space. For one thing, many of the interviewees reported a desire to have a permanent site for the Third Place program. This desire for an ongoing space to come together is particularly important since, as noted, public spaces have become less accessible to young people. One young woman's response at Third Place shows an awareness of the space's enabling function in allowing interactions that do not often take place in the outside community and shows her sadness that this space could not be permanently accessed:

> . . . I also learned that . . . you become a family here. And it's hard like when it comes to the end cuz you don't really see them anymore. (Maori female, 13)

Links between music, identity, and place can create possibilities for peacebuilding, but in cultures of violence such as Northern Ireland, these links can also lead to complications. As previously discussed, in Northern Ireland music has historically been used in a divisive political way. This suggests the link between space, music, and identity has potential to build more inclusive spaces and nonviolent identities, but can also be used in a way that creates spatial segregation and division that supports conflict identities.

For peacebuilding to occur, spaces need to be created, understood, and experienced as sites where exchanges across difference can occur without fear of violence or oppression. Such locations may be what program leaders are aiming to create when they cite the need for "safe spaces." However, I am not suggesting that the places where people in conflict interact ought to be safe in the sense of "comfortable" or merely affirming preexisting ways of knowing and being. These sorts of spaces should not be seen as totally free, as the programs are taking a clear stand against violence, requiring that the spaces be used for nonviolent interaction. Much of the important contribution to peacebuilding that can be made through creating these spaces is in fact based on the potential for the nonviolent challenging, resisting, or contesting of identities. Likewise, these spaces very much resemble what Fine, Weis, and Powell describe as "safe spaces," places where, while wider social inequality cannot be escaped, young people have been able to challenge hegemonic assumptions and imagine different ways of being and understanding.[42]

By coming together and sharing space through music participation, these youth may have the chance to see the identity of others as multiple and fluid, rather than singular and fixed. A young Northern Irish youth from a Protestant background, for example, could potentially learn to see a Northern Irish Catholic young person not as a representative of IRA ideology, but as a person with his or her own views, ideas, and abilities that do not necessarily have to be oppositional or oppressive. For such shifts to occur, space must first be made, creating the conditions for interactions between these two people in a way that is interactive and perhaps even cooperative, rather than hostile and oppositional.

While the creation of space is important for allowing identity shifts, this does not ensure consistently nonviolent responses. As the lead facilitator at Third Place noted, challenges remain. While the space may give participants room for seeing themselves differently, this is not a cure-all solution that can resolve all violent conflict in the community, or even for the young people involved in the project. As she explained, two of the participants missed the final performance for the workshops series because they had been involved in a fight in the neighborhood and been arrested. She recalled that when she asked one of the young men involved what happened, he replied:

> It's so different . . . when you're not at the space . . . I'm a different person when I'm in this space, but when

I leave it's so hard for me to try and contain myself or just . . . be that person that I am at this space.

The lead facilitator noted that the program leaders were working to find new ways to address these issues by offering the young people support outside the hours and location of the workshops. This awareness of the challenges is a major first step to adapting the program to meet the diverse needs of young people in the community.

Most of the youth respondents from both Australia and Northern Ireland reported that "everyone" would feel comfortable participating in the program space. And many youth who feel excluded in other forums did clearly feel welcome in the Third Place and Breaking Barriers projects; the space contributes to a sense of inclusiveness for many who often feel on the margins elsewhere. For example, after I had completed my research at Third Place, I went back to visit and found that several homeless young people had started coming along to the project. They appeared to be accepted by the other youth. One girl with whom I was familiar referred to her homeless friend and told me how he had taught her this song on piano and was really talented. This showed a level of respect. The friend seemed shy but happy in the space, and the kids who had been there longer seemed to be genuinely trying to include him and the other homeless youth who were participating. So the participants were actually creating space for others who often feel they have no space, such as refugees, immigrants, and homeless youth.

However, there were some limitations here, too. More critical engagement may be required for program planners, as the participants who have continued coming to the workshops may not be the best placed to explain why other youth have stopped participating or never started. This may apply, for example, to young people whose sexual orientations or identities place them in a minority category. Based on observing many interactions in both Third Place and Breaking Barriers, I noted several instances in which young male participants made derogatory comments and jokes about other boys present being gay. Practitioners planning peace projects also need to take into account the need for sensitivity training around issues of sexuality. The chief facilitator in the Australian project reported that they had done so in a previous project run by the organization, as two girls who openly identified as lesbians were participating, and she overheard some other participants making insensitive comments. This is commendable, showing that the issue has been considered before and was met with a response. However, adopting such initiatives only when a visible situation arises is probably inadequate. A more proactive approach may be needed to attempt to prevent such exclusions from the beginning. In the Northern Ireland program no attention appeared to be given to issues of inclusiveness regarding sexuality or gender. While I suggest that music programs can be a useful way of engaging youth in peacebuilding, to foster positive peace, program leaders must seriously and critically engage with the gendering of space through the music work in order to provide better support for inclusion for both boys and girls.

Conclusion

Given its links with other key issues, such as dialogue and identity, it is clear that space requires in-depth consideration when engaging in peacebuilding work, including with youth. Music may play a major role in transforming space, and the use of music may be well suited to projects that engage young people. Moreover, music may have an important role to play in peacebuilding, as it may alter spaces in such a way that makes contestations of conflict identities possible. Of course, there are limitations to what changes in space and identity can occur, as meanings are assigned to people and places from the outside, too. Nevertheless, young people can resist these identities imposed on themselves, their peers, and the spaces they inhabit.

7

Gendering the Jam

Possibilities and Prohibitions

Gender equality is a key factor in achieving positive peace, so evaluating prospects for democratizing gender roles and challenging gender norms is vital in any study of peacebuilding. Building sustainable positive peace with young people will require constant reflection and an awareness of processes of inclusion and exclusion to avoid merely reproducing dominant cultural norms that operate in a hierarchal way to exclude particular ideas and identities. Likewise, greater awareness is needed of how gender operates in cultures of violence, particularly when it comes to youth, as much of the research looking at youth in peacebuilding pays no attention to gender at all. In this study I have sought to learn more about the role of gender in how young people experience and respond to conflict as well as how gender norms may influence their participation in music-based peacebuilding.

Local gender orders can play a role in feeding conflict and making peace more elusive by encouraging youth, especially young men, to participate in violence while creating disincentives for youth, especially girls, to get involved in peace work. Women and girls are often deeply impacted by conflict and excluded from participation in peace processes. Attempts to address this often focus on "fixing" women's or girls' modes of interaction to teach them to engage with men or boys on their terms. But why not ask how boys might adapt to be more gender aware and inclusive of girls? By developing an awareness of these challenges and exclusionary discourses, and at the same time creatively employing resistant practices to challenge these norms, youth peacebuilders may push the boundaries of entrenched prohibitions and in doing so play an important role in building a culture of peace that is inclusive and gender just.

Key Concepts

Gender norms are an important ordering device in contemporary societies. Gender includes socially constructed norms and patterns of behavior between women and men, boys and girls. A dichotomy of "masculine" as opposed to "feminine" is constructed, wherein men are expected to display masculine characteristics and women feminine traits. These normative traits are specific to time and place. As an aspect of identity, gender is understood here as flexible and fluid rather than essential or fixed. Gender is also a compulsory performance; we are constantly required to work at the making of normal identity although the content of this can and does shift over time and in different contexts. In other words, masculinities are plural, as are femininities. Manhood (and womanhood) must be achieved by behaving in certain ways in front of one's social group, where one is judged on that performance.[1]

Furthermore, gender is decidedly political: gender acts as a symbol of the political and social order and controlling gendered behavior is a mechanism for controlling that order.[2] Boundaries of gender are inseparable from other political and social boundaries, as these gender borders express the most intensely embedded types of domination that offer "basic metaphors for others, and thus constitute the most intensely 'naturalised' of all our boundary making activities."[3]

There are a variety of forms of masculinity and femininity, and many ways of being a woman or a man, but there are certain forms of gendered identity that are culturally dominant and understood as the ideal standard.[4] This is the basis for Connell's understanding of "hegemonic masculinity," which I draw on here. Hegemonic masculinity is the prevailing ideal of masculinity in the hierarchy of gender.[5] Hegemonic masculinity suppresses other forms of masculinities and femininities, which can also pose challenges to it. Connell argues that most men receive what she calls the "patriarchal dividend," though some individuals may receive none, less, or more, based on where they sit in the current social order. So, not only are women oppressed by this gender hierarchy; men displaying other forms of masculinity, such as gay men, may also be subordinated. Indeed, most men and boys cannot or do not live up to the standards of ideal manhood constructed within and through hegemonic masculinity. In the modern Western world, hegemonic masculinity is generally identified with heterosexuality, power, strength, whiteness, and matrimony. The emphasis on attaining physical toughness and exercising authority can thus encourage men and boys to engage in violence in order to live up to these standards of masculinity. Thus, dismantling the current assumptions of hegemonic masculinity is an important political project, including in relation to boys' participation in violence.

Conflict is linked to the way genders are socially constructed, so gender must be given consideration when aiming to build peace. This requires analyzing the different roles women and men take on in violence and conflict in order to develop novel perspectives and gain understanding. One key goal is ensuring that the ideas of masculinity and femininity that are linked to violent behavior are not uncritically carried over in post-conflict situations as part of daily life.[6] In particular, men cannot be the sole decision-makers in attempts to build peace, especially since peace processes that include women are more likely to succeed.[7]

This study likewise asks questions about how this applies to youth such as: What are the gendered factors that influence responses to conflict for boys and girls? How might local gender regimes and notions of masculinity and femininity impact girls' and boys' decisions to take part in peace projects?; and, How can the violent notions of hegemonic masculinity be resisted or challenged within particular gender regimes?

Masculinity in Violent Conflict

The pressure on men to perform or prove their masculinity through participation in violence has played a serious role in starting, fueling, and prolonging violent conflict all around the world.[8] Power has frequently been linked to men's violence, as the essentialized view that women are delicate and submissive while men are superior and aggressive is often used by men who seek to legitimize violence against women.[9] In cases of war, governments, guerrillas, and warlords wishing to engage in violent conflict use the gender stereotypes that are available, manipulating masculinity for their own purposes to mobilize men into combat. In other cases where young men had to be taught to kill, leaders have marginalized different types of masculinity. To do so, they set militarism up as the standard of masculinity, and derogate any nonviolent conflict resolution as feminine.[10] Given this, men may gain standing in their communities by participating in political violence.

Parties to conflict can also produce oppressive gender roles, practices, and gendered discourses. These discourses might, for example, support men's authority in political decision-making and configure the roles of women as mostly family based.[11] In such circumstances, community programs working to end violence may seek to gain legitimacy, credibility, and respect by recruiting ex-combatants to join in their work.[12] While this is common practice, focusing on recruitment of male ex-combatants in peacebuilding work can lead to reinforcing norms of gendered exclusion in post-conflict societies. Privileging their participation can lead to issues of gender inequality being marginalized, while the notion that men should be heard and recognized is reinforced.[13] Indeed, most peace processes still take place between all-male representatives from the parties to conflict, with the number of women involved in peace negotiations worldwide amounting to a mere 4 percent.[14] With gender identities posing such issues in adult participation in peace processes, it is not surprising that they also influence youth participation in conflict as well as in peacebuilding.

Boys, Masculinity, and Violence

Gender is a key factor in how young men understand themselves and others. Barker's research shows that "young men frequently report a sense of being observed and watched to see if they measure up to culturally salient versions of manhood,"[15] so pressure to comply with local gender norms is high. Gendered differences in relation to violence are likewise apparent. For example, school settings are dominated by entrenched cultural images that link manhood to competition, violence, and courage.[16] This and other forms of gender socialization tend to consolidate negative masculinity models. This can be particularly relevant for poor boys, as "almost universally, cultures promote an achievement-oriented masculinity that emphasizes men's primary roles as providers (workers) and protectors."[17] This has drawn many young men from low-income families to be attracted to violent masculinities modeled through groups such as gangs that bring with them access to money and resources to attract girls.

Research conducted in diverse cultures around the world, including empirical studies, shows that compared to girls and young women, boys and young men have tended to be far more frequently involved in violence as participants/perpetrators. This is evident on the local interpersonal level as well as on the broader social level of involvement in gangs, militias, or formal military enlistment. Indeed, while war impacts everyone, young men make up the largest proportion of all people fighting in wars, and the majority of child soldiers worldwide are male. Boys involved in conflict often aspire to become powerful men by controlling a setting and exerting violence on those around them, as it can aid them in achieving and wielding power. These models of masculinity created by war and conflict often lead young male soldiers or combatants to rape women and girls.[18] This rigid structure of gender norms for boys can also lead to scenarios in which allegations of homophobia are used to criticize young men who do not act in traditional ways. The promotion of more gender-equitable actions is hindered, as are HIV prevention efforts.[19]

Perhaps because of these statistical observations, some scholars have proposed that where many male youth are present violence is inevitable.[20] However, these positions rely on essentialized views of gender that naturalize men and boys as inherently violent. Hegemonic masculinity has been upheld and reinforced through social gendered norms. Yet it is important to beware of casting all young men as perpetrators or potential perpetrators. After all, many boys are not violent and/or are mainly victims of violence from other men (and women). Many boys who have participated in violence have also been victims or witnesses. Because in many places boys are able to spend more time in public spaces than girls, they may be more frequently exposed to physical violence, not just as participants, but also as victims or witnesses.[21]

While the scenario I have set out regarding young men, violence, and masculinities paints a dismal picture of ideals of manhood encouraging violence and disrespect for women, it is important to recognize that there is also evidence that some young men in cultures of violence interact in ways that are less violent and more respectful. There are some young men who, for example, spend their time participating in nonviolent cultural activities, some of which even focus on peacebuilding.[22] Recognizing this, scholars and practitioners dealing with issues of peace and security need to pay attention to what conditions might support boys in adopting nonviolent modes of masculinity.

Little research exists to date on what alternatives have enabled young men to avoid involvement in violence. Barker's research in the United States and Brazil is an exception. He notes that boys who were not involved in gangs shared some similar characteristics, including (a) having one or more stable relationship(s) with someone who would be let down if the boy joined a gang; (b) being able to access some different sense of self that would be positively valued in his social environment, especially his group of male peers (such as being a good musician or a good student); (c) having the ability to reflect on the costs and risks that come with the violent masculinity gangs promote; and (d) locating a different group of male peers that offered positive reinforcement for male identities not associated with gangs.[23]

In his research in Brazil, Barker suggests that young men who were more gender equitable also shared certain factors, including (a) family members or other role models who presented alternative views of more equitable gender roles; (b) some experience of pain resulting from traditional masculinity (such as domestic violence or abandonment) and the ability to reflect on the negative results; and (c) locating a social space or a group of peers where alternative views on masculinity were put forth.[24]

Given this, in searching to build cultures of peace, it makes sense to pursue cultural transformation of hegemonic patterns of gender. One key aspect of this includes creating spaces where young men are able to engage critically with masculinity, including rehearsing alternative modes of masculinity that are not dependent on violent behavior. In this context, projects seeking to build peace with young people need to be constantly reflecting on whether their work is creating or sustaining spaces where young men can "try on" new forms of nonviolent masculinity in a supportive environment.

Finding the Girls in Conflict

While providing options for young men is important, it must also come with attention to the place of girls in conflict and in peacebuilding. As violence by females tends to be understood as "unnatural" or unfeminine, and male violence has been seen as a much larger problem, relatively little information has been collected about the ways girls engage in violence. One must be careful not to obscure the role of young women in violence and conflict. Research confirms that in conflict zones where child soldiers are present, girls account for 6–50 percent of child soldiers. Girls also regularly participate in violent behaviors in schools, including bullying, and some even bully boys. Girls may also regularly perpetrate indirect violence against other girls by socially alienating them, spreading rumors, or using other means to influence their peer group.[25] Indeed, research suggests that while boys are more likely to act as bullies and be directly bullied or attacked, girls are more vulnerable to being socially isolated and excluded from their peer group. Of course, some girls may be dissuaded from continued participation in direct violence because of social norms encouraging them to be more feminine and passive, which may discourage the use of physical violence. Yet it is clear that girls participate not only in verbal aggression and intimidation, but also in physical aggression and violence.[26]

Nevertheless, young women are often ignored when it comes to youth programs addressing violence. For example, when it comes to formal programs promoting reintegration of ex-combatants, female youth who have participated in military groups are often left out. Indeed, research conducted in 20 different countries impacted by war since the early 1990s has shown that young women and girls are the most regularly at-risk and overlooked group. It is often the case that the few programs that do exist for youth are dominated by boys, while women's organizations are often run by and geared toward older women.[27]

Key questions thus need to be continually posed about whether and how girls might be excluded from peace work. While modernity has created impediments for girls, including unequal opportunities, dominant discourses still purport that the sole requirements for success are ambition, effort, and good choices.[28] Thus, care needs to be taken to avoid blaming young women for their own exclusion; if girls fail to get involved in formal political action, it can easily be written off as individual weakness, rather than systematic exclusion. This is something I engage with and question in greater detail in the case studies section in the second half of this chapter, but suffice to say here that these sorts of narratives about girls make creating open and inclusive programs more difficult. Challenging gender assumptions is important, because girls are an important part of society and deserve to play a fair role in efforts focused on building cultures of peace. In fact, they must do so if any such change is to be sustainable.

Gender, Music, and Prospects for Peace

Given that this book focuses on the use of music in youth peacebuilding, it is necessary to question whether or how music may be used in ways that foster gender inclusion. First, it is important to recognize that music practices can be used to naturalize gender difference. Music performance is frequently an important way gender behavior is socialized and taught. For example, youth may be taught from a very early age that certain music practices are reserved for males or females only, and song lyrics may reinforce certain dominant ideas about gender roles. Dance can be an essential method of gender socialization and integral to the performance of femininity and masculinity at rituals and special occasions.[29]

Traditional gender norms can also be displayed and reinforced through music performance, as in the case of Northern Ireland's male-dominated, hard-line "Blood and Thunder" bands, which have been and are viewed as a display of masculinity in the Protestant community and have likewise aided in fulfilling the cultural, political, and social needs of male youth from working-class backgrounds.[30] Music can be and has been used in ways that exclude or marginalize girls' participation, as has been documented in numerous accounts in the literature, particularly those focused on hip-hop.

At the same time, music and dance may be utilized in contestations of the current gender order. They may do so by providing a space for expanding boundaries and exploring the borders that separate female from male. This can create ground on which it is possible to contest gender categories, as identity factors such as age, gender, and culture "hover around the musical space but can penetrate only very partially the moment of enactment of musical fellowship."[31]

Participation in music activity may, for example, be used to produce nonviolent alternative masculinities. While some Blood and Thunder bands in Northern Ireland have supported violence, many other "parading bands provided one of the few positive outlets for the expression of political discontent during the 'Troubles,'" and today some have been working to change the atmosphere of the parades from aggressive to enjoyable family-friendly environments.[32]

Young women's greater involvement in youth cultural work has also initiated the questioning of traditional gender roles. For example, girls' involvement in music such as the Riot Grrrl movement discussed earlier has provided the opportunity for girls to challenge hegemony and participate actively in creating new social identities.[33] Even when participating in male-dominated genres such as hip-hop, young women may potentially create a destabilizing minority[34] that can challenge the existing gender order.

Gender in the Case Studies

When asked, "[How] do you think being a boy/girl affects your ability to be a peacemaker or the ways you can be involved in making peace?" most of the participants in both case studies did not indicate an awareness of any direct impacts of gender on their involvement. However, gender differences often emerged in response to other questions, indicating that girls and boys do have different experiences with violence and experience different barriers to participation in peacebuilding activities, including those involving music and dance.

In nearly all of the interviews, youth participants were asked whether they thought boys or girls were more violent, or if they thought participation in violence was equal for males and females. At Third Place (Australia), half of the youth participants who were asked this question believed boys engaged in more violence. Other responses included one young man, who said there was no violence in his community (although in other questions he did mention involvement in violence with other boys at his school) and two young women and one young man, who said participation in violence was equal between boys and girls.

I asked this same question to youth participants at Breaking Barriers (Northern Ireland). Nine of 13 interviewees there said violence was equal between boys and girls. One interviewee said it depends on where the boys and girls live, two said boys are more involved, and one said it was about equal but that guys are more involved in direct violence rather than just having sectarian attitudes. These responses show an awareness that discrimination itself is a form of violence. In fact, observation of conflict in Northern Ireland suggested that more boys were involved in direct violence, but both girls and boys had a more developed understanding of conflict than the Australian participants. The experience in Northern Ireland of these young people living in a conflict zone meant that they had a broader view of what conflict and violence could mean beyond direct violence.

In the Australian case study, all but two youth interviewees said they had been involved in or affected by violence, with most of them having directly participated in violence, including some of the girls. In my interviews in Northern Ireland, boys were more likely than girls to say they had participated in violence/fighting/rioting, with five boys saying they had done so. Two boys said they had not participated in or been affected by violence or conflict. This is interesting, because it would be almost impossible to be completely unaffected given the ongoing nature of the conflict in Northern Ireland. It seems boys who did not directly participate in fighting were less likely to see it as affecting them. However, this was not the case for all boys. Three girls and two boys said they had experienced violence in the form of bullying or intimidation, and one girl said she had been affected when she was younger because her family could not visit certain places due to violence. However, this was not necessarily just a gendered difference, as all boys who admitted to participating in violence were from the same area with similar backgrounds, so there were certainly other factors at play.

When I delved into these issues with the youth participants in both contexts, their responses illuminated a link between boys' participation in violence and expectations of performing gender. In both case studies, young people from diverse backgrounds reported understanding masculinity as performed through violence:

I think there's more boys in conflict. . . . Cuz they think if you're a boy then you have to be more manly and tough . . . (White Australian male, 14)

. . . Guys are trouble in everywhere. . . . Cuz . . . in school they wanna be the man . . . they decide, because of small things, they wanna be you know, "I'm the man," "No, you're not the man," "No, you're not the man," "I'm the man!" . . . [i]t's about who's better and stuff. (White Slovenian female, 18)

. . . I mean where I'm from . . . it's mostly guys, but sometimes girls they go pretty hard, hey. . . . Most of the girls I know they kinda really hate violence. I mean it's even if they hate some girl they won't even go and confront them, pull their hair and shit, they'll just kinda talk about them to their friends. . . . Guys most of them you know they got their pride, a lot of pride, and they're like, "Ye-uh, you say something about me?" And they just wanna confront them like [pushing motion] that. Like confrontation . . . and do something like that . . . (Fijian/Indian male, 20)

I'd say the guys probably. . . . Cuz girls don't have conflict. (Northern Irish Protestant male, 14)

. . . [H]ere, it's probably like about equal. They may not so much like direct conflict but the whole, the idea of can I say sectarianism? . . . Is yeah, it's like boy or girl doesn't really matter, they all feel that way. But maybe not the direct conflict is . . . probably more of a male thing . . . maybe just cuz they're just more aggressive generally, or they're more violent than females. . . . It's just here. It's like stereotype. (Northern Irish Protestant male, 16)

Well boys being boys they probably create the conflict more than girls would, to be honest. But, everyone has the ability to, whether they choose not to is up to them.

> . . . Cuz they're not very, they're not as good at showing their emotions, it's just what girls would do. I mean like expressing how he feels he'd rather punch a guy in the face than say to him I don't like what you're doing. (Northern Irish Protestant female, 17)

Conversations with the young program leaders in Australia also provided insights based on their understandings from working in several communities and schools affected by violence. All three of the leaders interviewed stated that they believed young men to be more involved in violence in the local area. In Northern Ireland when I asked the program facilitators, "Do you think boys or girls are more involved in conflict or violence in your community, or that it's equal? Why do you think that is?" Of four leaders, two said boys were more involved, one said boys are more in direct violence but girls are behind the scenes, and one noted gender differences, but did not clearly articulate what they were. For example, one facilitator at Breaking Barriers explained her view that boys' greater level of involvement in violence is based on the way they have been socialized to masculinity in their culture.

> I don't think that in that case it's the genes, I think it's the culture. Boys . . . are told—all the time—to fight. To fight for your woman, to fight for the property, to fight for the paramilitary. We were told to be at home, not fight. To, you know, do peace at home. . . . When I was a child, I always was told that I had to negotiate and I had to talk and communicate and . . . try to avoid fights and problems and conflicts. . . . My brother when he has a problem and he fights with him, hits and pushing him, well it's okay because he's a boy . . . because we have base capacity to negotiate. . . . It's said that the best negotiators are women. (Colombian female, 31)

Moreover, like the young people interviewed, the program facilitators in Northern Ireland pointed out the complexity of violence and noted that while men and boys may be more likely to participate in direct violence, women and girls certainly still play roles in activities that hinder prospects for peace. As two of them explain here:

> [T]ypically like you always associate men doing that, boys too. You know boys will like be menaces. . . . So I suppose people stereotype, would think boys would get involved in rioting and like all that thing more, but people'd be surprised—the women do it too. But when there's news reports it's always . . . you'll see the men, but people don't see the women behind the scenes. . . . So . . . I think like predominantly yes males would probably do that and I think that because of the way women are . . . genetically they're meant to be softer and more caring. . . . Women do have a more caring nature, but then it depends on your background. Like you know if you're brought up to think like that and think you know oh we don't want peace, you know Northern Ireland will never have peace . . . you're gonna portray that to the children as well. So I don't know it's kinda hard to decide you know . . . with men and women . . . who would do more. I don't know. (Northern Irish Protestant female, 21)

> It's just a bit, probably equal, you know they say guys are guys or whatever and get in fights and that where girls have got more sort of behind the scenes you know . . . so they're just involved in different ways . . . (Northern Irish Protestant male, 31)

The young women program leaders at Third Place also stated that boys are more involved in violence. In fact, the lead facilitator asserted that research they had done in numerous schools in the area backed this up with data, explaining:

> [W]e did this cultural mapping process . . . where we went around . . . finding out what young people . . . see in their community . . . around gang violence and all that stuff . . . and the results from that . . . it's mostly the . . . male, or boys, who . . . are more in that kind

of situation of violence. (Samoan/German female from New Zealand, 25)

When the female program leaders were asked why they thought boys were more involved, one suggested:

> Growing up in [a nearby neighborhood] and always having the boys at school and meeting other boys from around the suburb, they tend to be rough . . . in just the way that they would speak to the girls and things like that, they would carry on . . . in a different way . . . in a more aggressive way than the girls would. (Samoan/Chinese female raised in Australia, 18)

When asked whether the young men expect each other to interact in that way, she stated that they do.

Another facilitator explained how performing dominant modes of violent masculinity can be seen as key to popularity and having friends. This is particularly important when looking at groups of youth that may be marginalized, such as refugees and other immigrant communities. She said:

> [O]ne of the little African boys that I interviewed, I asked him . . . why . . . he's always in fights, why [he] . . . wants to be in on gang violence, and . . . he expressed that . . . it makes him cool . . . it makes him popular . . . and, just he's really conscious of just not having friends. (Samoan/German female from New Zealand, 25)

When I inquired as to whether that was different for girls, she noted that popularity and acceptance for the girls was different, not based on whether they engage in fights:

> . . . It was more the girls that mentioned . . . that it was the boys kind of into gang violence and stuff, and . . . they're more into stopping it. . . . They don't like it. . . . There weren't very many probs. . . . I think the only problem with the girls was that they were feeling unsafe to walk from school, or walk, because of the

> gang violence. . . . They voiced their opinions, but . . . I haven't heard of any talks about girls getting into fights and stuff. . . . I remember . . . in one conversation that we had . . . that there was a fight they called a "chick fight" at the train station. . . . It's actually, yeah it's one mentioned that was pretty petty stuff, so it's not really that much of a problem. (Samoan/German female from New Zealand, 25)

This is interesting, as it seems to indicate that while there actually are violent interactions between young women, it is not seen as serious or threatening in the same way as when young men are involved. It would also be worth talking more with girls to gain further understandings of the race issues involved in girl-on-girl conflict, as two of the young women gave racialized accounts when describing physical violence between girls.

> I reckon they're sorta equal, but I've seen more fights about, more violence than, with girls than boys around here. . . . I always see the fights down at the station . . . with . . . Aboriginal girls. . . . Cuz too many other cultures diss their culture, so they end up in a fight. . . . I've seen heaps of those down there in the last week. . . . Like four or five. (Samoan/Maori female, 13)

> I'm not racist, but the Maori girls, they're really aggressive, they can be really aggressive if they want to . . . (White Slovenian female, 18)

These racialized accounts indicate the need for acknowledging and engaging with the links between various identity factors when looking at issues of conflict and gender.

Overall, in both the Australian and Northern Irish contexts, there were numerous instances in which I heard or observed ways in which boys' and girls' experiences of violence and identity differed based on gender. Peacebuilding projects need to take this into account. My findings suggest that gender-sensitive frameworks are needed for peacebuilding work to account for differences in a way that addresses violence as complex, multifaceted, and influenced by gender identities.

"It's More of a Guy Thing": Girls' Exclusion from Peacebuilding Activities

In both case studies, the evidence suggested that girls were often excluded from certain activities based on gender norms. At Third Place (Australia), three of the four girls interviewed did not participate as dancers in the workshops, yet all of them mentioned dance when asked about how they became interested in their art form or some other question. Obviously these girls like and enjoy dance. Yet, participating in dance at the workshops, where the crump group was all boys, and the breakdance group had only one girl, did not seem like an option for them. One young female facilitator explained how the girls attending were often less comfortable with performing in mixed-gender groups:

> I thought they were a whole lot more shy around the boys. And when they'll be with their girlfriends they'll be loud and out there. (Samoan/Chinese female raised in Australia, 18)

At Breaking Barriers (Northern Ireland), young women were also excluded from some parts of music programs, such as rapping or playing leading roles in rock music, which are seen to be masculine activities. In the YM program I observed, it went even further, with girls being formally excluded from participation. When we first got to the program site, three girls arrived and wanted to participate but were told by the center director that they could not; the program was only for the boys, and this was confirmed in my interviews. The boys told the girls to get out too, even though they were also flirting with them—so they still maintained it as an exclusive boys' space. Throughout the program, the girls entered several times wanting to join in, but even though they were only watching and not bothering anyone, the project manager told them to leave, and the boys all chimed in shouting, "Yeah, tell them!" The girls later told me the youth center director is going to book in a time for them to have their own workshop, but I have not heard of this happening to date. I also asked some questions about the gender makeup of other YM programs that I was unable to observe because they took place before my arrival. One boy who had participated in a previous program in Belfast stated:

> Well there was more boys than girls . . . I think cuz there was about three or four girls involved in it, but the rest were guys. (Northern Irish Protestant male, 12)

It is clear that gendered issues of identity can impact what roles young people may be interested in taking in peacebuilding programs, particularly those that use music and dance, and this may be magnified as youth reach the teenage years. As some of their facilitators at Breaking Barriers explained:

> I think there's still [a] stereotype where a band is men. . . . I think that's why we don't have a lot of women guitarists or women drummers because . . . you know it's a stereotype that that's what men do. . . . You very rarely see like a woman rock band or anything you know. But hopefully that'll change and hopefully like with my influence, I'll get more women involved in it, having a woman drummer and stuff. . . . I think it depends on the age. Like if it's quite a young group, boys and girls aren't really conscious of each other you know. But I think as children get older they do become more conscious of hang on, I'm a girl and you're a boy. . . . So I would think I suppose it depends on age. But if it's like 12- or 13-year-olds obviously the boys are gonna want to show off to impress the girls, so it's a different dynamic. Whilst the younger groups it's all just . . . let's play an instrument, let's have fun. (Northern Irish Protestant female, 21)

> I think it depends on the program you are offering. . . . You know if you're offering something really appealing toward the boys, more boys will come . . . and if you're

> offering something appealing to girls you'll get more girls . . . sometimes it's difficult to work with both . . . (Mexican female, 31)

Noticing these patterns, I wanted to know more about why girls might feel excluded. Thus, I began asking the youth participants and facilitators at Third Place: "This is a space with majority boys—why do you think that is? Do you think other girls would feel comfortable here? What do you think it would take to involve other girls? How would you design a project to include them?" Their responses portrayed a dominant view, evident across ethnic, class, and gender differences, that the problem is in the girls—they are not aware, interested, skilled, or confident enough to participate. None of the respondents mentioned anything indicating other (external) factors that might make the girls feel excluded. What does this mean for the young women taking part in music-based peacebuilding?

These findings relate to a growing body of literature exploring the impact of neoliberal discourse on understandings of gender. "Neoliberalism" is often used to describe a system of global economics that envisions market-based solutions as always preferable. Emerging strongly in Western developed countries in recent decades, this economic system was further entrenched globally by the IMF and World Bank mandating structural adjustment programs across the developing world. The outcome has often been particularly harmful for women, as neoliberalism has become so naturalized to the point that it is often seen as a neutral best practice for ordering government and economic systems. Under this paradigm, it is assumed that economics can generally be seen as separate from politics and culture, while any problems that could cross over will be best "corrected" by the free market. Likewise, the best and fairest way to organize societies is one that ignores or denies interventions to address intersecting structural inequalities, such as those related to gender, race, and class.[35] The term "neoliberalism" is used here to represent a related hegemonic political discourse that sees the world and interactions in it as characterized by freedom, privatization, individualization, and choice.[36] In this way, inequality is constituted as a personal issue, with the burden on individuals to overcome obstacles, rather than an issue potentially requiring changes to structures that may perpetuate the inequalities.

Rich argues that young women are often heavily influenced by neoliberal ideas, through which they understand themselves primarily as unconstrained individuals able to make free choices.[37] This may have some positive impacts for girls, affording them a sense of access to opportunities and a sense of agency. Indeed, this could arguably be seen as supporting activism associated with DIY (do-it-yourself) feminism, which underscored the Riot Grrrl movement and helped in popularizing some versions of third wave feminism.[38]

However, focusing on individual capacity and responsibility for improving one's own lot can simultaneously obscure structural and sociocultural gender-based inequalities. Girls may deny that they are personally influenced by gender, as occurred in this research. This denial can lead to girls seeing any failure, including their own, as caused solely by individual shortcomings. In short, they may see any inability to participate as their own fault. In seeking to avoid being positioned as "victims," girls often find themselves unable to acknowledge, engage, contest, and resist diverse manifestations of gender inequality.[39]

Comments by men and boys interviewed confirmed that their views were also shaped by these discourses. When asked why fewer girls participated or why they may not feel able to participate, "I don't know," was a very common response among male interviewees. Franzway et al. suggest that this kind of "not knowing" is a crucial part of the problem of women's low participation in male-dominated activities. This analysis can also be usefully applied to studies focused on youth. This kind of "ignorance," or "not knowing about gender and change," is influenced by gender politics. It is often framed by an invisible construction of girls as lacking aptitude, information, and authority. A gendered understanding of politics recognizes that masculine practices and concerns are understood as the norm and sheds light on "the invisibility of men's power [and boys'], which is constituted as the normal way of being."[40]

Refusing to recognize the role of gender politics in the organizational culture of peacebuilding programs can create a reluctance to reconsider entrenched practices and norms that privilege boys' participation over girls'. Consider these responses from male participants when asked why boys were more involved than girls in some activities:

> I'm not sure . . . originally there was a lot of boys who . . . were already dancing. . . . They probably wanna do it cuz of . . . like I don't know, skill. [You think that more guys already had skills in those areas and that's why they came?] Yeah. (White Australian male, 14)

> [T]he girls think it's . . . not for them. I don't know. Maybe they don't really like it. . . . They're not as interested. (Black African Liberian male, 16)

> I don't know. . . . I think it's just not many people know about it. But . . . when girls know about it they come to it. Like [girl break-dancer] she didn't hear about it until we told her and then she wanted to come. . . . Or maybe they just think it's more of a guys' thing . . . (White Australian male, 16)

> I don't know. I just think . . . there wasn't many girls knew about it . . . there wasn't many there. (Northern Irish Protestant male, 12)

> I don't really know but maybe it's just cuz they're . . . I don't like to stereotype . . . but maybe more like shy or . . . I don't know, more introvert with their . . . abilities and . . . I don't understand why . . . (Northern Irish Protestant male, 16)

These quotes show how boys in both case studies professed not knowing why few girls participated while at the same time they explained girls' nonparticipation as a deficiency on the part of the girls, painting them as unaware or unable to participate.

Since facilitators develop, implement, and adapt these projects, it is important to consider their views, too. Their responses also indicated a belief that the girls had some problem or lacked something needed for participating in the activities dominated by boys. When questioned about why some groups were majority boys, a male facilitator stated:

> I really don't know. . . . I think it probably comes back to a woman, I mean . . . I don't know why. (Tongan male raised in Australia, 24)

Girls participating also appeared to have accepted this discourse, noting their feelings of being unable to participate based on it being "a boys' thing."

> I wanted to do crumping but for me it was like, you know it's a boys' thing—can't really do it. . . . So I guess it was like for, as girls here, it's probably break dancing and crumping's for guys. So there's only singing left, so they're just singing . . . (Maori female, 13)

> Like I know [her friend] . . . she's too shamed. She can dance and crump, but she's too shamed. . . . [S]he doesn't have much confidence. . . . They do [want to crump]. . . . [T]hey tell me they do, but they're like scared. (Samoan/Maori female, 13)

The only girl who participated in the otherwise all-male break-dance group deemed herself a tomboy for doing so, identifying this as outside "normal" girl behavior. Indeed, she suggested that it may even be considered "manly" to be unafraid of trying new things.

> [T]here's a lot of girls that wanna sing. . . . But . . . their friends don't want to go to sing and then because of that they won't go. If I wanna do something and if my friend don't wanna go . . . I will say, "Why you don't wanna go?" and . . . I would go just to try it if nothing else. . . . Guys just try it, but girls . . . I'm not fully tomboy, but I am like in some ways . . . and I just . . . everything what's possible . . . you never know what

> you're good in. If you're not at one you try it . . . anyway. (White Slovenian female, 18)

Likewise, a young woman arts worker stated:

> [Y]ou don't find as much girls crumping . . . it's pretty rare. . . . I know a lot of young girls who would love to learn about crumping, but . . . sometimes I kind of look at it like, I noticed it from the last workshops . . . there seems to be . . . like some of the girls go . . . for the singing and song writing because they [are] . . . drawn to [female facilitator who raps, which is also in the singing room]. . . . They wanna go there because you know . . . they're so close to [her] . . . they just wanna be near her. Or they'll come to me if they wanna . . . hang out with me. . . . Sometimes that can be the case. . . . But I think the boys go to crumping because they like crumping . . . it's the in thing at the moment. . . . They kind of like to express themselves and just make yourself seen. . . . They've actually got a lot to say, a long story to turn into . . . just by looking at their actions they're really into it. . . . I think the boys go there . . . cuz they love it. . . . But I think some of the girls . . . could . . . go to an MC or song writing workshop because you know they wanna be near me and her . . . but also . . . I think there's a shame factor in there. (Samoan/German female from New Zealand, 25)

Because one young crump instructor originally had come to the project as a participant before becoming a leader, I also wanted to draw on her reflections of being a girl in that environment, asking what she had felt like as a participant in a majority-male space. She said:

> I was just really shamed . . . cause the dance was just all girls we had our own little room where we'd practice. . . . The boys were mainly . . . in the whole MC song writing, so they were in another room. And when it came to show and tell . . . I'd get shamed. . . . I was intimidated

> just knowing that the boys were around . . . watching. (Samoan/Chinese female raised in Australia, 18)

How had she overcome this, I wondered?

> I just pretty much tried to look away and just do what I do. (Samoan /Chinese female raised in Australia, 18)

In this way, she suggests that the onus was on the girls to fit in by individually overcoming barriers to their participation.

That these neoliberal understandings of gender were shared by young people and facilitators from such diverse backgrounds is a testament to how hegemonic the discourse has become globally, particularly in Western developed countries such as the two studied here. At the same time, different expectations around who could participate, and how, were influenced by other identity factors. Just as some types of music or instruments are often seen to be masculine or feminine, intersections with race and/or ethnicity can also impact participation. As noted in the case studies chapter, ethnopolitical identities are also ascribed to particular instruments or activities. For example, in Northern Ireland, one drum, the bodhrán, is seen as symbolizing the nationalist (Catholic) community, while another, the lambeg, automatically brings to mind marching bands and the Orange (Protestant) tradition, and contentions can and do arise about who plays what, when, and how. As also previously noted, oftentimes in Northern Ireland areas considered neutral for peacebuilding were experienced as less accessible to youth from lower socioeconomic-status backgrounds, so it is important to recognize that race and class intersect with gender in influencing who participates and how.

Assumptions of Individualization and the Construction of Girls as Deficient

The impact of neoliberal discourse, including the assumption of an existing equal playing field in which individual actors can and should take responsibility for securing their own positive outcomes was evident in the design and leadership styles of both programs. Was there something different about girls who did participate in masculine-identified practice? I was particularly interested to find out what made the only girl who participated in break dancing at Third Place feel able to do so. I later learned through interviews with one of the male breakdancers that she already knew him and his brothers, and they had directly invited her to come and participate in the group. So while she was an exceptional female for joining their group, she also had a connection and support network already in place with several of the boys in the otherwise all-male group. This most likely gave her an automatic "in" and a reason to feel comfortable that the other girls would not share. What then might help other girls feel included in the work?

When I asked female facilitators in Australia whether they had any ideas of what could be done to make the girls feel more comfortable, they both advocated "fixing" something in the girls, rather than any process that could include educating the boys on being more inclusive or adapting the structure of the programs:

> . . . [R]eally focusing on their shame factor . . . creating more activities about shame, just trying to eliminate it . . . (Samoan/Chinese female raised in Australia, 18)

> I'm trying to put some activities in place to try and eliminate their shame factor. . . . I didn't question why they weren't joining dance groups. . . . I assume that it's because they're a bit shy to just be around the guys and stuff. (Samoan/German female from New Zealand, 25)

It is commendable that these program leaders are thinking of ways to support girls' involvement, but this focus might not address the larger task of challenging gendered exclusions that may hinder peacebuilding. After the Third Place project I studied ended, I learned that a separate "hip-hop" dance group for girls was started. Many joined, as it had more "feminine" moves than crump or breaking and was thus seen as more acceptable. However, while this does offer girls a creative outlet for dance, it does not challenge the male ownership of particular musical activities or the essentialized gender identities associated with particular practices. This raises questions about when it might be worthwhile for youth peacebuilding projects to deconstruct the ways certain activities are (re)created as masculine domains and adopt methods that include reflection on the part of boys about creating or sustaining gendered exclusions, rather than regarding the problem as maladjustment on the part of young women that needs to be corrected.

In both case studies, interviewees talked about music participation involving merely "individual" preferences, yet it was also clear that many had frequently observed gender differences. This suggests a need to consider how dominant assumptions about gender in a given culture impact individual understandings of identity. It also merits some discussion and analysis of the impact of neoliberal discourse on program planning and implementation, including how this impacts prospects for peacebuilding. Questions must be asked about how gender-based exclusions can be mitigated. Facilitators at Breaking Barriers reported noting gender differences in participation and framed these in a way that made it seem that girls and women need extra help, direction, or protection, whereas boys could operate more independently. As two of them explained:

> I find the girls will be more willing to do it, but with instruction. They . . . wouldn't consciously go over and go "I wanna hit it." They'll do it if someone tells them to or if the boys are gonna go, "I don't wanna do that," but once they get started you see the boys and they're interacting more and they're enjoying it more than the girls. And half the time the girls will do it first and the boys don't want to, but then after they get involved it's totally changed . . . (Northern Irish Protestant female, 21)

> I'm quite wary . . . even to . . . bring a woman . . . with me . . . at the initial meeting. . . . Sometimes when we have a school that's all boys . . . it's just she could feel a bit uncomfortable with it . . . (Northern Irish Protestant male, 31)

At Breaking Barriers few girls participated, so it was difficult to gather girls' views. However, opportunities existed to learn more about the boys' views on gender. Based on observations and questions posed in the literature about gender in youth musical programs, I specifically asked the participants in boys-only programs if they preferred to have the workshops exclusively for boys. In their responses, one said he would like it sometimes mixed, sometimes not; one said something unclear; and four preferred gender-segregated programs. When I asked if they thought they would interact differently if the project included girls, five out of six said yes, with one boy specifically saying, "It'd be embarrassing."

In the Northern Irish context, when it came to questions of better including girls, boys and male facilitators favored the "do nothing" approach. For example, when I asked the project manager about gender ratios, he upheld his view that music is just more a "guy thing," an attitude I had encountered at times in my Australian case study:

> . . . [W]e haven't really tried to market it for being male or female, so just whoever took part took part that way. . . . Not to try to do a balance but it's something that we haven't really looked at. . . . If people don't wanna take part they don't wanna take part. . . . It just so happens to be that music does seem to attract more guys. . . . Whether it's a confidence thing or I don't know what. . . . And that's just kind of like a male thing . . . to beat the drum and to kind of show their . . . territory . . . (Northern Irish Protestant male, 31)

In short, he did not see the need to think or plan around gender issues. His view, which informed the program's design, favored ignoring gender in seeking to see everyone as the same:

> . . . We're quite good at working in a team and . . . if there's all girls . . . it just never crossed my mind that they were all girls. . . . They're just people . . . (Northern Irish Protestant male, 31)

The prospect of a gender-blind program may seem reasonable, but these findings pose serious questions about effectiveness and inclusion when ignoring gender is standard practice. Likewise, when I asked one participant if he could offer advice on ways to involve both girls and boys, he seemed to support the continuation of the "no-gender-plan model" espoused by the program director:

> I think it was just really by chance, I don't think it was . . . like we have to get this many girls and this many guys and have to have equal numbers. . . . Cuz [the program director] put up . . . notices and handed out application forms and it was just really who responded to that. . . . I don't think you can really control that apart from just how the individual is . . . (Northern Irish Protestant male, 16)

Of course, I also wanted to learn whether boys had felt excluded from any group based on gender. However, none of the young men currently involved in Third Place said they wanted to sing, which was the only girl-majority group. Still, it is likely that young men who might like to participate in such activities may feel unable to do so based on their need to avoid femininity and prove their masculinity. One older male participant reflected on his teen years and noted how boys' choices are also constrained or denigrated based on gendered assumptions:

> When I was young . . . I remember all the guys, I say I'm in the choir, and they're like, "That's gay, bro!" you know they're like, "What the hell are you in choir for?" I didn't give a shit. . . . Man I enjoy the singing . . . (Fijian/Indian male, 20)

I also did not observe any instances of boys being excluded in the Breaking Barriers programs, but one female facilitator shared a story of how she had observed this in other programs where she had worked prior to this job:

> [W]ith dance you always get more girls. And then . . . maybe like two or three boys that want to get involved

> but it's like a peer pressure. . . . And they think oh what are my friends gonna think? And sometimes you find them the first like two or three classes and after that they disappear because there's too much peer pressure. . . . Unless all of them decide to go together . . . so they'll go . . . (Mexican female, 31)

Addressing Exclusions

These findings point to the need for youth peacebuilding programs to not only acknowledge that gender matters, but also to critically engage with some key feminist debates around the equality/difference tension. These tensions have sparked years of debate in feminist circles, with some scholars arguing that equality feminism relies on masculine subjectivities that inherently subordinate women and can lead to their constructing "(other) women as other."[41] At the same time, some scholars have looked at difference in various ways and pointed out limitations and challenges associated with it from various feminist viewpoints. As Scott has convincingly argued, while doing so is common, conceptualizing equality and difference as dichotomous is problematic in creating a double bind in which women can only be understood as unequal based on their differences to men.[42] I suggest that this argument can also be applied to differences between girls and boys. Scott thus argues that difference is not antithetical to, but indeed essential to, achieving true equality. In other words, as Forcey puts it, "feminists need to recognize the antithesis of difference is not equality but rather sameness; and the antithesis of equality is not difference, but rather inequality."[43]

It is critical that peacebuilding programs consciously create reflexive frameworks for thinking about these activities in a way that foregrounds the idea that girls matter and their involvement in peacebuilding is essential. Moreover, while I did not observe any boys being or feeling excluded from feminine-identified practice, observations and responses indicate that truly gender-inclusive programming will require challenging gender-based exclusion however it may occur. Where boys may be absent from peacebuilding initiatives, programs must seek to address this by appealing to young men through offering relevant and accessible activities that provide attractive alternatives to violence.[44] Critically engaging with these issues on a practical level might include: pointed discussions around gender equality and difference in program planning and evaluation, experimental use of separate gendered spaces, and integration to coeducational programs to evaluate the possibilities and prohibitions posed by each.

Questions of gender mainstreaming have highlighted the need for addressing existing tensions as to whether gender equality should draw on concepts of "sameness," "difference," or "transformation." Walby thus urges the need to question whether gender equality can be separated from strategies for achieving it, or whether in fact notions of equality and strategic interventions must be constituent parts of the same process. At the same time, these questions are complicated by the need for addressing other intersecting inequalities, particularly those related to ethnicity and class.[45] Based on a cross-cultural analysis of young people's attitudes toward gender across 10 countries, Bulbeck suggests that Western feminists might discover a new set of possibilities by developing a vocabulary that allows equality to be asserted at the same time as difference is demanded. This, she suggests, might facilitate the pursuit of gender-differentiated projects in some cases.[46]

Responses by some of the girls I interviewed suggested they would appreciate such work. At the end of each interview, I asked, "Do you have any suggestions for how the program should be changed to make it better, or overall comments?" The responses of two of the four young female participants at Third Place suggested the need for girl-specific programming:

> I reckon add a bit more dancing—for girls—like more activities . . . (Maori female, 13)

> . . . I would probably put hip-hop in because there are a lot of girls that dance to hip-hop, but they're not interested in break dance. (White Slovenian female, 18)

These comments indicate that some young women would prefer programs directed at them, and imply that single-sex programs may offer some prospects. Likewise, Schell-Faucon suggests that "gender-specific learning" is the best approach in youth peacebuilding programs and argues that because in some societies girls cannot attend camps with boys and because girls have "different experiences of, and reactions to, conflict and violence," gender-specific work is very important in encouraging their participation and meeting their needs.[47] In certain circumstances gender-segregated groups could be appropriate. For example, in some locations certain cultural or religious protocols may limit or prohibit boys and girls from participating in particular activities together. In such circumstances, gender-segregated groups may be beneficial or even necessary, at least initially, in youth peacebuilding programs. For example, they may be used where activities seen as predominantly masculine, such as sports, are a key feature.

However, separating girls and boys is not necessarily a long-term solution, particularly as it can leave girls without the opportunity to work with other leaders in their artistic field who happen to be males. Thus, Baker and Cohen[48] suggest that while initially girls may prefer to have a "safe space" for learning skills in male-dominated activities, they may later benefit from program integration. Of the four young people I interviewed who had participated in the Breaking Barriers program at their coeducational school, they all supported gender integration, with one girl even saying:

> It's . . . so much better cuz you don't wanna always just be with girls, and boys are really cool as well. (Northern Irish Catholic female, 13)

Many facilitators would not see any need for gender-sensitive programming, as they may think that the projects are successful and thus assume that no alterations are needed. For example, while acknowledging the different experiences of violence for young men and women, when asked whether he had noticed any differences at Third Place in how they interacted with each other, a male facilitator reported seeing none:

> Nah, I think it was quite good. . . . I think they . . . worked well together . . . really team-like, which we

> were really happy with. (Tongan male raised in Australia, 24)

My observations supported this view; there were many examples of young men and women supporting one another. For instance, when one girl joined the break-dance group, the boys all encouraged her even though she was new and inexperienced. At the same time, I wonder how much this was influenced by her status as a group insider, as previously noted. Thus, their interaction with her may be different from how they would engage with an unfamiliar girl wishing to participate. Likewise, it is worth further examining what could make male-dominated activities more welcoming and inclusive environments for girls interested in participating.

In this case I have looked at mixed-gender groups and noted prospects for improved gender relations through this work, but many difficulties remain. Thus, more research is needed on what gender inclusiveness would look like in peacebuilding practice. One girl who sang in the project said she had become involved because some facilitators approached her one day as she was walking home from school and directly asked her if she would sing with them. To learn more, I asked participants and facilitators what methods they might envision could be used to create more inclusive programming to involve girls. The female break-dancer, when asked how to attract more girls, advocated a similar approach of reaching out to them:

> . . . I would go [say to] each of them . . . , "Listen, it's for free, I'm going to teach you . . . I can pick you up . . ." whatever is necessary just to try to show them. . . . If it's necessary I would . . . go to each of them to ask if they wanna go. (White Slovenian female, 18)

I also asked a young male facilitator if he could imagine ways to involve more girls. He suggested:

> An idea would probably be to have . . . facilitators who, a guy and a girl, you know partnering . . . (Tongan male raised in Australia, 24)

A young woman participant echoed this view, suggesting that the program:

> Have . . . girl teachers . . . have them as a girl instead of a boy. . . . And then heaps of girls would do it. (Samoan/Maori female, 13)

Interviewees also suggested individually encouraging people to get involved, saying:

> . . . You could maybe get more girls by like getting more people to start learning music . . . and start learning to play instruments. . . . Enjoying music. (Northern Irish Protestant male, 12)

> . . . It's good to have mixed workshops because some of . . . the kids who were very confident . . . I've seen . . . the kids would actually see talents in other kids and be like, "You're a very good singer. We'd like you to be our singer." And they'd . . . probably kind of shrink into themselves, but probably by the end of the week they're the ones that are sitting in the spotlight. . . . So that's what I like to see. (Northern Irish Protestant female, 17)

Another facilitator suggested that gender inclusivity might be achieved by:

> [U]sing different approaches . . . you can work with something that is fashionable like hip-hop . . . something very approachable . . . and from that you can develop . . . something positive. (Mexican female, 31)

These responses indicate that working with boys and girls simultaneously is possible, but not necessarily easy. Creative, innovative frameworks are required to ensure that both young men and young women feel they can participate and develop their skills in peacebuilding.

Positive Prospects

While challenges exist, I want to highlight here that the evidence gathered suggests that girls who overcame the barriers to participation in coeducational programs experienced positive outcomes that may make their continued involvement in peacebuilding more likely. Of all the girls interviewed in both programs, only one had ever previously participated in a peacebuilding project, so having a positive experience at the program could generate further interest in peacebuilding. All the girls involved said they believed this experience would make it easier for them to take part in peacebuilding in the future. At both programs, all girls interviewed said music had been a useful way for them to get involved in peacebuilding, while about half of them said they would not have attended a peacebuilding program if it had not involved music. When the girls were asked how, if at all, the program had changed the way they see themselves, their answers included statements about increased confidence and self-respect. Moreover, all of the girls in both projects said they had learned skills that they could use to address future conflict nonviolently, and they all said they would keep using the skills learned in the workshops to continue to make peace in their communities. It thus appears that musical projects can help prepare girls for action and leadership in other peacebuilding initiatives.

While several gendered issues complicate the capacity for youth to make peace, I am not suggesting that young men and women cannot work together, nor that peace can be achieved without the inclusion and participation of youth from various cultures and genders. Finding novel ways to build understanding and foster cooperation between boys and girls is an integral part of creating more peaceful, gender-just societies. This may occur through building new relationships with boys and girls working collaboratively. One of the girls in the Australian case study explained how her participation in the music-based project had changed her relationship with the boys:

> . . . For me it's kind of brought . . . me closer to the guys . . . become friends and stuff. . . . Like forget about like,

> "Oh guys suck!" . . . For me it shows . . . another side to guys like. . . . There's always friends there that you can have . . . (Maori female, 13)

In response to a question of how she overcame feeling "shamed" in her past experience as a participant, one female leader expressed similar sentiments:

> I just got used to it, but then at the same time I was also building up friendship with the fellas . . . (Samoan/Chinese female raised in Australia, 18)

These remarks indicate that there are some prospects for youth to carry out peacebuilding work productively in mixed-gender environments. Girls may build confidence working with boys; and, by working with girls in music-based projects, boys may learn to be noncompetitive in a way that creates new modes of nonviolent masculinities they may not have seen as options in other settings. While I did not see any clear evidence of this taking place in these case studies, future research should consider this. Asking such questions is important because dominant notions of masculinity as violent can impede peace while excluding girls from certain masculine-identified musical activities. By challenging exclusive male ownership of such activities and spaces, peacebuilding projects may benefit boys and girls through supporting more democratic interactions across gender.

Individuals crossing gender boundaries in musical practice do not necessarily imply some sweeping change. However, individual work could eventually lead to wider change over time that could have implications for the existence of sexism, racism, and homophobia. To foster this, peacebuilding organizations could take a more explicit stance against exclusive practices by being proactive as opposed to reactive, adopting policies that are antiracist, antisexist, and antihomophobic. Still, many questions remain about how best to implement such programming. Should more girls-only programs be created? Or should coeducational programs be modified to create more gender-inclusive spaces? My suggestion is that both are needed.

Conclusion

A feminist research ethic requires asking questions about inclusion and exclusion, and such work is desperately needed in peacebuilding research. Programs geared toward youth are no exception. More research is needed in this area, including looking at who leaves the projects, when, why, and how, as well as engagement with young people not participating to learn more about why that may be. In short, we need to be learning more about whether or not some young people will be accepted for involvement in musical peacebuilding projects, and gender is clearly an area that merits study as part of this equation. The mixed understandings and responses documented in these case studies give reason to examine further the concepts of difference, sameness, and equality in regard to the impact of gender on participation in peacebuilding programs. Critical reflection is needed on all of the key themes discussed in this chapter.

Gender is a major influence on the lives of young people, and it plays a significant role in conflict. Thus, scholars and practitioners wishing to address the international political problem of conflict can learn important lessons by looking at how gender politics takes placein the context of youth peacebuilding programs. Girls are often excluded from peace processes, so further investigation is needed of how and why this occurs. The data gathered through these case studies revealed a tendency to rely on neoliberal discourses in ignoring the gendered dimensions of participation, while seeing exclusion as a lack on the part of the individual girls. These assumptions must be uncovered and critically interrogated in order to create more inclusive peacebuilding programs for youth. Doing so will require rejecting discourses that paint girls as unskilled and uninterested and acknowledging their creativity and capacity for peacebuilding. These findings suggest that the connection between organizational choices and unequal gender participation should be adequately acknowledged and addressed when planning youth peacebuilding projects. Further research should tackle important questions of whether peacebuilding activities ought to reflect or challenge accepted notions of which activities are masculine or feminine, as well as identifying the conditions under which these projects should feature gender-segregated or integrated activities.

Postlude

In this research, I have found that music can be a particularly useful way to engage youth in peacebuilding. Youth participants themselves confirmed this—when asked whether they thought music had been a useful tool for their involvement in peacebuilding, all of them said it had. Moreover, music emerged as key to involving these youth in peacebuilding. Most of the young people I interviewed said they would not have been interested in participating in a peacebuilding program that did not include music or dance. However, many of those same youth, after being drawn in by the music, reported that they had become inspired to continue working to build peace in some capacity.

For the youth participants in these programs, music became a useful tool for building peace by: offering a mechanism for engaging in dialogue across difference, providing a performative framework for challenging essentialist notions of conflict identities, and presenting an opportunity for (re) creating spaces as more open and inclusive for youth. These are all important prospects that merit further research and consideration.

First, one way in which music is useful for engaging youth in peacebuilding is that it has the capacity for facilitating dialogue. In the two case studies, young people and facilitators demonstrated several ways that music can serve as a form of dialogue for building peace. Music could do so, they suggested, by offering new modes of expression and enabling communication across difference, even in conflict settings. Moreover, music-based dialogue can offer a nonviolent mechanism for sharing meaning—many youth participants said they could use music when faced with conflict instead of resorting to violence. At the same time, interviewees also recognized the importance of traditional modes of dialogue. Many said taking part in these music-based peacebuilding programs had given them a chance to develop and hone skills in "talking things out." These programs are important for the young people who participate in them, but they can also have a broader impact. The findings suggest that music is particularly useful for engaging people outside the program in this musical dialogue by conveying the youth's message in a way that encourages the development of a culture of peace. Furthermore, many participants said they had told or would tell others about their musical activities in an attempt to get more people involved in promoting a culture of peace through music. Not all musical activities will constitute an act or dialogue, nor will they all promote peace, but these findings suggest that musical activities can be a relevant and effective way to engage youth in a dialogue for peace.

Music-based peacebuilding programs for youth can also help encourage identity work that supports the formation of cultures of peace. The research presented here suggests that music can play a major role in encouraging identity work that may offer alternative understandings of identity for youth, both of themselves and of others. Although it is limited, the evidence suggests that music may be useful for developing more peaceful understandings of the self, developing greater self-esteem, and aiding in healing. This musical work across difference can also enable youth to develop different understandings of the identities of others, including challenging stereotypes through collaborative work. While these outcomes differed across the two programs, they were evident to some degree in both. Even in short-term projects some level of change occurred in youth participants' understandings of their own identities as well as those of others. I am not implying that identity issues around violence, stereotypes, or confidence have been permanently addressed or "fixed" by these programs. Instead, the evidence suggests that music can be adapted to youth peacebuilding work in a way that gives participants the opportunity to imagine and experience alternative, more peaceful identities for themselves and others. This process requires continual attention, but for many participants this was their introduction to peace work and it provided them with a lived experience of identities that they may draw on in future identity constructions. Overall, these findings suggest that music can be a potentially powerful resource for unsettling identities in a way that may offer alternative nonviolent responses to conflict and difference.

Another related aspect of the usefulness of music for engaging youth in peacebuilding is based on the role of music in perceptions of space. Given its links with dialogue and identity, space has been given serious consideration in this research. The data collected from the case studies suggests that the (re)creation of particular kinds of spaces for music-based peacebuilding can make dialogue and identity work more accessible for youth. Young people are informed and molded by the local places and spaces where they live and interact. They can also play a role in (re)producing these locales through their cultural work, such as participation in music-making. In doing so, they may aid in endowing place with meaning that is more peaceful, inclusive, and safe. Indeed, they may contribute to changing the landscape as experienced by the people who encounter it, both themselves and outsiders. They may also take part in making space for understanding and encounters across difference. Of course, there are limitations to what changes in space and identity can occur, as meanings are assigned to people and places from the outside, too. Nevertheless, young people can resist the identities imposed on themselves, their peers, and the spaces they inhabit. In summary, music-based programs can play a role in (re)constructing spaces that support and encourage interaction across difference in peaceful, nonviolent ways, and may even contribute to changing perceptions of a local area more broadly, which can aid in building wider cultures of peace.

While these prospects for supporting dialogue, enabling identity work, and (re)creating space are important, I am not suggesting that all issues of inclusion have been addressed. Concerns remain, particularly when it comes to realizing a gender-equitable framework, which is necessary for sustainable peace. As I have outlined, music may in some instances be more gendered, or even sexist, than other media, which can undermine its capacity to contribute to building cultures of peace. Indeed, it was clear that when programs relied primarily on certain masculine-identified music and dance genres, girls often felt excluded from these peacebuilding activities. In the few instances where this was even acknowledged, the typical response was to attempt to "fix" the girls by teaching them to engage in a more masculine fashion.

Nevertheless, while girls constituted a minority at most of the workshops I observed, the young women who did manage to overcome the barriers to participation reported important gains. These included: greater self-confidence, enhanced artistic skills that could be used in addressing conflict nonviolently, and a sense that this experience would leave them better placed to get involved in peacebuilding in the future. These observations suggest that music can be a useful way to engage both girls and boys in peace work, but they also make it clear that critically engaging with gender throughout program planning and implementation is necessary to foster greater inclusion and thus support the creation of cultures of peace.

Having reviewed these key ideas, it is necessary here to outline and reiterate some caveats, challenges, and limitations to the positions I have taken. First of all, there are limits to the research design employed here. For one thing, it does not provide a strong sense of the process through which young people who originally came to these projects solely to participate in music activities transformed into youth who see themselves as peacebuilders. Moreover, as it provides no comparison with youth programs that use other methods to engage in peacebuilding, it does not allow me to claim that the particular changes (such as in identity, levels of violence, etc.) would only have occurred in a music-based program. Indeed, I do not suggest that music is the only way such changes can occur, nor do I argue that it will always be the best medium for engaging young people in peacebuilding. As I have discussed earlier, music is not inherently peaceful and therefore can be used to confirm exclusive or xenophobic identities. Thus, in at least some instances, it may be necessary to combine musical participation with other activities that critically engage more directly with issues of injustice. More investigation is certainly needed of how music can best be used to engage and include a diverse group of youth. Moreover, while existing literature does make a preliminary case for the role of self-confidence and self-esteem in reducing violence by and against youth, further critical examination is needed to better analyze whether and how this contributes to building a culture of peace.

Nonetheless, based on this research, I do think there are some particular things music can offer to youth peacebuilding programs that other forms of communication often do not. For example, in some cases it can be more inclusive, such as instances in which some participants cannot read, cannot or do not like to take part in other activities like sport, or do not already consider themselves politically engaged. Compared to traditional forms of political engagement, music-based activities are likely to appeal to young people as enjoyable, thus making political involvement more popular and possibly lending greater energy to that involvement. Because music is more emotional and corporeal than most existing forms of peacebuilding, it can also play a role in shifting identities in different ways than other mediums, such as the written word. The accessibility of music also enhances the capacity for messages to be spread rapidly, which makes it an effective way to disseminate ideas supporting a culture of peace. Finally, through working together in music-making, youth may develop skills needed for building peace, including capacities in negotiation and teamwork, although this may also be the case for other collaborative activities.

My observations in this research suggest that young people's tolerance of diverse others may require, or at least be enhanced by, exposure to people, especially other youth, who embody the kinds of difference associated with the conflict, such as ethnic or religious difference. Such experiences may thus be necessary or at least beneficial to the prospects for musical programs to engage effectively in peacebuilding. In the programs studied here it appears that program leaders wished to promote liberal tolerance demonstrating to the youth participants the inclusivity of their shared humanity. Many participants reported learning this universal humanity message and as a result suggested they were better able to tolerate and understand people from different ethnic backgrounds. However, it should be noted that there are limits to the capacity for liberal tolerance to promote peace.[1] It is also clear that mere exposure to difference does not inevitably lead to acceptance of difference. For example, the data gathered here indicate that exposure to gender differences and sexuality differences often does not result in changes in attitude. This implies that exposure to differences may not impact attitudes unless attention is also given to challenging stereotypes. It can thus be surmised that for music to lead to successful peacebuilding, programs ought to include at least some discussions or activities focused on breaking down stereotypes and exposing inequalities associated with difference.

Before moving forward to questions for future research, it is worth taking the time to reflect on the framing of this project. To reiterate, my aim has not been to formally evaluate the projects studied. Still, I identified several signs of effectiveness in these music-based peacebuilding programs. The successes of these organizations in using music to engage youth in peacebuilding further strengthens the case for trying related activities in other projects. For example, recall the story I shared of the boys participating in a music project in Northern Ireland. When faced with friends calling to ask them to join in violent sectarian riots, the boys chose instead to stay and take part in the program, because they preferred the music-making. This could be interpreted as directly reducing youth participation in violence across political divides. At the same time, remember the young woman in the Australian program, who through her dance participation had come to understand her identity in a new way that merited self-respect and confidence. In her case a very different specific act of violence, self-harm, was halted.

Program leaders also played significant roles in engaging the general public in ways that encourage support or involvement in creating peace. While this is important, I believe youth peacebuilding programs should also include deep involvement of participants, including peer leadership. As I have noted, the existing literature suggests that youth leadership can be key to engaging young people in peacebuilding. Based on my observations in these two programs, one that featured youth leaders and one that did not, it does appear that young people in the program with youth leadership felt a much greater sense of ownership in and commitment to the program and ensuring its sustainability. Results from two case studies alone do not provide conclusive generalizable evidence on this issue, but they do suggest that the existing literature on this topic is correct about the value of youth leadership and its impact on sustainability.

This project grew out of a lifelong love of music and dance, an ongoing dedication to working for peace, and a commitment to acknowledging the work of youth, who often inspire me with their innovative and imaginative ways of engaging in political action. All this led me to a curiosity about whether music might be a useful way to engage young people in peacebuilding. Investigating that question led me on a journey that took me from the south-side cityscape of Brisbane, Australia, to small country towns in Northern Ireland. I met young people and youth workers from diverse backgrounds: immigrants, refugees, Indigenous people, working poor, middle class, well-to-do, girls, boys, women, men, Protestant, Catholic, atheist, Muslim, emerging artists, professional musicians, dreamers, planners, doers. I entered their world and embarked on an expedition that would take me a little over three years, only to leave me wishing I could do it all over again, to hear, see, and learn more about how these diverse individuals and groups are using music to build cultures of peace.

Please do not misunderstand me—in this initial journey I have been successful at meeting my research goals: I answered my key question, I gathered substantial supporting evidence, and I critically engaged with the issues at hand. And yet, because I see such promise and challenge in this work, I long for the chance to jump right in again to attempt to explore some of the questions that remain unanswered because they fell outside the scope of this project. Alas, those questions at present must wait for another day. Still, it is worth posing some of them here to stimulate engagement and discussion on how best to deal with these issues in a way that supports the efforts of young people, scholars, and youth workers striving to build cultures of peace.

- What impact does youth leadership have on outcomes of youth peacebuilding programs?
- How does program duration impact on the results in programs like this? What are the longer-term impacts on participants and their communities?
- What practical actions could be implemented to create more inclusive settings for programs engaging youth in peacebuilding? What kind of inclusion training might aid these youth in their peacebuilding work and political education?
- How can youth who leave these programs early be engaged to learn more about why they chose to leave or lost interest? What can their experiences tell us about creating more engaging and inclusive programming?
- How might different genres of music and dance be used together or separately to draw interest from different individuals or groups? How can music that is often seen as "belonging" to one group (such as hip-hop being seen as owned by men and boys) be adapted to a more diverse group of participants?
- What are some specific ways young people from a dominant culture can take part in using music to challenge cultural hegemony (e.g., challenging the dominance of "whiteness")? What are some concrete ways young men can take part in using music to challenge current gender norms in an effort to democratize gender and include girls?
- What other ways are young people getting involved in peacebuilding work through culture?
- How can government policy recognize and financially support youth peacebuilding efforts while maintaining leadership on the part of the youth cultural producers?

- Would the introduction of such programs to schools and other formal settings be a useful way to engage more young people in peacebuilding in a way that is more open to all youth? Or would they be discouraged by the formal structure?

Obviously this list of questions is not exhaustive, but I think it offers much to be considered and will hopefully stimulate discussion and collaboration around these issues for scholars, practitioners, and activists working in the field of peace and conflict.

While conflict regularly impacts the lives of young people, they have often been forgotten by scholarship and programs focused on dealing with conflict. Moreover, when youth have been given attention, portrayals have often tended to essentialize them as perpetrators or victims. Depictions such as these ignore the fact that young people are also active in peacebuilding. I do not mean to imply here that these are three distinct groups of youth: the violent, the weak, and the activists. Instead, throughout this study I have sought to shed light on what may motivate young people to get involved in building peace and sustain their interest in continued peacebuilding work. This is important because youth are often denied access to formal peacebuilding work, even though they are an important part of communities experiencing conflict. Despite this exclusion, many young people are involved in peace work, particularly in areas focused on building a culture of peace. Through this involvement youth may use their knowledge and skills to engage in a way that is relevant to their lives. This book is but one humble attempt to recognize, support, and encourage the participation of youth in peacebuilding. To the young people who inspired it—may your talent, creativity, and passion for peace inspire all who cross your path—you have certainly brightened mine.

Appendices

Appendix 1.
Third Place Respondent Demographics

Black African Sudanese female, 15 years old, singer, self-supporting

White Australian male, 14 years old, break-dancer, says his mom looks after his little brother and sister (unclear, as his older brother said she's a journalist)

Male of Samoan and Maori heritage, 14 years old, crumper, parents own a resort in Samoa

Maori female, 13 years old, singer, parents are both factory workers

Black African Liberian male, 16 years old, crumper, did not know what his mom does for work

White Australian male, 16 years old, break-dancer, mom is a journalist? (older brother of 14-year-old break-dancer)

White Australian male, 17 years old, break-dancer, mom does payroll for a pest control company, stepfather works for the railway, father works at the Port Authority

Samoan/Maori female, 13 years old, singer, lives with her aunt and uncle, who are both factory workers

Slovenian (white, Eastern European), 18 years old, break-dancer, father is a house painter, mom is retraining as a nurse because her Slovenian papers are not accepted in Australia

Fijian/Indian male, 20 years old, MC, father works in a company's laser computer operations division

Appendix 2.
Third Place Participant Interview Schedule

- Name, age, school
- Family/cultural background (English at home?)
- Parents' current and past occupation? (Indicator of class)

1. What made you want to get involved with [Third Place]?
2. What does "peace" mean to you?
3. Were you involved in any peacebuilding activities before joining this project?
4. Do you think music/dance has been a useful tool for your involvement in peacebuilding? How?
5. Would you have participated in a peace workshop without the music/dance?
6. How did you get interested in [your art form]?
7. Do you feel being involved in this project will make it easier for you to be formally involved in peacebuilding in the future? For example, did it help you develop leadership skills?
8. How do you think being a boy/girl affects your ability to be a peacemaker or the ways you can be involved in making peace?
9. Do you think boys or girls are more involved in conflict or violence in your community, or is it all the same? Why do you think that is?
10. At [Third Place], did being a boy/girl play a role in how you were able to interact in the group? (For girls saying not affected: This is a space with majority boys—why do you think that is? Do you think other girls would feel comfortable here? What do you think it would take to involve other girls? How would you design the project to include them?)
11. Did you interact with people from different backgrounds than your own? Did that change any of your views? Would you continue to hang out with that person or people after the project?
12. Do you think there are any kids who would have trouble fitting in here? (Gay kids, disabled, other cultural groups?)

13. Have there been any times that you have been involved in or affected by violence or conflict in your community? Can you tell me what happened?
14. What skills, if any, have you learned in this project that can help you address future conflict nonviolently?
15. How, if at all, has being part of [Third Place] changed the way you see yourself? How has it changed the way you see others?
16. Has being part of [Third Place] made you feel empowered? How?
17. Will you continue to use the skills you've gained here to make peace? How? Will you tell others about what you've learned?
18. Do you think [Third Place] can help reduce the violent events in your community?
19. Do you have any suggestions for how the program should be changed to make it better?

Appendix 3.
Third Place Facilitator Demographics

Indigenous Australian female, MC, 24
*Samoan female from New Zealand, singer/crew leader, 25
*Samoan/Chinese female raised in Australia, crump dancer, 18
Samoan male from New Zealand, crump dancer, 21
*Tongan male raised in Australia, singer, 24
White Australian male, break-dancer, 20

* *Denotes the facilitators I was able to interview.*

Appendix 4.
Third Place Facilitator Interview Schedule

- Name, age, work, education
- Family/cultural background (English at home?)

- Parents' current and past occupation? (Indicator of class)
- What made you want to get involved with [Third Place]?

1. What does "peace" mean to you?
2. Were you involved in any peacebuilding activities before joining this project?
3. What do you think it is about music/dance that makes it such a useful tool for your involvement in peacebuilding?
4. Would you have been interested in facilitating peace workshops without the music/dance? Or is that the best way you feel you can be involved?
5. How did you get interested in [your art form]?
6. Do you feel being involved in this project will make it easier for you to be formally involved in peacebuilding in the future? Did it help you develop leadership skills?
7. As a leader in this project, have you made any links with the general public (those not participating in this project) that encourage their support or involvement in building peace? Is there anything, do you think, that is unique to music and dance that can be particularly useful in engaging people outside the program?
8. How do you think being a young wo/man affects your ability to be a peacemaker or the ways you can be involved in making peace?
9. Do you think boys or girls are more involved in conflict or violence in your community, or that it is equal? Why do you think that is?
10. At [Third Place], did being a young wo/man play a role in how you were able to interact in the group? Have you noticed any differences in the way young participants interact or participate based on gender?
11. Most groups (dancing and MCs) were majority boys throughout the workshops—why do you think that is? Do you think other girls would feel comfortable here? What do you think it would take to involve other girls? How would you design the project to include them?

12. Did you interact with people from different backgrounds than your own? Did that change any of your views? Would you continue to hang out with that person or people after the project?
13. Do you think there are any kids who would have trouble fitting in here? (Specify and directly ask about: gay kids, disabled, other culture cultural groups?)
14. Have there been any times that you have been involved in or affected by violence or conflict in your community? Can you tell me what happened?
15. What skills, if any, have you learned/taught in this project that can help you address future conflict nonviolently?
16. Has being part of [Third Place] changed the way you see yourself? How?
17. Has it changed the way you see others?
18. Has being part of this project made you feel empowered in any way? How?
19. Will you continue to use the skills you've gained here to make peace? How?
20. Do you think [Third Place] can help reduce or has already reduced the violent events in the local communities? How?
21. Do you have any suggestions for how the program should be changed to make it better? Any issues you feel need to be addressed?

Appendix 5.
Breaking Barriers Respondent Demographics

Northern Irish Protestant female, 17 years old, guitarist, has participated in Breaking Barriers workshops and is now on their board, middle-class parents

Northern Irish Protestant male, 16 years old, drummer, has participated in Breaking Barriers workshops and now helps by playing music in some of their programs, middle-class parents

Northern Irish Protestant male, 12 years old, participated in Breaking Barriers workshops as a rapper but usually does other music work, middle-class parents

Northern Irish Protestant male, 14 years old, participated in Breaking Barriers workshops at his school's youth club, working-class parents

Northern Irish Protestant male, 14 years old, participated in Breaking Barriers workshops at his school's youth club, working-class parents

Northern Irish Protestant male, 14 years old, participated in Breaking Barriers workshops at his school's youth club, working-class parents

Northern Irish Protestant male, 14 years old, participated in Breaking Barriers workshops at his school's youth club, working-class parents

Northern Irish Protestant male, 14 years old, participated in Breaking Barriers workshops at his school's youth club, working-class parents

Northern Irish Protestant male, 14 years old, participated in Breaking Barriers workshops at his school's youth club, working-class parents

(Joint interview) Northern Irish Catholic females, 13 years old, participated in Breaking Barriers workshops at their school, middle-class parents

(Joint interview) Northern Irish Catholic, female and male, 13 years old, participated in Breaking Barriers workshops at their school, middle-class parents

Appendix 6. Breaking Barriers Youth Participant Interview Schedule

Background:

- Name, age, school
- Family/cultural background (English at home?)
- Parents' current and past occupation? (Indicator of class)

1. What made you want to get involved with [Breaking Barriers]?
2. What does "peace" mean to you?
3. Were you involved in any peacebuilding activities before

joining this project?

4. Do you think music/dance has been a useful tool for your involvement in peacebuilding? How?
5. Would you have participated in a peace program without the music/dance?
6. How did you get interested in [your art form]?
7. Do you feel being involved in this project will make it easier for you to be formally involved in peacebuilding in the future? For example, did it help you develop leadership skills?
8. How do you think being a boy/girl affects your ability to be a peacemaker or the ways you can be involved in making peace?
9. Do you think boys or girls are more involved in conflict or violence in your community, or is it all the same? Why do you think that is?
10. Participants in these programs are majority boys—why do you think that is? Do you think other girls would feel comfortable here? What do you think it would take to involve other girls? How would you design the project to include them?
11. At [Breaking Barriers], did being a boy/girl play a role in how you were able to interact in the group?
12. Did you interact with people from different backgrounds than your own? Did that change any of your views? Would you continue to hang out with that person or people after the project?
13. Do you think there are any kids who would have trouble fitting in here? (Gay kids, disabled, other cultural groups?)
14. Have there been any times that you have been involved in or affected by violence or conflict in your community? Can you tell me what happened?
15. What skills, if any, have you learned in this project that can help you address future conflict nonviolently?
16. How, if at all, has being part of this project changed the way you see yourself? How has it changed the way you see others?
17. Has being part of this project made you feel empowered? How?

18. Will you continue to use the skills you've gained here to make peace? How? Will you tell others about what you've learned?
19. Do you think [Breaking Barriers] can help reduce the violent events in your community?
20. Do you have any suggestions for how the program should be changed to make it better?

Appendix 7.
Breaking Barriers Facilitator Demographics

Northern Irish Protestant male, 31 years old, Breaking Barriers project manager (director), middle class

Colombian female, 31 years old, facilitates at some of Breaking Barriers workshops on global issues and fair trade, not a trained musician herself, but she plays along with percussion hand instruments and mainly does the talking parts, middle class

Mexican female, 31 years old, a musician working with Breaking Barriers youth projects (also teaches dance to kids in her own work), from a well-to-do background

Northern Irish Protestant female, 21 years old, assistant project manager at Breaking Barriers, works mainly in the office in planning as she learns more about how to run things, but she does go along to some of the projects to watch, middle class

Appendix 8.
Breaking Barriers Facilitators Interview Schedule

Background:

- Name, age, work, education
- Family/cultural background (English at home?)
- Parents' current and past occupation? (Indicator of class)

1. What made you want to get involved with [Breaking Barriers]?

2. What does "peace" mean to you?
3. Were you involved in any peacebuilding activities before joining this project?
4. What do you think it is about music/dance that makes it such a useful tool for building peace?
5. Would you have been interested in facilitating peace workshops without the music/dance? Or is that the best way you feel you can be involved?
6. How did you get interested in [your art form]?
7. Do you feel being involved in this project will make it easier for you to be formally involved in peacebuilding in the future? Did it help you develop leadership skills?
8. As a leader in this project, have you made any links with the general public (those not participating in this project) that encourage their support or involvement in building peace?
9. Is there anything, do you think, that is unique to music and dance that can be particularly useful in engaging people outside the program?
10. How do you think being a young wo/man affects your ability to be a peacemaker or the ways you can be involved in making peace?
11. Do you think boys or girls are more involved in conflict or violence in your community, or that it is equal? Why do you think that is?
12. At [Breaking Barriers], does being a young wo/man play a role in how you were able to interact in the group? Have you noticed any differences in the way young participants interact or participate based on gender? Have you observed any gendered differences in your career as an arts worker?
13. The majority of participants in community youth arts programs tend to be boys (The [Project Movement] band is almost all men)—why do you think that is? Do you think other girls would feel comfortable here? What do you think it would take to involve other girls? How would you design the project to include them?
14. Did you interact with people from different backgrounds than your own? Did that change any of your views? Would you continue to hang out with that person or people after the project?
15. Do you think there are any kids who would have trouble

fitting in here? (Specify and directly ask about: gay kids, disabled, other culture cultural groups?)

16. Have there been any times that you personally have been involved in or affected by violence or conflict in your community? Can you tell me what happened?
17. What skills, if any, have you learned/taught in this project that can help you address future conflict nonviolently?
18. Has being part of [Breaking Barriers] changed the way you see yourself? How?
19. Has it changed the way you see others?
20. Has being part of this project made you feel empowered in any way? How?
21. Will you continue to use the skills you've gained here to make peace? How?
22. Do you think [Breaking Barriers] can help reduce or has already reduced the violent events in local communities? How?
23. Do you have any suggestions for how the program should be changed to make it better? Any issues you feel need to be addressed? If anything were an option, how would you design or alter it?

Notes

Introduction

1. See for example: Siobhán McEvoy, "Communities and Peace: Catholic Youth in Northern Ireland," *Journal of Peace Research* 37, no. 1 (2000); Siobhán McEvoy-Levy, "Youth as Social and Political Agents: Issues in Post-Settlement Peace Building," in *Kroc Institute Occasional Paper #21:OP:2* (Kroc Institute's Research Initiative on the Resolution of Ethnic Conflict [RIREC], 2001); Celina Del Felice and Andria Wisler, "The Unexplored Power and Potential of Youth as Peace-Builders," *Journal of Peace and Conflict Development*, no. 11 (2007); Tristan Anne Borer, John Darby, and Siobhán McEvoy-Levy, "Caught between Child Rights and Security: Youth and Postwar Reconstruction," in *Peacebuilding after Peace Accords: The Challenges of Violence, Truth, and Youth*, ed. Tristan Anne Borer, John Darby, and Siobhán McEvoy-Levy (Notre Dame, IN: University of Notre Dame Press, 2006); Leonisa Ardizzone, "Generating Peace: A Study of Nonformal Youth Organizations," *Peace and Change* 28, no. 3 (2003); Leonisa Ardizzone, *Gettin' My Word Out* (Albany: State University of New York Press, 2007); Paula Green, "Contact: Training a New Generation of Peacebuilders," *Peace and Change* 27, no. 1 (2002); Jennifer Hanis Dé Bryant and Charles Stoner, "Special Needs, Special Measures: Working with Homeless and Poor Youth," in *Peacebuilding for Adolescents: Strategies for Educators and Community Leaders*,

ed. Linda Rennie Forcey and Ian Murray Harris (New York: Peter Lang Publishing, 1999); Sandra Botero and Astrid Zacipa, "Colombia's Children: Agents of a New Culture of Peace," in *Children and Peacebuilding: Experiences and Perspectives*, ed. Heather Elliot (Melbourne: World Vision Australia, 2001); Angela McIntyre and Thokozani Thusi, "Children and Youth in Sierra Leone's Peace-Building Process," *African Security Review* 12, no. 2 (2003); Shelley Anderson, ed., *Girls Change the World! International Women's Day for Peace and Disarmament May 24, 2007* (Geneva: International Peace Bureau, 2007).

2. Stephanie Schell-Faucon, "Conflict Transformation through Educational and Youth Programmes" (Berlin: Berghof Research Center for Constructive Conflict Management, 2001), 2.
3. Borer, Darby, and McEvoy-Levy, "Caught between Child Rights and Security: Youth and Postwar Reconstruction," 50.
4. Ho-Won Jeong, *Peacebuilding in Postconflict Societies: Strategy and Process* (Boulder: Lynne Rienner Publishers, 2005).
5. Craig Zelizer and Robert A. Rubinstein, eds., *Building Peace: Practical Reflections from the Field* (Sterling, VA: Kumarian Press, 2009).
7. The 14th Dalai Lama, "Nobel Lecture" (paper presented at the Nobel Peace Prize Nobel Lecture, December 11, 1989); Stuart Rees, *Passion for Peace: Exercising Power Creatively* (Sydney: University of New South Wales Press, 2003).
8. Elisabeth Porter, "Women, Political Decision-Making, and Peace-Building," *Global Change, Peace & Security* 15, no. 3 (2003): 255–256.
9. Dé Bryant and Stoner, "Special Needs, Special Measures: Working with Homeless and Poor Youth," 268.
10. Boulding cited in: Joseph De Rivera, "Assessing the Basis for a Culture of Peace in Contemporary Societies," *Journal of Peace Research* 41, no. 5 (2004): 546.
11. Kenneth Bush, "Field Notes: Fighting Commodification and Disempowerment in the Development Industry: Things I Learned About PCIA in Habarana and Mindanao" (Berlin: Berghof Research Centre for Constructive Conflict Management, 2005), 12.

12. This built on A/RES/52/13, the resolution on a culture of peace adopted the previous year. De Rivera, "Assessing the Basis for a Culture of Peace in Contemporary Societies," 531.
13. UNESCO, "Culture of Peace: Peace Is in Our Hands," http://www3.unesco.org/iycp/uk/uk_sum_cp.htm.
14. De Rivera, "Assessing the Basis for a Culture of Peace in Contemporary Societies," 535.

Chapter 1. Youth in Peace and Conflict

1. Borer, Darby, and McEvoy-Levy, "Caught between Child Rights and Security: Youth and Postwar Reconstruction," 41.
2. Heather Elliot, ed., *Children and Peacebuilding: Experiences and Perspectives* (Melbourne: WorldVision Australia, 2001), 2.
3. John Paul Lederach, *The Moral Imagination: The Art and Soul of Building Peace* (Oxford: Oxford University Press, 2005), 122.
4. McEvoy-Levy, "Youth as Social and Political Agents: Issues in Post-Settlement Peace Building"; Johan Galtung, "Violence, Peace and Peace Research," *Journal of Peace Research* 6, no. 3 (1969).
5. McEvoy-Levy, "Youth as Social and Political Agents: Issues in Post-Settlement Peace Building," 23, 2.
6. Borer, Darby, and McEvoy-Levy, "Caught between Child Rights and Security: Youth and Postwar Reconstruction," 59.
7. Karen Hein, "Young People as Assets: A Foundation View," *Social Policy* 30, no. 1 (1999): 23.
8. Del Felice and Wisler, "The Unexplored Power and Potential of Youth as Peace-Builders," 13–20.
9. Stephanie Schwartz, *Youth and Post-Conflict Reconstruction: Agents of Change* (Washington, DC: United States Institute of Peace Press, 2010).
10. Ardizzone, "Generating Peace: A Study of Nonformal Youth Organizations."

11. Ibid., 423.
12. Christine Griffin, "Troubled Teens: Managing Disorders of Transition and Consumption," *Feminist Review* 55(1997).
13. Ardizzone, "Generating Peace: A Study of Nonformal Youth Organizations," 421, 24.
14. Ibid.
15. Hein, "Young People as Assets: A Foundation View," 25–27.
16. Peter G. Christenson and Donald F. Roberts, *It's Not Only Rock & Roll: Popular Music in the Lives of Adolescents* (Cresskill, NJ: Hampton Press, 1998), 19–21.
17. Andreana Clay, "All I Need Is One Mic: Mobilizing Youth for Social Change in the Post-Civil Rights Era," *Social Justice* 33, no. 2 (2006): 111.
18. Catherine Clark et al., "Media Portrayal of Young People—Impact and Influences" (London: National Children's Bureau, The National Youth Agency—Young Researcher Network, 2009).
19. ActNow, "Portrayal of Young People by the Media," The Inspire Foundation, http://www.actnow.com.au/Issues/Portrayal of young people by the media.aspx; Louise Merrington, "Here's a Generation Wanting to Be Heard," *The Age*, August 31, 2004; Sunanda Creag, "Consuming Identity: Are Young Voices Being Marginalised and Trivialised?" *M/C Reviews* (1999).
20. Anita Harris, *Future Girl* (New York and London: Routledge, 2004), 134.
21. Ibid.
22. Shannon Stewart, "All-Ages Movement Project: Project Report," 2006, http://www.allagesmovementproject.org.
23. Harris, *Future Girl*, 158.
24. Del Felice and Wisler, "The Unexplored Power and Potential of Youth as Peace-Builders," 12–13.
25. McIntyre and Thusi, "Children and Youth in Sierra Leone's Peace-Building Process"; Borer, Darby, and McEvoy-Levy, "Caught between Child Rights and Security: Youth and Postwar Reconstruction," 59.
26. John Paul Lederach, *Preparing for Peace: Conflict Transformation across Cultures* (Syracuse, NY: Syracuse University Press, 1995), 26, 83.

27. Huseyn Aliyev, "Peace-Building from the Bottom: A Case Study of the North Caucasus," *Caucasian Review of International Affairs* 4, no. 4 (2010): 325–341.
28. Ibid.
29. Mads Frilander and Hannah Stogdon, "Engaging with the Grassroots: Humanitarian Decision-Making, Conflict Sensitivity, and Somali 'Non-State Actors' Platforms" (Nairobi, Kenya: Safer World UK, 2011).
30. Lederach, *Preparing for Peace: Conflict Transformation across Cultures*, 81.
31. Ibid.
32. Harris, *Future Girl*, 146.
33. Lisa Schirch, *Ritual and Symbol in Peacebuilding* (Bloomfield, CT: Kumarian Press, 2005), 17.
34. Ibid., 2.
35. Ibid., 35.
36. Lederach, *The Moral Imagination: The Art and Soul of Building Peace*, 38.
37. Ibid., 69.
38. Cheryl de la Rey and Susan McKay, "Peacebuilding as a Gendered Process," *Journal of Social Issues* 6, no. 1 (2006); Azza Karam, "Women in War and Peace-Building: The Roads Traversed, the Challenges Ahead," *International Feminist Journal of Politics* 3, no. 1 (2001); Gender and Peacebuilding Working Group of the Canadian Peacebuilding Coordinating Committee (CPCC), "Fact Sheet: Resolution 1325 for Girls and Young Women," http://www.peacebuild.ca/upload/fact_sheet.pdf; Porter, "Women, Political Decision-Making, and Peace-Building"; Donna Pankhurst, "The 'Sex War' and Other Wars: Towards a Feminist Approach to Peace Building," *Development in Practice* 13, no. 2 (2003); Donna Pankhurst, "Women, Gender and Peacebuilding" (Bradford: University of Bradford, Centre for Conflict Resolution: Department of Peace Studies, 2000); Ciara Daniels, "Filling the Gaps: A Virtual Discussion of Gender, Peace and Security Research—Summary of Dialogue" (New York: United Nations International Research and Training Institute for the Advancement of Women, 2008): Australian Government, "Background Paper:

Women's Equal Participation in Conflict Prevention, Conflict Management and Conflict Resolution in Post-Conflict Peace-Building," ed. Office on the Status of Women (Canberra: Australian Government, 2004); Donna Pankhurst, "Mainstreaming Gender in Peacebuilding—A Framework for Action: From the Village Council to the Negotiating Table: The International Campaign to Promote the Role of Women in Peacebuilding" (London: International Alert, 2000); Phyllis Ghim Lian Chew, "The Challenge of Unity: Women, Peace and Power," *International Journal on World Peace* 15, no. 4 (1998); Ho-Won Jeong, *Peace and Conflict Studies: An Introduction* (Aldershot: Ashgate Publishing Limited, 2000); Mary Caprioli, "Gendered Conflict," *Journal of Peace Research* 37, no. 1 (2000); Elisabeth Rehn and Ellen Johnson Sirleaf, "Executive Summary—Women War Peace: The Independent Experts' Assessment," in *Progress of the World's Women 2002* (Washington, DC: UNIFEM, 2002).

39. Pankhurst, "The 'Sex War' and Other Wars: Towards a Feminist Approach to Peace Building," 156.
40. Ibid., 153.
41. Porter, "Women, Political Decision-Making, and Peace-Building," 248.
42. de la Rey and McKay, "Peacebuilding as a Gendered Process," 141.
43. Pankhurst, "The 'Sex War' and Other Wars: Towards a Feminist Approach to Peace Building."
44. UNFPA, "Homepage," http://www.unfpa.org/adolescents/index.htm; http://www.unfpa.org/adolescents/about.htm.
45. J. Ann Tickner, *Gendering World Politics: Issues and Approaches in the Post-Cold War Era* (New York: Columbia University Press, 2001).
46. J. Ann Tickner, *Gender in International Relations: Feminist Perspectives on Achieving Global Security* (New York: Columbia University Press, 1992), 40.
47. Carol Cohn, "Wars, Wimps, and Women: Talking Gender and Thinking War," in *Gendering War Talk*, ed. Miriam Cooke and Angela Woolacott (Princeton, NJ: Princeton University Press, 1993), 238.
48. Rela Mazali, "And What About the Girls? What a Culture of

War Genders Out of View," *Journal of Jewish Women's Studies and Gender Issues* , no. 6 (Fall/5764 2003): 48.

49. Gender and Peacebuilding Working Group of the Canadian Peacebuilding Coordinating Committee (CPCC), "How Can We Use Resolution 1325?" http://www.peacebuild.ca/upload/fact_sheet_new.pdf.
50. Anita Harris, "Revisiting Bedroom Culture: New Spaces for Young Women's Politics," *Hecate: An Interdisciplinary Journal of Women's Liberation* 27, no. 1 (2001). Citing Debi Roker.
51. Harris, *Future Girl*, 134.
52. Graeme Stuart, "Conflict Resolution & Non-Violence Workshops with Young People," *Youth Studies Australia* 18, no. 2 (1999): 39.
53. R. W. Connell, "Change among the Gatekeepers: Men, Masculinities, and Gender Equality in the Global Arena," *Signs: Journal of Women in Culture and Society* 30, no. 3 (2005).

Chapter 2. Music Makes the (Young) People Come Together?

1. Ajay Heble, "Take Two/Rebel Musics: Human Rights, Resistant Sounds, and the Politics of Music Making," in *Rebel Musics: Human Rights, Resistant Sounds, and the Politics of Music Making*, ed. Daniel Fischlin and Ajay Heble (Montreal: Black Rose Books, 2003); John Sloboda, *Exploring the Musical Mind* (Oxford: Oxford University Press, 2005); Simon Frith, "Music and Identity," in *Questions of Cultural Identity*, ed. Stuart Hall and Paul du Gay (London: Sage, 1996), 118; Anthony Storr, *Music and the Mind* (London: HarperCollins Publishers, 1992).
2. Nancy Love, "'Singing for Our Lives': Women's Music and Democratic Politics," *Hypatia* 17, no. 4 (2002). Quoting Derk Richardson 1990: 61.
3. Marie Boti et al., "Making Rebel Musics: The Films," in *Rebel Musics: Human Rights, Resistant Sounds, and the Politics of Music Making*, ed. Daniel Fischlin and Ajay Heble (Montreal: Black Rose Books, 2003), 5; Daniel Fischlin, "Take One/Rebel Musics: Human Rights, Resistant Sounds, and the Politics of Music Making," in *Rebel Musics: Human Rights,*

Resistant Sounds, and the Politics of Music Making, ed. Daniel Fischlin and Ajay Heble (Montreal: Black Rose Books, 2003).

4. Karlene Faith, "Reflections on Inside/Out Organizing," *Social Justice* 27, no. 3 (2000): 163; Ben Shepard, "The Use of Joyfulness as a Community Organizing Strategy," *Peace and Change* 30, no. 4 (2005).
5. David Kinnaman and Gabe Lyons, *Unchristian: What a New Generation Thinks About Christianity . . . And Why It Matters* (Grand Rapids, MI: Baker Books, 2007), 171. Quoting Michelangelo.
6. Michael Frost, *Exiles: Living Missionally in a Post-Christian Culture* (Peabody, MA: Hendrickson Publishers, 2006), 318.
7. Clay, "All I Need Is One Mic: Mobilizing Youth for Social Change in the Post-Civil Rights Era," 109. Citing Fine 1995.
8. Rob Bell, *Sex God: Exploring the Endless Connections between Sexuality and Spirituality* (Grand Rapids: Zondervan, 2007), 41.
9. Shepard, "The Use of Joyfulness as a Community Organizing Strategy."
10. Love, "'Singing for Our Lives': Women's Music and Democratic Politics," 84–86.
11. Jennifer Rycenga, "Lesbian Compositional Practice: One Lover-Composer's Perspective," in *Queering the Pitch: The New Gay and Lesbian Musicology*, ed. Phillip Brett, Elizabeth Wood, and Gary C. Thomas (New York: Routledge, 1994), 283–284. As cited in: Love, "'Singing for Our Lives': Women's Music and Democratic Politics," 78.
12. Rycenga, "Lesbian Compositional Practice: One Lover-Composer's Perspective," 283–284. (As cited in: Love, "'Singing for Our Lives': Women's Music and Democratic Politics," 78.)
13. Frith, "Music and Identity," 118.
14. Ibid., 114–115.
15. Heble, "Take Two/Rebel Musics: Human Rights, Resistant Sounds, and the Politics of Music Making," 236; Christenson and Roberts, *It's Not Only Rock & Roll: Popular Music in the Lives of Adolescents*, 116.
16. Germán Munõz and Martha Marín, "Music Is the

Connection: Youth Cultures in Colombia," in *Global Youth? Hybrid Identities, Plural Worlds*, ed. Pam Nilan and Carles Feixa (London and New York: Routledge, 2006), 130–131.

17. Ibid., 132.
18. Ibid., 147.
19. Ibid.
20. Lederach, *The Moral Imagination: The Art and Soul of Building Peace.*
21. John Paul Lederach and Angela Jill Lederach, *When Blood and Bones Cry Out: Journeys through the Soundscape of Healing and Reconciliation*, ed. Kevin P. Clements, New Approaches to Peace and Conflict (Brisbane: University of Queensland Press, 2010).
22. June Boyce-Tillman, *Constructing Musical Healing: The Wounds That Sing* (London and Philadelphia: Jessica Kingsley Publishers, 2000).
23. Roland Bleiker, ed., "Painting Politics: Editor's Introduction," *Social Alternatives* 20, no. 4 (2001): 7; Roland Bleiker, *Aesthetics and World Politics*, ed. Oliver P. Richmond, Rethinking Peace and Conflict Studies (New York: Palgrave Macmillan, 2009).
24. Heble, "Take Two/Rebel Musics: Human Rights, Resistant Sounds, and the Politics of Music Making," 235.
25. Ibid.
26. Frost, *Exiles: Living Missionally in a Post-Christian Culture*, 116.
27. Fischlin, "Take One/Rebel Musics: Human Rights, Resistant Sounds, and the Politics of Music Making," 21.
28. Ardizzone, "Generating Peace: A Study of Nonformal Youth Organizations," 432.
29. Harris, *Future Girl.*
30. Stewart, "All-Ages Movement Project: Project Report."
31. Schell-Faucon, "Conflict Transformation through Educational and Youth Programmes," 5.
32. Rees, *Passion for Peace: Exercising Power Creatively*, 26.
33. Gerald Phillips, "Can There Be 'Music for Peace'?" *International Journal on World Peace* 21, no. 2 (2004).
34. Some authors also argue that this has been the case in the social sciences more generally. See for example: Munõz

and Marín, "Music Is the Connection: Youth Cultures in Colombia," 130–131.

35. Christenson and Roberts, *It's Not Only Rock & Roll: Popular Music in the Lives of Adolescents,* 12.
36. Ibid., 41.
37. Susan Hopkins, "Hole Lotta Attitude: Courtney Love and Guitar Feminism," *Social Alternatives* 18, no. 2 (1999): 14.
38. Christenson and Roberts, *It's Not Only Rock & Roll: Popular Music in the Lives of Adolescents,* 6.
39. Ibid., 3.
40. Fischlin, "Take One/Rebel Musics: Human Rights, Resistant Sounds, and the Politics of Music Making," 30.
41. Del Felice and Wisler, "The Unexplored Power and Potential of Youth as Peace-Builders," 19.
42. Jeff Zimbalist and Matt Mochary, *Favela Rising* (US: Thinkfilm, 2005).
43. Ibid.
44. Thomas L. Jipping, "Heavy Metal, Rap, and America's Youth: Issues and Alternatives (2nd edition). A Special Report of the Free Congress Foundation" (Washington, DC: Free Congress Foundation, 1990), 3.
45. Sarah Baker and Bruce M. Z. Cohen, "From Snuggling and Snogging to Sampling and Scratching: Girls' Nonparticipation in Community-Based Music Activities," *Youth & Society* 39, no. 3 (2008): 316.
46. Ibid., 316–317.
47. Clay, "All I Need Is One Mic: Mobilizing Youth for Social Change in the Post-Civil Rights Era," 106.
48. Christenson and Roberts, *It's Not Only Rock & Roll: Popular Music in the Lives of Adolescents,* 7.
49. Ibid.
50. Munõz and Marín, "Music Is the Connection: Youth Cultures in Colombia," 141.
51. Harris, *Future Girl,* 163.
52. Clay, "All I Need Is One Mic: Mobilizing Youth for Social Change in the Post-Civil Rights Era."
53. Chilla Bulbeck, "The 'White Worrier' in South Australia: Attitudes to Multiculturalism, Immigration and Reconciliation," *Journal of Sociology* 40, no. 4 (2004).

54. Munõz and Marín, "Music Is the Connection: Youth Cultures in Colombia," 130–131.
55. Ibid.
56. Roland Bleiker, "The Changing Speed of Dissent Politics," *Social Alternatives* 19, no. 1 (2000).
57. Munõz and Marín, "Music Is the Connection: Youth Cultures in Colombia," 130–131.
58. Lena Slachmuijlder, "The Rhythm of Reconciliation: A Reflection on Drumming as a Contribution to Reconciliation Processes in Burundi and South Africa" (Waltham, MA: Brandeis University Press, 2005), 21–22.
59. Mavis Bayton, *Frock Rock* (Oxford: Oxford University Press, 1998), 1. As cited in: Baker and Cohen, "From Snuggling and Snogging to Sampling and Scratching: Girls' Nonparticipation in Community-Based Music Activities," 319.
60. Baker and Cohen, "From Snuggling and Snogging to Sampling and Scratching: Girls' Nonparticipation in Community-Based Music Activities," 319.
61. John Connell and Chris Gibson, *Sound Tracks: Popular Music, Identity and Place* (London: Routledge, 2003), 210.
62. Bonnie C. Wade, *Thinking Musically: Experiencing Music, Expressing Culture* (New York, Oxford: Oxford University Press, 2004), 39.
63. Christenson and Roberts, *It's Not Only Rock & Roll: Popular Music in the Lives of Adolescents*, 143.
64. Reebee Garofalo, *Rockin' the Boat: Mass Music & Mass Movements* (Cambridge, MA: South End Press, 1999), 11.
65. Lisa Gilman and John Fenn, "Dance, Gender, and Popular Music in Malawi: The Case of Rap and Ragga," *Popular Music* 25, no. 3 (2006): 375.
66. Avelardo Valdez and Jeffrey A. Halley, "Gender in the Culture of Mexican American Conjunto Music," *Gender and Society* 10, no. 2 (1996): 149.
67. Ibid.
68. Love, "'Singing for Our Lives': Women's Music and Democratic Politics," 71.
69. Ibid., 72–73.
70. Ibid., 77.
71. John Shepherd, "Difference and Power in Music," in

Musicology and Difference: Gender and Sexuality in Music Scholarship, ed. Ruth A. Solie (Berkeley: University of California Press, 1993), 50. As cited in: Love, "'Singing for Our Lives': Women's Music and Democratic Politics," 77.

72. Love, "'Singing for Our Lives': Women's Music and Democratic Politics," 78–79.
73. Connell and Gibson, *Sound Tracks: Popular Music, Identity and Place*, 209.
74. Nicola Dibben, "Representations of Femininity in Popular Music," *Popular Music* 18, no. 3 (1999): 352.
75. Joanne Hollows, *Feminism, Femininity and Popular Culture* (Manchester: Manchester University Press, 2000), 184; Bettina Fritzsche, "Spicy Strategies: Pop Feminist and Other Empowerments in Girl Culture," in *All About the Girl: Culture, Power, and Identity*, ed. Anita Harris (New York, London: Routledge, 2004).
76. Gayle Wald, "Just a Girl? Rock Music, Feminism, and the Cultural Construction of Female Youth," *Signs* 23, no. 3 (1998).
77. Dafna Lemish, "Spice World: Constructing Femininity the Popular Way," *Popular Music and Society* 26, no. 1 (2003): 25, 27; Fritzsche, "Spicy Strategies: Pop Feminist and Other Empowerments in Girl Culture."
78. Fritzsche, "Spicy Strategies: Pop Feminist and Other Empowerments in Girl Culture," 155.
79. Debbie Weekes, "Where My Girls At? Black Girls and the Construction of the Sexual," in *All About the Girl: Culture, Power, and Identity*, ed. Anita Harris (New York, London: Routledge, 2004).
80. Joan Morgan, *When Chickenheads Come Home to Roost: A Hip-Hop Feminist Breaks It Down* (New York: Simon & Schuster, 1999).
81. Gwendolyn D. Pough, *Check It While I Wreck It: Black Womanhood, Hip-Hop Culture, and the Public Sphere* (Boston: Northeastern University Press, 2004).
82. Michael Jeffries, "Re: Definitions: The Name and Game of Hip-Hop Feminism," in *Home Girls Make Some Noise: Hip Hop Feminism Anthology*, ed. Gwendolyn D. Pough, Elaine Richardson, Aisha Durham, and Rachel Raimist (Mira Loma, CA: Parker Publishing, 2007), 217.

83. Alesha Dominek Washington, "Not the Average Girl from the Videos: B-Girls Defining Their Space in Hip-Hop Culture," in *Home Girls Make Some Noise: Hip Hop Feminism Anthology*, ed. Gwendolyn D. Pough, Elaine Richardson, Aisha Durham, and Rachel Raimist (Mira Loma, CA: Parker Publishing, 2007); Sujatha Fernandes, "Proven Presence: The Emergence of a Feminist Politics in Cuban Hip-Hop," in *Home Girls Make Some Noise: Hip Hop Feminism Anthology*, ed. Gwendolyn D. Pough, Elaine Richardson, Aisha Durham, and Rachel Raimist (Mira Loma, CA: Parker Publishing, 2007); Eric Darnell Pritchard and Maria L. Bibbs, "Sista' Outsider: Queer Women of Color and Hip Hop," in *Home Girls Make Some Noise: Hip Hop Feminism Anthology*, ed. Gwendolyn D. Pough, Elaine Richardson, Aisha Durham, and Rachel Raimist (Mira Loma, CA: Parker Publishing, 2007).
84. Mimi Schippers, "The Social Organization of Sexuality and Gender in Alternative Hard Rock: An Analysis of Intersectionality," *Gender and Society* 14, no. 6 (2000).
85. Rachel L. Einwohner, Jocelyn A. Hollander, and Toska Olson, "Engendering Social Movements: Cultural Images and Movement Dynamics," *Gender and Society* 14, no. 5 (2000).
86. Mary Anne Clawson, "When Women Play the Bass: Instrument Specialization and Gender Interpretation in Alternative Rock Music," *Gender and Society* 13, no. 2 (1999).
87. UNESCO, "Gender Dynamics of Conflict, Peace-Building, and Reconstruction," http://portal.unesco.org/shs/en/ev.phpURL_ID=7839&URL_DO=DO_TOPIC&URL_SECTION=201.html; Gender and Peacebuilding Working Group of the Canadian Peacebuilding Coordinating Committee (CPCC), "Fact Sheet: Understanding United Nations Security Council Resolution 1325," http://www.peacebuild.ca/upload/fact_sheet_new.pdf.
88. Anderson, ed., *Girls Change the World! International Women's Day for Peace and Disarmament May 24, 2007*, 2.
89. Marc Sommers, "Fearing Africa's Young Men: Male Youth, Conflict, Urbanization, and the Case of Rwanda," in *The Other Half of Gender: Men's Issues in Development*, ed. Ian Bannon and Maria C. Correia (Washington, DC: The World Bank, 2006), 157.

90. Rana A. Emerson, "'Where My Girls At?' Negotiating Black Womanhood in Music Videos," *Gender and Society* 16, no. 1 (2002).
91. Gilman and Fenn, "Dance, Gender, and Popular Music in Malawi: The Case of Rap and Ragga," 379.
92. Christenson and Roberts, *It's Not Only Rock & Roll: Popular Music in the Lives of Adolescents*, 39, 92.
93. Arun Saldanha, "Music, Space, Identity Global Youth/ Local Others in Bangalore, India," Brussels: Center for Media Sociology (1998), http://www.cia.com.au/peril/ youth/arun-msi.pdf.
94. Randall Everett Allsup, "Mutual Learning and Democratic Action in Instrumental Music Education," *Journal of Research in Music Education* 51, no. 1 (2003): 33.
95. Baker and Cohen, "From Snuggling and Snogging to Sampling and Scratching: Girls' Nonparticipation in Community-Based Music Activities," 325.
96. Ibid., 333.
97. Ibid., 331.
98. Ibid., 334.
99. Harris, *Future Girl*, 159.
100. Sandra Renew, "The Social Construction of Gender, Violence and Schools," *Redress* (November 1995): 7.
101. Angus Tulley, "Masculinities and Violence," *Changing Education: A Journal for Teachers and Administrators* 4 no. 2&3 (1997): 1.
102. Renew, "The Social Construction of Gender, Violence and Schools," 8.
103. R. W. Connell, *Gender, Polity Short Introductions* (Cambridge: Polity Press, 2002), 53.
104. Amanda Keddie and Martin Mills, "Teaching for Gender Justice," *Australian Journal of Education* 51, no. 2 (2007).
105. Ibid., 23.
106. Maree Hedemann, "Gender & Violence," *Redress* (September 1998): 21.
107. Wesley Imms, "Boys Talk About 'Doing Art': Some Implications for Masculinity Discussion," *Australian Art Education* 26, no. 1 (2003): 29.

108. Michael Flood, "Why Violence against Women and Girls Happens, and How to Prevent It: A Framework and Some Key Strategies," *Redress*, no. 13–19 (August 2007): 14.
109. Ibid., 18.
110. Gary Barker, "Growing Up Poor and Male in the Americas: Reflections from Research and Practice with Young Men in Low-Income Communities in Rio De Janeiro," in *The Other Half of Gender: Men's Issues in Development,* ed. Ian Bannon and Maria C. Correia (Washington, DC: The World Bank, 2006), 112.
111. Paul Richards, "Young Men and Gender in War and Postwar Reconstruction: Some Comparative Findings from Liberia and Sierra Leone," in *The Other Half of Gender: Men's Issues in Development,* ed. Ian Bannon and Maria C. Correia (Washington, DC: The World Bank, 2006), 196.
112. Barker, "Growing Up Poor and Male in the Americas: Reflections from Research and Practice with Young Men in Low-Income Communities in Rio De Janeiro," 112.
113. Sommers, "Fearing Africa's Young Men: Male Youth, Conflict, Urbanization, and the Case of Rwanda," 139–141.
114. Gary Barker and Christine Ricardo, "Young Men and the Construction of Masculinity in Sub-Saharan Africa: Implications for HIV/AIDS, Conflict, and Violence," in *The Other Half of Gender: Men's Issues in Development,* ed. Ian Bannon and Maria C. Correia (Washington, DC: The World Bank, 2006), 173.
115. Fredy Alcaraz, Hernan Gomez, and Carlos Ivan Garcia Suarez, "Masculinity and Violence in Colombia: Deconstructing the Conventional Way of Becoming a Man," in *The Other Half of Gender: Men's Issues in Development,* ed. Ian Bannon and Maria C. Correia (Washington, DC: The World Bank, 2006), 108.
116. Barker and Ricardo, "Young Men and the Construction of Masculinity in Sub-Saharan Africa: Implications for HIV/AIDS, Conflict, and Violence," 165.
117. Alcaraz, Gomez, and Suarez, "Masculinity and Violence in Colombia: Deconstructing the Conventional Way of Becoming a Man," 102.

118. Barker and Ricardo, "Young Men and the Construction of Masculinity in Sub-Saharan Africa: Implications for HIV/AIDS, Conflict, and Violence," 161.
119. Barker, "Growing Up Poor and Male in the Americas: Reflections from Research and Practice with Young Men in Low-Income Communities in Rio De Janeiro," 117.
120. Alcaraz, Gomez, and Suarez, "Masculinity and Violence in Colombia: Deconstructing the Conventional Way of Becoming a Man," 107–109.
121. Barker, "Growing Up Poor and Male in the Americas: Reflections from Research and Practice with Young Men in Low-Income Communities in Rio De Janeiro," 120.
122. Flood, "Why Violence against Women and Girls Happens, and How to Prevent It: A Framework and Some Key Strategies," 15.
123. Connell, *Gender*, 14.
124. R. W. Connell, "Men, Masculinities and Feminism," *Social Alternatives* 16, no. 3 (1997): 9.
125. Barker, "Growing Up Poor and Male in the Americas: Reflections from Research and Practice with Young Men in Low-Income Communities in Rio De Janeiro," 131.
126. Barker and Ricardo, "Young Men and the Construction of Masculinity in Sub-Saharan Africa: Implications for HIV/AIDS, Conflict, and Violence," 189.

Chapter 3. The Beat on the Ground: Introducing the Case Studies

1. Bruce Hayllar and Tony Veal, *Pathways to Research* (Port Melbourne: Rigby Heinemann, Reed International Books, 1996); Pranee Liamputtong and Douglas Ezzy, *Qualitative Research Methods*, 2nd ed. (New York: Oxford University Press, 2005).
2. Gayle Letherby, *Feminist Research in Theory and Practice* (Buckingham: Open University Press, 2003), 73.
3. Nancy Naples, *Feminism and Method: Ethnography, Discourse Analysis, and Activist Research* (New York: Routledge, 2003), 3.
4. Brooke Ackerly and Jacqui True, *Doing Feminist Research in*

Political and Social Sciences (New York: Palgrave, 2010).

5. Joey Sprague, *Feminist Methodologies for Critical Researchers: Bridging Differences* (Walnut Creek, CA: AltaMira Press, 2005), 126. Citing Riessman 1993.
6. Kate Donelan, "'Overlapping Spheres' and 'Blurred Spaces': Mapping Cultural Interactions in Drama and Theatre with Young People," *NJ (Drama Australia Journal)* 28, no. 1 (2004): 15.
7. DFAT (Department of Foreign Affairs and Trade), "A Diverse People," Australian Government.
8. Mohammed El-Leissy, "Young People's Experiences of Racism in Australia," *Australian Mosaic*, no. 16 (2007): 38.
9. Phil Mercer, "Indian Students Claim Epidemic of Racist Violence in Australia," Voice of America News, 4 June 2009.
10. El-Leissy, "Young People's Experiences of Racism in Australia," 38.
11. UNFPA, "Gender-Based Violence: A Price Too High," in *State of World Population* (New York: United Nations, 2005).
12. Andrew Jakubowicz, "Hobbits and Orcs: The Street Politics of Race and Masculinity," *Australian Options* 44(2006): 2.
13. Shane Homan, "Youth, Live Music and Urban Leisure: Geographies of Noise," *Youth Studies Australia* 22, no. 2 (2003): 17.
14. Tony Mitchell, "Australian Hip Hop as a Subculture," *Youth Studies Australia* 22, no. 2 (2003): 41.
15. Katrin Lock, "Who Is Listening? Hip Hop Culture in Sierra Leone, Liberia and Senegal," in *Resounding International Relations: On Music, Culture and Politics*, ed. M. I. Franklin (New York: Palgrave Macmillan, 2005), 145.
16. Jan Jagodzinski, *Music in Youth Culture: A Lacanian Approach* (New York: Palgrave Macmillan, 2005), 64.
17. Lock, "Who Is Listening? Hip Hop Culture in Sierra Leone, Liberia and Senegal," 144.
18. Abdoulaye Niang, "Bboys: Hip-Hop Culture in Dakar, Senegal," in *Global Youth? Hybrid Identities, Plural Worlds*, ed. Pam Nilan and Carles Feixa (London and New York: Routledge, 2006), 173.
19. Munõz and Marín, "Music Is the Connection: Youth Cultures in Colombia," 133.

20. Christenson and Roberts, *It's Not Only Rock & Roll: Popular Music in the Lives of Adolescents*, 43.
21. Saldanha, "Music, Space, Identity Global Youth/Local Others in Bangalore, India"; Tara Brabazon, "Dancing through the Revolution," *Youth Studies Australia* 21, no. 1 (2002).
22. Brabazon, "Dancing through the Revolution," 19.
23. UNICEF, "Report Card 7 Child Poverty in Perspective: An Overview of Child Well-Being in Rich Countries: A Comprehensive Assessment of the Lives and Well-Being of Children and Adolescents in the Economically Advanced Nations," in *Innocenti Report Cards* (Florence, Italy: UNICEF Innocenti Research Center, 2007).
24. Landon E. Hancock, "The Northern Irish Peace Process: From Top to Bottom," *International Studies Review* 10 (2008): 203.
25. McEvoy-Levy, "Youth as Social and Political Agents: Issues in Post-Settlement Peace Building," 19–20.
26. Marina Monteith and Eithne McLaughlin, "Severe Child Poverty in Northern Ireland: Key Research Findings" (Washington, DC: Save the Children, 2004), 6.
27. BBC News, "Racism Growing in NI," *BBC News*, 14 April 2000. However, this government report was based on interview surveys, so it may merely indicate that people in Northern Ireland found it "easier" to talk about issues of racism than of sectarianism.
28. David McKittrick, "Racism 'Is the New Terrorism' as Attacks Rise in Ulster," *The Independent*, 16 October 2004.
29. McEvoy-Levy, "Youth as Social and Political Agents: Issues in Post-Settlement Peace Building," 20.
30. Paul Connolly and Paul McGinn, "Sectarianism, Children and Community Relations in Northern Ireland" (Coleraine: Centre for the Study of Conflict/University of Ulster, 1999). As cited in: McEvoy-Levy, "Youth as Social and Political Agents: Issues in Post-Settlement Peace Building," 20.
31. Sean Byrne, *Growing Up in a Divided Society: The Influence of Conflict on Belfast Schoolchildren* (London: Associated University Presses, 1997); Connolly and McGinn, "Sectarianism, Children and Community Relations in Northern Ireland." As cited in: McEvoy-Levy, "Youth as Social and Political

Agents: Issues in Post-Settlement Peace Building," 21.

32. McEvoy-Levy, "Youth as Social and Political Agents: Issues in Post-Settlement Peace Building," 21.
33. Department of Education, "Peace II Programme: The EU Programme for Peace and Reconciliation in Northern Ireland and the Border Region of Ireland 2000–2004 (Peace II)," ed. Department of Education (Belfast: Northern Ireland Government, 2009).
34. Flashpoints: World Conflicts, "Northern Ireland," http://www.flashpoints.info/countries-conflicts/Northern_Ireland-web/n-ireland_briefing.html.

Chapter 4. Building Peace Through a Musical Dialogue

1. Akbar Ahmed and Brian Forst, eds., *After Terror* (Cambridge: Polity, 2005); Edward (Edy) Kaufman, "Dialogue-Based Processes: A Vehicle for Peacebuilding," in *People Building Peace II: Successful Stories of Civil Society*, ed. Paul van Tongeren, Malin Brenk, Marte Hellema, and Juliette Verhoeven (Boulder, London: Lynne Rienner Publishers, 2005), 473; J. Martin Ramirez, "Peace Through Dialogue," *International Journal on World Peace* 24, no. 1 (2007); Liz Karagianis, "The Art of Dialogue," *Spectrum* (online) Winter 2001(2001); Kwame Anthony Appiah, *Cosmopolitanism: Ethics in a World of Strangers* (London: Allen Lane, 2006), 85; Leslie Beyer-Hermsen, "Can We Talk? Citizens' Voices in Search of Sustainable Peace," *Peace and Conflict: Journal of Peace Psychology* 7, no. 4 (2001): 362; Schirch, *Ritual and Symbol in Peacebuilding*; Lederach, *The Moral Imagination: The Art and Soul of Building Peace.*
2. David Bohm, *On Dialogue*, ed. Lee Nichol (London: Routledge, 1996). As cited in: Glenna Gerard, "Creating New Connections: Dialogue and Improv," in *Dialogue as a Means of Collective Communication*, ed. Bela H. Banathy and Patrick M. Jenlink (New York: Kluwer Academic/Plenum Publishers, 2005), 336.
3. Schirch, *Ritual and Symbol in Peacebuilding*, 60.
4. Molly Andrews, "Grand National Narratives and the Project

of Truth Commissions: A Comparative Analysis," *Media Culture Society* 25, no. 1 (2003).

5. Jessica Senehi and Sean Byrne, "From Violence toward Peace: The Role of Storytelling for Youth Healing and Political Empowerment after Conflict," in *Troublemakers or Peacemakers? Youth and Post-Accord Peace Building*, ed. Siobhán McEvoy-Levy (South Bend, IN: University of Notre Dame Press, 2006).
6. Oliver Ramsbotham, Tom Woodhouse, and Hugh Miall, *Contemporary Conflict Resolution: The Prevention, Management and Transformation of Deadly Conflicts*, 2nd ed. (Cambridge: Polity, 2005), 295.
7. Lederach, *The Moral Imagination: The Art and Soul of Building Peace*, 49.
8. Ibid.
9. Jan Blommaert, Mary Bock, and Kay McCormick, "Narrative Inequality in the TRC Hearings: On the Hearability of Hidden Transcripts," *Journal of Language and Politics* 5, no. 1 (2006): 39.
10. Peter M. Kellett, *Conflict Dialogue: Working with Layers of Meaning for Productive Relationships* (Thousand Oaks, London, New Delhi: Sage Publications, 2007), 67.
11. Lederach, *The Moral Imagination: The Art and Soul of Building Peace*, 57.
12. Allsup, "Mutual Learning and Democratic Action in Instrumental Music Education," 30. Citing Eisner 2001: 22.
13. Mary Ann Hunter, "Of Peacebuilding and Performance: Contact Inc's 'Third Space' of Intercultural Collaboration," *Australasian Drama Studies* 47, no. October 2005 (2005): 140; Mehri Madarshahi, "Mission: Mehri Madarshahi's Speech at the UNESCO Conference in Rabat (2005)"; David Oddie, "Conquering Conflict," *the wee can* (Autumn 2005); Donelan, "'Overlapping Spheres' and 'Blurred Spaces': Mapping Cultural Interactions in Drama and Theatre with Young People," 16.
14. Schirch, *Ritual and Symbol in Peacebuilding*, 82.
15. Clay, "All I Need Is One Mic: Mobilizing Youth for Social Change in the Post-Civil Rights Era," 113.

16. Munõz and Marín, "Music Is the Connection: Youth Cultures in Colombia," 132.
17. For further historical background and information, see the documentary film *Rize* (2005) from David LaChapelle Studio.

Chapter 5. Shifting Identities, Performing Peace

1. John Baily, "The Role of Music in the Creation of an Afghan National Identity, 1923–1973," in *Ethnicity, Identity and Music: The Musical Construction of Place*, ed. Martin Stokes, Ethnic Identities (Oxford, New York: Berg, 1994); Diana Francis, *People, Peace and Power: Conflict Transformation in Action* (London; Sterling, VA: Pluto Press, 2002); Schirch, *Ritual and Symbol in Peacebuilding*; Anna C. Snyder, *Setting the Agenda for Global Peace: Conflict and Consensus Building* (Aldershot: Ashgate, 2003); Lederach, *Preparing for Peace: Conflict Transformation across Cultures*; Jodi Halpern and Harvey M. Weinstein, "Rehumanizing the Other: Empathy and Reconciliation," *Human Rights Quarterly* 26, no. 3 (2004); Green, "Contact: Training a New Generation of Peacebuilders"; Ervin Staub et al., "Healing, Reconciliation, Forgiving and the Prevention of Violence after Genocide or Mass Killing: An Intervention and Its Experimental Evaluation in Rwanda," *Journal of Social & Clinical Psychology* 24, no. 3 (2005); Paul van Tongeren, Juliette Verhoeven, and Jim Wake, "People Building Peace: Key Messages and Essential Findings," in *People Building Peace II: Successful Stories of Civil Society*, ed. Paul van Tongeren, Malin Brenk, Marte Hellema, and Juliette Verhoeven (Boulder, London: Lynne Rienner Publishers, 2005).
2. Baily, "The Role of Music in the Creation of an Afghan National Identity, 1923–1973," 45.
3. Francis, *People, Peace and Power: Conflict Transformation in Action*, 4.
4. Dan Smith, "Trends and Causes of Armed Conflict" (Berlin: Berghof Research Centre, 2005), 10.

5. Mats Berdal, "How 'New' Are 'New Wars'? Global Economic Change and the Study of Civil War," *Global Governance* 9, no. 2003 (2003): 487.
6. John Mueller, "The Banality Of 'Ethnic War,'" *International Security* 25, no. 1 (2000): 62.
7. Smith, "Trends and Causes of Armed Conflict," 11.
8. Chris Hedges, "War Is a Force That Gives Us Meaning," in *Approaches to Peace: A Reader in Peace Studies*, ed. David Barash (New York: Oxford University Press, 2010 [2002]), 26; Sigmund Freud, "Why War?" in *Approaches to Peace: A Reader in Peace Studies*, ed. David Barash (New York: Oxford University Press, 2010 [1959]), 9; Irving Janis, "Victims of Groupthink," in *Approaches to Peace: A Reader in Peace Studies*, ed. David Barash (New York: Oxford University Press, 2010 [1982]), 31.
9. Margaret Mead, "Warfare Is Only an Invention—Not a Biological Necessity," in *Approaches to Peace: A Reader in Peace Studies*, ed. David Barash (New York: Oxford University Press, 2010 [1940]), 20.
10. Smith, "Trends and Causes of Armed Conflict," 13.
11. Francis, *People, Peace and Power: Conflict Transformation in Action*, 98; Lederach, *Preparing for Peace: Conflict Transformation across Cultures.*
12. Halpern and Weinstein, "Rehumanizing the Other: Empathy and Reconciliation," 566–567.
13. Ibid., 562.
14. Green, "Contact: Training a New Generation of Peacebuilders," 99.
15. Baily, "The Role of Music in the Creation of an Afghan National Identity, 1923–1973"; Francis, *People, Peace and Power: Conflict Transformation in Action*; Schirch, *Ritual and Symbol in Peacebuilding*; Snyder, *Setting the Agenda for Global Peace: Conflict and Consensus Building*; Lederach, *Preparing for Peace: Conflict Transformation across Cultures*; Halpern and Weinstein, "Rehumanizing the Other: Empathy and Reconciliation"; Green, "Contact: Training a New Generation of Peacebuilders"; Staub et al., "Healing, Reconciliation, Forgiving and the Prevention of Violence after Genocide

or Mass Killing: An Intervention and Its Experimental Evaluation in Rwanda"; van Tongeren, Verhoeven, and Wake, "People Building Peace: Key Messages and Essential Findings."

16. Dibben, "Representations of Femininity in Popular Music," 331; Stan Hawkins, *Settling the Pop Score: Pop Texts and Identity Politics* (Burlington, VT: Ashgate Publishing, 2002), 18; Connell and Gibson, *Sound Tracks: Popular Music, Identity and Place*, 117.
17. Donelan, "'Overlapping Spheres' and 'Blurred Spaces': Mapping Cultural Interactions in Drama and Theatre with Young People," 28.
18. Halpern and Weinstein, "Rehumanizing the Other: Empathy and Reconciliation."
19. Green, "Contact: Training a New Generation of Peacebuilders," 101.
20. Snyder, *Setting the Agenda for Global Peace: Conflict and Consensus Building*, 66.
21. Staub et al., "Healing, Reconciliation, Forgiving and the Prevention of Violence after Genocide or Mass Killing: An Intervention and Its Experimental Evaluation in Rwanda," 302.
22. Michael Keith, *After the Cosmopolitan: Multicultural Cities and the Future of Racism* (London: Routledge, 2005), 164.
23. Frith, "Music and Identity," 110.
24. Mark Slobin, *Subculture Sounds: Micromusic of the West* (Hanover and London: Wesleyan University Press, 1993), 41. As cited in: Frith, "Music and Identity," 110.
25. Connell and Gibson, *Sound Tracks: Popular Music, Identity and Place*, 117; Clay, "All I Need Is One Mic: Mobilizing Youth for Social Change in the Post-Civil Rights Era," 106.
26. Tia DeNora, *Music in Everyday Life* (Cambridge: Cambridge University Press, 2000), 40.
27. Frith, "Music and Identity," 111.
28. John Miller Chernoff, *African Rhythm and African Sensibility: Aesthetics and Sensibility in African Musical Idioms* (Chicago: University of Chicago Press, 1979). As cited in: Frith, "Music and Identity."

29. Ibid., 124.
30. Diane M. Daane, "Child and Adolescent Violence," *Orthopaedic Nursing* 22, no. 1 (2003); M. Brent Donnellan et al., "Low Self-Esteem Is Related to Aggression, Antisocial Behavior, and Delinquency," *Psychological Science* 16, no. 4 (2005).
31. P. L. Ellickson and K. A. McGuigan, "Early Predictors of Adolescent Violence," *American Journal of Public Health* 90, no. 4 (2000).
32. Hallam Hurt et al., "Exposure to Violence: Psychological and Academic Correlates in Child Witnesses," *Archives of Pediatrics and Adolescent Medicine* 155, no. 12 (2001); Matthew W. Reynolds et al., "The Relationship between Gender, Depression, and Self-Esteem in Children Who Have Witnessed Domestic Violence," *Child Abuse & Neglect* 25, no. 9 (2001); Daniel W. L. Lai, "Violence Exposure and Mental Health of Adolescents in Small Towns: An Exploratory Study," *Canadian Journal of Public Health* (May–June 1999).
33. Michael Cascardi and K. Daniel O'Leary, "Depressive Symptomatology, Self-Esteem, and Self-Blame in Battered Women," *Journal of Family Violence* 7, no. 4 (1992); Michelle R. Callahan, Richard M. Tolman, and Daniel G. Saunders, "Adolescent Dating Violence Victimization and Psychological Well-Being," *Journal of Adolescent Research* 18, no. 6 (2003): 666.
34. Kurt Naumann, "Briefing Paper: Bullying," ed. U.S. Department of Justice (School Violence Resource Center, 2001).
35. Deborah Prothrow-Stith and Sher Quaday, "Hidden Casualties: The Relationship between Violence and Learning," *Streamlined Seminar: National Association of Elementary School Principals* 14, no. 2 (1995).
36. Elissa Emerson and Deborah Shelton, "Using Creative Arts to Build Coping Skills to Reduce Domestic Violence in the Lives of Female Juvenile Offenders," *Issues in Mental Health Nursing* 22 (2001): 189.
37. M. Isolina Ferré, "Prevention and Control of Violence through Community Revitalization, Individual Dignity, and Personal Self-Confidence," *Annals of the American Academy of Political and Social Science* 494 (1987).

38. DeNora, *Music in Everyday Life*, 81.
39. Alan Lomax, "Folk Song Style," *American Anthropologist* 61, no. 6 (1959): 929. As cited in: Baily, "The Role of Music in the Creation of an Afghan National Identity, 1923–1973," 47.
40. Donelan, "'Overlapping Spheres' and 'Blurred Spaces': Mapping Cultural Interactions in Drama and Theatre with Young People," 19.
41. Christenson and Roberts, *It's Not Only Rock & Roll: Popular Music in the Lives of Adolescents*, 247.
42. Clay, "All I Need Is One Mic: Mobilizing Youth for Social Change in the Post-Civil Rights Era," 107.
43. Ibid., 108.

Chapter 6. Making Space, Creating Common Ground

1. Michel Foucault, "Of Other Spaces," *Diacritics* 16, no. 1 (1986).
2. Henri Lefebvre, *The Production of Space*, trans. Donald Nicholson-Smith (Oxford: Blackwell Publishing, 1991 [1974]).
3. Edward Soja, *Thirdspace: Journeys to Los Angeles and Other Real-and-Imagined Places* (Oxford: Blackwell Publishing, 1996); Lefebvre, *The Production of Space*; Rick Allen, "What Space Makes of Us: Thirdspace, Identity Politics, and Multiculturalism," in *Annual Meeting of the American Educational Research Association* (Chicago, IL: Educational Resources Information Center [ERIC], 1997).
4. Lefebvre, *The Production of Space*; Soja, *Thirdspace: Journeys to Los Angeles and Other Real-and-Imagined Places*; Saldanha, "Music, Space, Identity Global Youth/Local Others in Bangalore, India"; Allen, "What Space Makes of Us: Thirdspace, Identity Politics, and Multiculturalism."
5. Allen, "What Space Makes of Us: Thirdspace, Identity Politics, and Multiculturalism," 2; Saldanha, "Music, Space, Identity Global Youth/Local Others in Bangalore, India."
6. Sara Cohen, "Identity, Place and the 'Liverpool Sound,'" in *Ethnicity, Identity and Music: The Musical Construction of Place*, ed. Martin Stokes, Ethnic Identities (Oxford, New

York: Berg, 1994), 129. Connell and Gibson, *Sound Tracks: Popular Music, Identity and Place*, 193; Martin Stokes, "Introduction: Ethnicity, Identity and Music," in *Ethnicity, Identity and Music: The Musical Construction of Place*, ed. Martin Stokes, Ethnic Identities (Oxford, New York: Berg, 1994), 5; Stokes, "Introduction: Ethnicity, Identity and Music," 3.

7. Foucault, "Of Other Spaces," 25.
8. Ibid., 24.
9. Stokes, "Introduction: Ethnicity, Identity and Music," 4.
10. DeNora, *Music in Everyday Life*, 123; Connell and Gibson, *Sound Tracks: Popular Music, Identity and Place*, 192.
11. DeNora, *Music in Everyday Life*, 60.
12. Lederach, *The Moral Imagination: The Art and Soul of Building Peace*, 146.
13. Mary Ann Cejka and Thomas Bainat, *Artisans of Peace: Grassroots Peacemaking among Christian Communities* (Maryknoll, NY: Orbis, 2003). As cited in: Lederach, *The Moral Imagination: The Art and Soul of Building Peace*, 165. Quoting researcher John Brewer from Northern Ireland.
14. Lederach, *The Moral Imagination: The Art and Soul of Building Peace*, 77.
15. Schirch, *Ritual and Symbol in Peacebuilding*, 68.
16. John Paul Lederach, *Building Peace: Sustainable Reconciliation in Divided Societies* (Washington, DC: United States Institute of Peace, 1997), 35.
17. Lederach, *The Moral Imagination: The Art and Soul of Building Peace*, 98.
18. Schirch, *Ritual and Symbol in Peacebuilding*, 68.
19. Ibid. (Citing Yarbrough and Wilmot's *Artful Mediation: Constructive Conflict at Work*). While not focused specifically on peacebuilding, Wise's work on sharing space is also relevant here, as she supports Schirch's points by arguing that sharing actual places, which she terms "contact zones," often can be difficult. These contact zones she speaks of can be understood as relational spaces. See Amanda Wise, "Sensuous Multiculturalism: Emotional Landscapes of Interethnic Living in Australian Suburbia," *Journal of Ethnic and Migration Studies* (2010): 37. NB: "Contact Zones" is a term coined by Mary Louise Pratt. See Mary Louise Pratt,

"Arts of the Contact Zone," in *Profession 91* (New York: MLA, 1991).

20. Schirch, *Ritual and Symbol in Peacebuilding*, 164.
21. Schell-Faucon, "Conflict Transformation through Educational and Youth Programmes," 12.
22. Harris, *Future Girl*, 120.
23. Paul Chatterton and Robert Hollands, *Urban Nightscapes: Youth Cultures, Pleasure Spaces and Corporate Power*, ed. Tracey Skelton and Gill Valentine, Critical Geographies (London, New York: Routledge, 2003), 194.
24. Murray Forman, *The 'Hood Comes First: Race, Space, and Place in Rap and Hip-Hop* (Middleton, CT: Wesleyan University Press, 2002), 8. Chatterton and Hollands, *Urban Nightscapes: Youth Cultures, Pleasure Spaces and Corporate Power*, 194.
25. Forman, *The 'Hood Comes First: Race, Space, and Place in Rap and Hip-Hop*, 344.
26. Ibid., 142.
27. Connell and Gibson, *Sound Tracks: Popular Music, Identity and Place*, 208.
28. Ibid.
29. Baker and Cohen, "From Snuggling and Snogging to Sampling and Scratching: Girls' Nonparticipation in Community-Based Music Activities," 321.
30. Chatterton and Hollands, *Urban Nightscapes: Youth Cultures, Pleasure Spaces and Corporate Power*, 154.
31. Sue Lees, *Sugar and Spice: Sexuality and Adolescent Girls* (London: Penguin, 1993), 69. As cited in: Chatterton and Hollands, *Urban Nightscapes: Youth Cultures, Pleasure Spaces and Corporate Power*, 154.
32. Chatterton and Hollands, *Urban Nightscapes: Youth Cultures, Pleasure Spaces and Corporate Power*, 154.
33. Sarah Cohen, "Men Making a Scene: Rock Music and the Production of Gender," in *Sexing the Groove*, ed. Sheila Whiteley (London: Routledge, 1997). As cited in: Baker and Cohen, "From Snuggling and Snogging to Sampling and Scratching: Girls' Nonparticipation in Community-Based Music Activities," 320.
34. Cohen, "Men Making a Scene: Rock Music and the Production of Gender," 31. As cited in: Baker and Cohen, "From

Snuggling and Snogging to Sampling and Scratching: Girls' Nonparticipation in Community-Based Music Activities," 320.

35. Baker and Cohen, "From Snuggling and Snogging to Sampling and Scratching: Girls' Nonparticipation in Community-Based Music Activities," 321.
36. Ibid., 320.
37. Gilman and Fenn, "Dance, Gender, and Popular Music in Malawi: The Case of Rap and Ragga," 371.
38. Cohen, "Men Making a Scene: Rock Music and the Production of Gender." As cited in: Baker and Cohen, "From Snuggling and Snogging to Sampling and Scratching: Girls' Nonparticipation in Community-Based Music Activities," 320.
39. Baker and Cohen, "From Snuggling and Snogging to Sampling and Scratching: Girls' Nonparticipation in Community-Based Music Activities," 320.
40. Arun Saldanha, "Music, Space, Identity Global Youth / Local Others in Bangalore, India," Brussels: Center for Media Sociology (1998), http://www.cia.com.au/peril/youth/arun-msi.pdf.
41. Tara Brabazon and Amanda Evans, "I'll Never Be Your Woman: The Spice Girls and New Flavours of Feminism," *Social Alternatives* 17, no. 2 (1998): 40.
42. Michelle Fine, Lois Weis, and Linda C. Powell, "Communities of Difference," in *Critical Ethnicity: Countering the Waves of Identity Politics*, ed. Robert H. Tai and Mary L. Kenyatta (Lanham, MD: Rowman & Littlefield Publishers, 1999).

Chapter 7. Gendering the Jam: Possibilities and Prohibitions

1. R. W. Connell, *Masculinities* (St. Leonards: Allen & Unwin, 1995); Barker and Ricardo, "Young Men and the Construction of Masculinity in Sub-Saharan Africa: Implications for HIV/AIDS Conflict, and Violence," 160; Rita Schäfer, "Masculinity and Civil Wars in Africa: New Approaches to Overcoming Sexual Violence in War," ed. Jörg-Werner Haas (Eschborn, Germany: Federal Ministry for Economic

Cooperation and Development: Program Promoting Gender Equality and Women's Rights, 2009); Tickner, *Gendering World Politics: Issues and Approaches in the Post-Cold War Era*; Tickner, *Gender in International Relations: Feminist Perspectives on Achieving Global Security*; Connell, *Gender*; Judith Butler, "Sexual Inversions," in *Feminist Interpretations of Michel Foucault*, ed. Susan J. Hekman (University Park, PA: The Pennsylvania State University Press, 1996); Judith Butler, *Gender Trouble: Feminism and the Subversion of Identity* (New York: Routledge, 1999); Ash Amin, "Ethnicity and the Multicultural City: Living with Diversity," *Environment and Planning A* 34 (2002); Barker and Ricardo, "Young Men and the Construction of Masculinity in Sub-Saharan Africa: Implications for HIV/AIDS, Conflict, and Violence."

2. Connell, *Gender*; R. W. Connell, *Gender and Power: Society, the Person and Sexual Politics* (Oxford: Polity, 1987); Stokes, "Introduction: Ethnicity, Identity and Music," 22.
3. Stokes, "Introduction: Ethnicity, Identity and Music," 22.
4. Connell, *Gender and Power: Society, the Person and Sexual Politics.*
5. Connell, *Masculinities*; Connell, *Gender.*
6. Schäfer, "Masculinity and Civil Wars in Africa: New Approaches to Overcoming Sexual Violence in War," 3.
7. Donald Steinberg, "Beyond Victimhood: Engaging Women in the Pursuit of Peace, Testimony to the House of Representatives Committee on Foreign Affairs, by Donald Steinberg, Deputy President, International Crisis Group (ICC), to Subcommittee on International Organizations, Human Rights and Oversight, 15 May 2008" (Washington, DC: 2008).
8. Barker and Ricardo, "Young Men and the Construction of Masculinity in Sub-Saharan Africa: Implications for HIV/AIDS, Conflict, and Violence," 159; Schäfer, "Masculinity and Civil Wars in Africa: New Approaches to Overcoming Sexual Violence in War" (see for several African examples); Fidelma Ashe, "The Gender Politics of De-Militarising Northern Ireland: Theorising Gender Power in the Context of Conflict Transformation" (Jordanstown: University of Ulster, 2009) (see for Northern Ireland example);

Barker, "Growing Up Poor and Male in the Americas: Reflections from Research and Practice with Young Men in Low-Income Communities in Rio De Janeiro" (see for Brazil and U.S. examples)

9. Alcaraz, Gomez, and Suarez, "Masculinity and Violence in Colombia: Deconstructing the Conventional Way of Becoming a Man," 102.
10. Schäfer, "Masculinity and Civil Wars in Africa: New Approaches to Overcoming Sexual Violence in War," 4.
11. Ashe, "The Gender Politics of De-Militarising Northern Ireland: Theorising Gender Power in the Context of Conflict Transformation," 14.
12. Kieran McEvoy and Anna Eriksson, "Restorative Justice in Transition: Ownership, Leadership, and 'Bottom-up' Human Rights," in *Handbook of Restorative Justice*, ed. Dennis Sullivan and Larry Tifft (London and New York: Routledge, 2006), 326. As cited in: Ashe, "The Gender Politics of De-Militarising Northern Ireland: Theorising Gender Power in the Context of Conflict Transformation," 9.
13. Ashe, "The Gender Politics of De-Militarising Northern Ireland: Theorising Gender Power in the Context of Conflict Transformation," 14.
14. Schäfer, "Masculinity and Civil Wars in Africa: New Approaches to Overcoming Sexual Violence in War," 6.
15. Barker and Ricardo, "Young Men and the Construction of Masculinity in Sub-Saharan Africa: Implications for HIV/AIDS, Conflict, and Violence," 160. (Cf. Barker 2005.)
16. Alcaraz, Gomez, and Suarez, "Masculinity and Violence in Colombia: Deconstructing the Conventional Way of Becoming a Man," 102.
17. Barker, "Growing Up Poor and Male in the Americas: Reflections from Research and Practice with Young Men in Low-Income Communities in Rio De Janeiro," 118.
18. Schäfer, "Masculinity and Civil Wars in Africa: New Approaches to Overcoming Sexual Violence in War," 5.
19. Barker, "Growing Up Poor and Male in the Americas: Reflections from Research and Practice with Young Men in Low-Income Communities in Rio De Janeiro," 129–130.
20. Sommers, "Fearing Africa's Young Men: Male Youth,

Conflict, Urbanization, and the Case of Rwanda," 139.

21. Barker, "Growing Up Poor and Male in the Americas: Reflections from Research and Practice with Young Men in Low-Income Communities in Rio De Janeiro," 112; Borer, Darby, and McEvoy-Levy, "Caught between Child Rights and Security: Youth and Postwar Reconstruction" (see for critiques of these views).
22. Such as the example of the Brazilian youth music groups documented in the film *Favela Rising*.
23. Barker, "Growing Up Poor and Male in the Americas: Reflections from Research and Practice with Young Men in Low-Income Communities in Rio De Janeiro," 120.
24. Ibid., 131.
25. Wanda Boyer, "Girl-to-Girl Violence: The Voice of the Victims," *Childhood Education* 84, no. 6 (2008): 344.
26. Coretta Phillips, "Who's Who in the Pecking Order? Aggression and 'Normal Violence' in the Lives of Girls and Boys," *The British Journal of Criminology* 43, no. 4 (2003): 716–718.
27. Sommers, "Fearing Africa's Young Men: Male Youth, Conflict, Urbanization, and the Case of Rwanda," 157.
28. Harris, *Future Girl*, 16.
29. Stokes, "Introduction: Ethnicity, Identity and Music," 22.
30. Jacqueline Witherow, "'The War on Terrorism' and Parading Bands in Northern Ireland," 2009, http://www.qub.ac.uk/sites/QUEST/FileStore/Filetoupload,25795,en.pdf.
31. Frith, "Music and Identity," 110; Stokes, "Introduction: Ethnicity, Identity and Music."
32. Witherow, "'The War on Terrorism' and Parading Bands in Northern Ireland."
33. Jessica Rosenberg and Gitana Garofalo, "Riot Grrrl: Revolutions from Within," *Signs* 23, no. 3 (1998).
34. Mitchell, "Australian Hip Hop as a Subculture," 44.
35. See Lisa Duggan, *The Twilight of Equality: Neoliberalism, Cultural Politics, and the Attack on Democracy* (Boston: Beacon Press, 2004).
36. Nick Couldry, *Why Voice Matters: Culture and Politics after Neoliberalism* (London: Sage Publications, 2010).
37. Emma Rich, "Young Women, Feminist Identities and

Neo-Liberalism," *Women's Studies International Forum* 28, no. 6 (2005).

38. Kathy Bail, ed., *DIY Feminism* (St. Leonards: Allen and Unwin, 1996); Rosenberg and Garofalo, "Riot Grrrl: Revolutions from Within"; Jennifer Baumgardner and Amy Richards, *Manifesta: Young Women, Feminism, and the Future* (New York: Farrar, Straus and Giroux, 2000).
39. Rich, "Young Women, Feminist Identities and Neo-Liberalism."
40. Suzanne Franzway et al., "Engineering Ignorance: The Problem of Gender Equity in Engineering," *Frontiers: A Journal of Women Studies* 30, no. 1 (2009): 10.
41. Nadine Changfoot, "The Second Sex's Continued Relevance for Equality and Difference Feminisms," *European Journal of Women's Studies* 16, no. 1 (2009).
42. Joan W. Scott, *Gender and the Politics of History* (New York: Columbia University Press, 1999); Joan W. Scott, "Deconstructing Equality-Versus-Difference: Or, the Uses of Poststructuralist Theory for Feminism," *Feminist Studies* 14, no. 1 (1988).
43. Linda Rennie Forcey, "Feminist and Peace Perspectives on Women," in *Encyclopedia of Violence, Peace & Conflict*, ed. Lester R Kurtz and Jennifer E Turpin (Waltham, MA: Academic Press, 1999), 17.
44. Ken Harland, "Violent Youth Culture in Northern Ireland: Young Men, Violence, and the Challenges of Peacebuilding," *Youth & Society* 32, no. 2 (2011).
45. Sylvia Walby, "Gender Mainstreaming: Productive Tensions in Theory and Practice," *Social Politics* 12, no. 3 (2005).
46. Chilla Bulbeck, "'If Most Men Are against Us, Can We Call Ourselves Feminists?': Young People's Views of Feminism—East and West," *PORTAL Journal of Multidisciplinary International Studies* 3, no. 2 (2006); Chilla Bulbeck, *Sex, Love and Feminism in the Asia Pacific: A Cross-Cultural Study of Young People's Attitudes*, ASAA Women in Asia Series (New York: Routledge, 2008).
47. Schell-Faucon, "Conflict Transformation through Educational and Youth Programmes," 13.

48. Baker and Cohen, "From Snuggling and Snogging to Sampling and Scratching: Girls' Nonparticipation in Community-Based Music Activities."

Postlude

1. For a discussion on the limits of liberal tolerance, see Charles Taylor, "The Politics of Recognition," in *Multiculturalism and the Politics of Recognition*, ed. Charles Taylor, et al. (Princeton: Princeton University Press, 1994).

Bibliography

Ackerly, Brooke, and Jacqui True. *Doing Feminist Research in Political and Social Sciences.* New York: Palgrave, 2010.

ActNow. "Portrayal of Young People by the Media." The Inspire Foundation. http://www.actnow.com.au/Issues/Portrayal_of_young_people_by_the_media.aspx.

AFP (Alliance for Peace). "Alliance for Peace." http://www.allianceforpeacebuilding.org/peacebuilding.htm.

Ahmed, Akbar, and Brian Forst, eds. *After Terror.* Cambridge: Polity, 2005.

Alcaraz, Fredy, Hernan Gomez, and Carlos Ivan Garcia Suarez. "Masculinity and Violence in Colombia: Deconstructing the Conventional Way of Becoming a Man." In *The Other Half of Gender: Men's Issues in Development,* edited by Ian Bannon and Maria C. Correia, 93–110. Washington, DC: The World Bank, 2006.

Aliyev, Huseyn. "Peace-Building from the Bottom: A Case Study of the North Caucasus." *Caucasian Review of International Affairs* 4, no. 4 (2010): 325–341.

Allen, Rick. "What Space Makes of Us: Thirdspace, Identity Politics, and Multiculturalism." In *Annual Meeting of the American Educational Research Association.* Chicago, IL: Educational Resources Information Center (ERIC), 1997. Available at: http://www.eric.ed.gov/PDFS/ED409409.pdf.

Allsup, Randall Everett. "Mutual Learning and Democratic Action in Instrumental Music Education." *Journal of Research in Music Education* 51, no. 1 (2003): 24–37.

Amin, Ash. "Ethnicity and the Multicultural City: Living with Diversity." *Environment and Planning A* 34 (2002): 959–980.

Anderson, Shelley, ed. *Girls Change the World! International Women's Day for Peace and Disarmament May 24, 2007.* Geneva: International Peace Bureau, 2007.

Andrews, Molly. "Grand National Narratives and the Project of Truth Commissions: A Comparative Analysis." *Media Culture Society* 25, no. 1 (2003): 45–65.

Appiah, Kwame Anthony. *Cosmopolitanism: Ethics in a World of Strangers.* London: Allen Lane, 2006.

Ardizzone, Leonisa. *Gettin' My Word Out.* Albany: State University of New York Press, 2007.

Ardizzone, Leonisa. "Generating Peace: A Study of Nonformal Youth Organizations." *Peace and Change* 28, no. 3 (2003): 420–445.

Ashe, Fidelma. "The Gender Politics of De-Militarising Northern Ireland: Theorising Gender Power in the Context of Conflict Transformation." University of Ulster, 2009. Available at: http://www.hannashouse.ie/PDFs/Ashe.pdf.

Australian Government. "Background Paper: Women's Equal Participation in Conflict Prevention, Conflict Management and Conflict Resolution in Post-Conflict Peace-Building." Edited by Office on the Status of Women. Canberra: Australian Government, 2004. Available at: http://www.fahcsia.gov.au/our-responsibilities/women/programs-services/international-engagement/united-nations-commission-on-the-status-of-women/background-paper-womens-equal-participation-in-conflict-prevention.

Bail, Kathy, ed. *DIY Feminism.* St. Leonards: Allen and Unwin, 1996.

Baily, John. "The Role of Music in the Creation of an Afghan National Identity, 1923–1973." In *Ethnicity, Identity and Music: The Musical Construction of Place,* edited by Martin Stokes, 45–60. Oxford, New York: Berg, 1994.

Baker, Sarah, and Bruce M. Z. Cohen. "From Snuggling and Snogging to Sampling and Scratching: Girls' Nonparticipation in Community-Based Music Activities." *Youth & Society* 39, no. 3 (2008): 316–339.

Barker, Gary Thomas. *Dying to Be Men: Youth, Masculinity and*

Social Exclusion. New York: Routledge, 2005.

Barker, Gary. "Growing Up Poor and Male in the Americas: Reflections from Research and Practice with Young Men in Low-Income Communities in Rio De Janeiro." In *The Other Half of Gender: Men's Issues in Development*, edited by Ian Bannon and Maria C. Correia, 111–136. Washington, DC: The World Bank, 2006.

Barker, Gary, and Christine Ricardo. "Young Men and the Construction of Masculinity in Sub-Saharan Africa: Implications for HIV/Aids, Conflict, and Violence." In *The Other Half of Gender: Men's Issues in Development*, edited by Ian Bannon and Maria C. Correia, 159–194. Washington, DC: The World Bank, 2006.

Baumgardner, Jennifer, and Amy Richards. *Manifesta: Young Women, Feminism, and the Future*. New York: Farrar, Straus and Giroux, 2000.

Bayton, Mavis. *Frock Rock*. Oxford: Oxford University Press, 1998.

BBC News. "Racism Growing in NI." *BBC News*, 14 April 2000.

Bell, Rob. *Sex God: Exploring the Endless Connections between Sexuality and Spirituality*. Grand Rapids: Zondervan, 2007.

Berdal, Mats. "How 'New' Are 'New Wars'? Global Economic Change and the Study of Civil War." *Global Governance* 9 (2003): 477–502.

Beyer-Hermsen, Leslie. "Can We Talk? Citizens' Voices in Search of Sustainable Peace." *Peace and Conflict: Journal of Peace Psychology* 7, no. 4 (2001): 361–364.

Bleiker, Roland. *Aesthetics and World Politics*. Edited by Oliver P. Richmond, Rethinking Peace and Conflict Studies. New York: Palgrave Macmillan, 2009.

Bleiker, Roland. "The Changing Speed of Dissent Politics." *Social Alternatives* 19, no. 1 (2000): 9–14.

Bleiker, Roland, ed. "Painting Politics: Editor's Introduction." *Social Alternatives* 20 no. 4 (2001): 3–9.

Blommaert, Jan, Mary Bock, and Kay McCormick. "Narrative Inequality in the TRC Hearings: On the Hearability of Hidden Transcripts." *Journal of Language and Politics* 5, no. 1 (2006): 37–70.

Bohm, David. *On Dialogue*. Edited by Lee Nichol. London: Routledge, 1996.

Borer, Tristan Anne, John Darby, and Siobhán McEvoy-Levy. "Caught between Child Rights and Security: Youth and Postwar Reconstruction." In *Peacebuilding after Peace Accords: The Challenges of Violence, Truth, and Youth*, edited by Tristan Anne Borer, John Darby, and Siobhán McEvoy-Levy, 41–67. Notre Dame, IN: University of Notre Dame Press, 2006.

Botero, Sandra, and Astrid Zacipa. "Colombia's Children: Agents of a New Culture of Peace." In *Children and Peacebuilding: Experiences and Perspectives*, edited by Heather Elliot, 22–27. Melbourne: World Vision Australia, 2001.

Boti, Marie, Malcolm Guy, Elysee Nouvet, and Hind Benchekroun. "Making Rebel Musics: The Films." In *Rebel Musics: Human Rights, Resistant Sounds, and the Politics of Music Making*, edited by Daniel Fischlin and Ajay Heble, 68–87. Montreal: Black Rose Books, 2003.

Boyce-Tillman, June. *Constructing Musical Healing: The Wounds That Sing*. London and Philadelphia: Jessica Kingsley Publishers, 2000.

Boyer, Wanda. "Girl-to-Girl Violence: The Voice of the Victims." *Childhood Education* 84, no. 6 (2008): 344–350.

Brabazon, Tara. "Dancing through the Revolution." *Youth Studies Australia* 21, no. 1 (2002): 19-24.

Brabazon, Tara, and Amanda Evans. "I'll Never Be Your Woman: The Spice Girls and New Flavours of Feminism." *Social Alternatives* 17, no. 2 (1998): 39–42.

Bulbeck, Chilla. *Sex, Love and Feminism in the Asia Pacific: A Cross-Cultural Study of Young People's Attitudes*, ASAA Women in Asia Series. New York: Routledge, 2008.

Bulbeck, Chilla. "'If Most Men Are against Us, Can We Call Ourselves Feminists?' Young People's Views of Feminism—East and West." *PORTAL Journal of Multidisciplinary International Studies* 3, no. 2 (2006): 1–28.

Bulbeck, Chilla. "The 'White Worrier' in South Australia: Attitudes to Multiculturalism, Immigration and Reconciliation." *Journal of Sociology* 40, no. 4 (2004): 341–361.

Bush, Kenneth. "Field Notes: Fighting Commodification and Disempowerment in the Development Industry: Things I

Learned About PCIA in Habarana and Mindanao." Berlin: Berghof Research Centre for Constructive Conflict Management, 2005.

Butler, Judith. *Gender Trouble: Feminism and the Subversion of Identity*. New York: Routledge, 1999.

Butler, Judith. "Sexual Inversions." In *Feminist Interpretations of Michel Foucault*, edited by Susan J. Hekman, 59–76. University Park, PA: The Pennsylvania State University Press, 1996.

Byrne, Sean. *Growing Up in a Divided Society. The Influence of Conflict on Belfast Schoolchildren*. London: Associated University Presses, 1997.

Callahan, Michelle R., Richard M. Tolman, and Daniel G. Saunders. "Adolescent Dating Violence Victimization and Psychological Well-Being." *Journal of Adolescent Research* 18, no. 6 (2003): 664–681.

Caprioli, Mary. "Gendered Conflict." *Journal of Peace Research* 37, no. 1 (2000): 53–68.

Cascardi, Michael, and K. Daniel O'Leary. "Depressive Symptomatology, Self-Esteem, and Self-Blame in Battered Women." *Journal of Family Violence* 7, no. 4 (1992): 249–259.

Cejka, Mary Ann, and Thomas Bainat. *Artisans of Peace: Grassroots Peacemaking among Christian Communities*. Maryknoll, NY: Orbis, 2003.

Changfoot, Nadine. "The Second Sex's Continued Relevance for Equality and Difference Feminisms." *European Journal of Women's Studies* 16, no. 1 (2009): 11–31.

Chatterton, Paul, and Robert Hollands. *Urban Nightscapes: Youth Cultures, Pleasure Spaces and Corporate Power*. Edited by Tracey Skelton and Gill Valentine, Critical Geographies. London, New York: Routledge, 2003.

Christenson, Peter G., and Donald F. Roberts. *It's Not Only Rock & Roll: Popular Music in the Lives of Adolescents*. Cresskill, NJ: Hampton Press, 1998.

Clark, Catherine, Amrita Ghosh, Emrys Green, and Naushin Shariff. "Media Portrayal of Young People: Impact and Influences." Washington, DC: National Children's Bureau, The National Youth Agency—Young Researcher Network, 2009.

Clawson, Mary Anne. "When Women Play the Bass: Instrument Specialization and Gender Interpretation in Alternative Rock Music." *Gender and Society* 13, no. 2 (1999): 193–210.

Clay, Andreana. "All I Need Is One Mic: Mobilizing Youth for Social Change in the Post-Civil Rights Era." *Social Justice* 33, no. 2 (2006): 105–119.

Cohen, Sara. "Identity, Place and the 'Liverpool Sound.'" In *Ethnicity, Identity and Music: The Musical Construction of Place*, edited by Martin Stokes, 117–134. Oxford, New York: Berg, 1994.

Cohen, Sarah. "Men Making a Scene: Rock Music and the Production of Gender." In *Sexing the Groove*, edited by Sheila Whiteley, 17–36. London: Routledge, 1997.

Cohn, Carol. "Wars, Wimps, and Women: Talking Gender and Thinking War." In *Gendering War Talk*, edited by Miriam Cooke and Angela Woolacott, 227–248. Princeton, NJ: Princeton University Press, 1993.

Connell, John, and Chris Gibson. *Sound Tracks: Popular Music, Identity and Place*. London: Routledge, 2003.

Connell, R. W. "Change among the Gatekeepers: Men, Masculinities, and Gender Equality in the Global Arena." *Signs: Journal of Women in Culture and Society* 30, no. 3 (2005): 1801–1825.

Connell, R. W. *Gender*. Polity Short Introductions. Cambridge: Polity Press, 2002.

Connell, R. W. "Men, Masculinities and Feminism." *Social Alternatives* 16, no. 3 (1997): 7–10.

Connell, R. W. *Masculinities*. St. Leonards: Allen & Unwin, 1995.

Connell, R. W. *Gender and Power: Society, the Person and Sexual Politics*. Oxford: Polity, 1987.

Connolly, Paul, and Paul McGinn. "Sectarianism, Children and Community Relations in Northern Ireland." Coleraine: Centre for the Study of Conflict/University of Ulster, 1999.

Couldry, Nick. *Why Voice Matters: Culture and Politics after Neoliberalism*. London: Sage Publications, 2010.

Creag, Sunanda. "Consuming Identity: Are Young Voices Being Marginalised and Trivialised?" *M/C Reviews* (1999). Available at: http://reveiws.media-culture.org.au/modules.php?name=News&file=article&sid=1720.

Daane, Diane M. "Child and Adolescent Violence." *Orthopaedic Nursing* 22, no. 1 (2003): 23–29.

Daniels, Ciara. "Filling the Gaps: A Virtual Discussion of Gender, Peace and Security Research—Summary of Dialogue." New York: United Nations International Research and Training Institute for the Advancement of Women, 2008.

Dé Bryant, Jennifer Hanis, and Charles Stoner. "Special Needs, Special Measures: Working with Homeless and Poor Youth." In *Peacebuilding for Adolescents: Strategies for Educators and Community Leaders*, edited by Linda Rennie Forcey and Ian Murray Harris, 263–288. New York: Peter Lang Publishing, 1999.

de la Rey, Cheryl, and Susan McKay. "Peacebuilding as a Gendered Process." *Journal of Social Issues* 6, no. 1 (2006): 141–153.

De Rivera, Joseph. "Assessing the Basis for a Culture of Peace in Contemporary Societies." *Journal of Peace Research* 41, no. 5 (2004): 531–548.

Del Felice, Celina, and Andria Wisler. "The Unexplored Power and Potential of Youth as Peace-Builders." *Journal of Peace and Conflict Development*, no. 11 (2007): 1–29. Available at: http://www.peacestudiesjournal.org.uk/dl/PCD%20ISSUE%2011%20ARTICLE-The%20Unexplored%20Power%20and%20Potential%20of%20Youth%20as%20Peace-Builders_Celina%20Del%20Felice%20and%20Andria%20Wisler.pdf.

DeNora, Tia. *Music in Everyday Life.* Cambridge: Cambridge University Press, 2000.

Department of Education. "Peace II Programme: The EU Programme for Peace and Reconciliation in Northern Ireland and the Border Region of Ireland 2000–2004 (Peace II)." Edited by Department of Education. Belfast: Northern Ireland Government, 2009.

DFAT (Department of Foreign Affairs and Trade). "A Diverse People." Canberra: Australian Government, 2007. See the updated page, available at: http://www.dfat.gov.au/facts/people culture.html.

Dibben, Nicola. "Representations of Femininity in Popular Music." *Popular Music* 18, no. 3 (1999): 331–355.

Donelan, Kate. "'Overlapping Spheres' and 'Blurred Spaces':

Mapping Cultural Interactions in Drama and Theatre with Young People." *NJ (Drama Australia Journal)* 28, no. 1 (2004): 15–33.

Donnellan, M. Brent, Kali H. Trzesniewski, Richard W. Robins, Terrie E. Moffit, and Avshalom Caspi. "Low Self-Esteem Is Related to Aggression, Antisocial Behavior, and Delinquency." *Psychological Science* 16, no. 4 (2005): 328–335.

Duggan, Lisa. *The Twilight of Equality: Neoliberalism, Cultural Politics, and the Attack on Democracy*. Boston: Beacon Press, 2004.

Einwohner, Rachel L., Jocelyn A. Hollander, and Toska Olson. "Engendering Social Movements: Cultural Images and Movement Dynamics." *Gender and Society* 14, no. 5 (2000): 679–699.

El-Leissy, Mohammed. "Young People's Experiences of Racism in Australia." *Australian Mosaic*, no. 16 (2007): 38–39.

Ellickson, P. L., and K. A. McGuigan. "Early Predictors of Adolescent Violence." *American Journal of Public Health* 90, no. 4 (2000): 566–572.

Elliot, Heather, ed. *Children and Peacebuilding: Experiences and Perspectives*. Melbourne: WorldVision Australia, 2001.

Emerson, Elissa, and Deborah Shelton. "Using Creative Arts to Build Coping Skills to Reduce Domestic Violence in the Lives of Female Juvenile Offenders." *Issues in Mental Health Nursing* 22 (2001): 181–195.

Emerson, Rana A. "'Where My Girls At?' Negotiating Black Womanhood in Music Videos." *Gender and Society* 16, no. 1 (2002): 115–135.

Faith, Karlene. "Reflections on Inside/Out Organizing." *Social Justice* 27, no. 3 (2000): 158–168.

Fernandes, Sujatha. "Proven Presence: The Emergence of a Feminist Politics in Cuban Hip-Hop." In *Home Girls Make Some Noise: Hip Hop Feminism Anthology*, edited by Gwendolyn D. Pough, Elaine Richardson, Aisha Durham, and Rachel Raimist, 5–18. Mira Loma, CA: Parker Publishing, 2007.

Ferré, M. Isolina. "Prevention and Control of Violence through Community Revitalization, Individual Dignity, and Personal Self-Confidence." *Annals of the American Academy of Political and Social Science* 494 (1987): 27–36.

Fine, Michelle, Lois Weis, and Linda C. Powell. "Communities of Difference." In *Critical Ethnicity: Countering the Waves of Identity Politics*, edited by Robert H. Tai and Mary L. Kenyatta, 21–64. Lanham, MD: Rowman & Littlefield Publishers, 1999.

Fischlin, Daniel. "Take One/Rebel Musics: Human Rights, Resistant Sounds, and the Politics of Music Making." In *Rebel Musics: Human Rights, Resistant Sounds, and the Politics of Music Making*, edited by Daniel Fischlin and Ajay Heble, 10–43. Montreal: Black Rose Books, 2003.

Flashpoints: World Conflicts. "Northern Ireland." http://www.flashpoints.info/countries-conflicts/Northern_Ireland-web/n-ireland_briefing.html.

Flood, Michael. "Why Violence against Women and Girls Happens, and How to Prevent It: A Framework and Some Key Strategies." *Redress*, no. 13–19 (August 2007): 13–19.

Forcey, Linda Rennie. "Feminist and Peace Perspectives on Women." In *Encyclopedia of Violence, Peace & Conflict*, edited by Lester R. Kurtz and Jennifer E. Turpin, 13–20. Waltham, MA: Academic Press, 1999.

Forman, Murray. *The 'Hood Comes First: Race, Space, and Place in Rap and Hip-Hop*. Middleton, CT: Wesleyan University Press, 2002.

Foucault, Michel. "Of Other Spaces." *Diacritics* 16, no. 1 (1986): 22–27.

Francis, Diana. *People, Peace and Power: Conflict Transformation in Action*. London; Sterling, VA: Pluto Press, 2002.

Franzway, Suzanne, Rhonda Sharp, Julie E. Mills, and Judith Gill. "Engineering Ignorance: The Problem of Gender Equity in Engineering." *Frontiers: A Journal of Women Studies* 30, no. 1 (2009): 89–106.

Freud, Sigmund. "Why War?" In *Approaches to Peace: A Reader in Peace Studies*, edited by David Barash. New York: Oxford University Press, 2010 (1959).

Frilander, Mads, and Hannah Stogdon. "Engaging with the Grassroots: Humanitarian Decision-Making, Conflict Sensitivity, and Somali 'Non-State Actors' Platforms." Nairobi, Kenya: Safer World UK, 2011.

Frith, Simon. "Music and Identity." In *Questions of Cultural*

Identity, edited by Stuart Hall and Paul du Gay, 108–127. London: Sage, 1996.

Fritzsche, Bettina. "Spicy Strategies: Pop Feminist and Other Empowerments in Girl Culture." In *All About the Girl: Culture, Power, and Identity*, edited by Anita Harris, 155–162. New York, London: Routledge, 2004.

Frost, Michael. *Exiles: Living Missionally in a Post-Christian Culture.* Peabody, MA: Hendrickson Publishers, 2006.

Galtung, Johan. "Violence, Peace and Peace Research." *Journal of Peace Research* 6, no. 3 (1969): 167–191.

Garofalo, Reebee. *Rockin' the Boat: Mass Music & Mass Movements.* Cambridge, MA: South End Press, 1999.

Gender and Peacebuilding Working Group of the Canadian Peacebuilding Coordinating Committee (CPCC). "Fact Sheet: Resolution 1325 for Girls and Young Women." http://www.peacebuild.ca/upload/fact_sheet.pdf.

Gender and Peacebuilding Working Group of the Canadian Peacebuilding Coordinating Committee (CPCC). "Fact Sheet: Understanding United Nations Security Council Resolution 1325." http://www.peacebuild.ca/upload/fact_sheet_new.pdf.

Gender and Peacebuilding Working Group of the Canadian Peacebuilding Coordinating Committee (CPCC). "How Can We Use Resolution 1325?" http://www.peacebuild.ca/upload/fact_sheet_new.pdf.

Gerard, Glenna. "Creating New Connections: Dialogue and Improv." In *Dialogue as a Means of Collective Communication*, edited by Bela H. Banathy and Patrick M. Jenlink, 333–356. New York: Kluwer Academic / Plenum Publishers, 2005.

Ghim Lian Chew, Phyllis. "The Challenge of Unity: Women, Peace and Power." *International Journal on World Peace* 15, no. 4 (1998): 29–42.

Gilman, Lisa, and John Fenn. "Dance, Gender, and Popular Music in Malawi: The Case of Rap and Ragga." *Popular Music* 25, no. 3 (2006): 369–381.

Green, Paula. "Contact: Training a New Generation of Peacebuilders." *Peace and Change* 27, no. 1 (2002): 97–105.

Griffin, Christine. "Troubled Teens: Managing Disorders of Transition and Consumption." *Feminist Review* 55 (1997): 4–22.

Halpern, Jodi, and Harvey M. Weinstein. "Rehumanizing the Other: Empathy and Reconciliation." *Human Rights Quarterly* 26, no. 3 (2004): 561–583.

Hancock, Landon E. "The Northern Irish Peace Process: From Top to Bottom." *International Studies Review* 10 (2008): 203–238.

Harland, Ken. "Violent Youth Culture in Northern Ireland: Young Men, Violence, and the Challenges of Peacebuilding." *Youth & Society* 32, no. 2 (2011): 414–432.

Harris, Anita. *Future Girl.* New York and London: Routledge, 2004.

Harris, Anita. "Revisiting Bedroom Culture: New Spaces for Young Women's Politics." *Hecate: An Interdisciplinary Journal of Women's Liberation* 27, no. 1 (2001): 128–138.

Hawkins, Stan. *Settling the Pop Score: Pop Texts and Identity Politics.* Burlington, VT: Ashgate Publishing, 2002.

Hayllar, Bruce, and Tony Veal. *Pathways to Research.* Port Melbourne: Rigby Heinemann, Reed International Books, 1996.

Heble, Ajay. "Take Two/Rebel Musics: Human Rights, Resistant Sounds, and the Politics of Music Making." In *Rebel Musics: Human Rights, Resistant Sounds, and the Politics of Music Making,* edited by Daniel Fischlin and Ajay Heble, 232–248. Montreal: Black Rose Books, 2003.

Hedemann, Maree. "Gender & Violence." *Redress* (September 1998): 16–24.

Hedges, Chris. "War Is a Force That Gives Us Meaning." In *Approaches to Peace: A Reader in Peace Studies,* edited by David Barash, 24–26. New York: Oxford University Press, 2010 (2002).

Hein, Karen. "Young People as Assets: A Foundation View." *Social Policy* 30, no. 1 (1999): 20–30.

Hollows, Joanne. *Feminism, Femininity and Popular Culture.* Manchester: Manchester University Press, 2000.

Homan, Shane. "Youth, Live Music and Urban Leisure: Geographies of Noise." *Youth Studies Australia* 22, no. 2 (2003): 12–18.

Hopkins, Susan. "Hole Lotta Attitude: Courtney Love and Guitar Feminism." *Social Alternatives* 18, no. 2 (1999): 11–14.

Hunter, Mary Ann. "Of Peacebuilding and Performance:

Contact Inc.'s 'Third Space' of Intercultural Collaboration." *Australasian Drama Studies* 47, no. October 2005 (2005): 140–158.

Hurt, Hallam, Elsa Malmud, Nancy L. Brodsky, and Joan Giannetta. "Exposure to Violence: Psychological and Academic Correlates in Child Witnesses." *Archives of Pediatrics and Adolescent Medicine* 155, no. 12 (2001): 1351–1356.

Imms, Wesley. "Boys Talk About 'Doing Art': Some Implications for Masculinity Discussion." *Australian Art Education* 26, no. 1 (2003): 29–37.

Jagodzinski, Jan. *Music in Youth Culture: A Lacanian Approach.* New York: Palgrave Macmillan, 2005.

Jakubowicz, Andrew. "Hobbits and Orcs: The Street Politics of Race and Masculinity." *Australian Options* 44 (2006): 2–5.

Janis, Irving. "Victims of Groupthink." In *Approaches to Peace: A Reader in Peace Studies,* edited by David Barash, 31–37. New York: Oxford University Press, 2010 (1982).

Jeffries, Michael. "Re: Definitions: The Name and Game of Hip-Hop Feminism." In *Home Girls Make Some Noise: Hip Hop Feminism Anthology,* edited by Gwendolyn D. Pough, Elaine Richardson, Aisha Durham, and Rachel Raimist, 208–227. Mira Loma, CA: Parker Publishing, 2007.

Jeong, Ho-Won. *Peace and Conflict Studies: An Introduction.* Aldershot: Ashgate Publishing Limited, 2000.

Jeong, Ho-Won. *Peacebuilding in Postconflict Societies: Strategy and Process.* Boulder: Lynne Rienner Publishers, 2005.

Jipping, Thomas L. "Heavy Metal, Rap, and America's Youth: Issues and Alternatives (2nd Edition). A Special Report of the Free Congress Foundation." Washington, DC: Free Congress Foundation, 1990.

Karagianis, Liz. "The Art of Dialogue." Spectrum (online) (Winter 2001). http://*spectrum.mit.edu/articles/intro/the-art-of-dialogue.*

Karam, Azza. "Women in War and Peace-Building: The Roads Traversed, the Challenges Ahead." *International Feminist Journal of Politics* 3, no. 1 (2001): 2–25.

Kaufman, Edward (Edy). "Dialogue-Based Processes: A Vehicle for Peacebuilding." In *People Building Peace II: Successful Stories of Civil Society,* edited by Paul van Tongeren, Malin

Brenk, Marte Hellema, and Juliette Verhoeven, 473–487. Boulder, London: Lynne Rienner Publishers, 2005.

Keddie, Amanda, and Martin Mills. "Teaching for Gender Justice." *Australian Journal of Education* 51, no. 2 (2007): 205–219.

Keith, Michael. *After the Cosmopolitan: Multicultural Cities and the Future of Racism.* London: Routledge, 2005.

Kellett, Peter M. *Conflict Dialogue: Working with Layers of Meaning for Productive Relationships.* Thousand Oaks, London, New Delhi: Sage Publications, 2007.

Kinnaman, David, and Gabe Lyons. *Unchristian: What a New Generation Thinks About Christianity . . . And Why It Matters.* Grand Rapids, MI: Baker Books, 2007.

Lai, Daniel W. L. "Violence Exposure and Mental Health of Adolescents in Small Towns: An Exploratory Study." *Canadian Journal of Public Health* May–June 1999 (1999): 181–185.

Lederach, John Paul. *The Moral Imagination: The Art and Soul of Building Peace.* Oxford: Oxford University Press, 2005.

Lederach, John Paul. *Building Peace: Sustainable Reconciliation in Divided Societies.* Washington, DC: United States Institute of Peace, 1997.

Lederach, John Paul. *Preparing for Peace: Conflict Transformation across Cultures.* Syracuse, NY: Syracuse University Press, 1995.

Lederach, John Paul, and Angela Jill Lederach. *When Blood and Bones Cry Out: Journeys through the Soundscape of Healing and Reconciliation.* Edited by Kevin P. Clements, New Approaches to Peace and Conflict. Brisbane: University of Queensland Press, 2010.

Lees, Sue. *Sugar and Spice: Sexuality and Adolescent Girls.* London: Penguin, 1993.

Lefebvre, Henri. *The Production of Space.* Translated by Donald Nicholson-Smith. Oxford: Blackwell Publishing, 1991 (1974).

Lemish, Dafna. "Spice World: Constructing Femininity the Popular Way." *Popular Music and Society* 26, no. 1 (2003): 17–29.

Lennon, John, and Paul McCartney. "With a Little Help from My Friends." Parlophone, 1967.

Letherby, Gayle. *Feminist Research in Theory and Practice.* Buckingham: Open University Press, 2003.

Liamputtong, Pranee, and Douglas Ezzy. *Qualitative Research Methods.* 2nd edition. New York: Oxford University Press, 2005.

Lock, Katrin. "Who Is Listening? Hip Hop Culture in Sierra Leone, Liberia and Senegal." In *Resounding International Relations: On Music, Culture and Politics,* edited by M. I. Franklin, 141–160. New York: Palgrave Macmillan, 2005.

Lomax, Alan. "Folk Song Style." *American Anthropologist* 61, no. 6 (1959): 927–954.

Love, Nancy. "'Singing for Our Lives': Women's Music and Democratic Politics." *Hypatia* 17, no. 4 (2002): 71–94.

Madarshahi, Mehri. "Mission: Mehri Madarshahi's Speech at the UNESCO Conference in Rabat (2005)." Rabat, Morocco. Available at: http://unesdoc.unexco.org/images/0015/001541/154100e.pdf from UNESCO.

Mazali, Rela. "And What About the Girls? What a Culture of War Genders Out of View." *Journal of Jewish Women's Studies and Gender Issues,* no. 6 (2003): 39–50.

McEvoy, Kieran, and Anna Eriksson. "Restorative Justice in Transition: Ownership, Leadership, and 'Bottom-Up' Human Rights." In *Handbook of Restorative Justice,* edited by Dennis Sullivan and Larry Tifft, 321–335. London and New York: Routledge, 2006.

McEvoy, Siobhán. "Communities and Peace: Catholic Youth in Northern Ireland." *Journal of Peace Research* 37, no. 1 (2000): 87–103.

McEvoy-Levy, Siobhán. "Youth as Social and Political Agents: Issues in Post-Settlement Peace Building." In *Kroc Institute Occasional Paper #21:OP:2*: Kroc Institute's Research Initiative on the Resolution of Ethnic Conflict (RIREC), 2001.

McIntyre, Angela, and Thokozani Thusi. "Children and Youth in Sierra Leone's Peace-Building Process." *African Security Review* 12, no. 2 (2003). http://www.iss.co.za/pubs/asr/12No2/E2.html.

McKittrick, David. "Racism 'Is the New Terrorism' as Attacks Rise in Ulster." *The Independent,* 16 October 2004.

Mead, Margaret. "Warfare Is Only an Invention—Not a

Biological Necessity." In *Approaches to Peace: A Reader in Peace Studies*, edited by David Barash, 19–22. New York: Oxford University Press, 2010 (1940).

Mercer, Phil. "Indian Students Claim Epidemic of Racist Violence in Australia." *Voice of America News*, 4 June 2009.

Merrington, Louise. "Here's a Generation Wanting to Be Heard." *The Age*, 31 August 2004.

Mitchell, Tony. "Australian Hip Hop as a Subculture." *Youth Studies Australia* 22, no. 2 (2003): 40–47.

Monteith, Marina, and Eithne McLaughlin. "Severe Child Poverty in Northern Ireland: Key Research Findings." Washington, DC; Save the Children, 2004.

Morgan, Joan. *When Chickenheads Come Home to Roost: A Hip-Hop Feminist Breaks It Down.* New York: Simon & Schuster, 1999.

Mueller, John. "The Banality of 'Ethnic War.'" *International Security* 25, no. 1 (2000): 42–70.

Munõz, Germán, and Martha Marín. "Music Is the Connection: Youth Cultures in Colombia." In *Global Youth? Hybrid Identities, Plural Worlds*, edited by Pam Nilan and Carles Feixa, 130–148. London and New York: Routledge, 2006.

Naples, Nancy. *Feminism and Method: Ethnography, Discourse Analysis, and Activist Research.* New York: Routledge, 2003.

Naumann, Kurt. "Briefing Paper: Bullying." Edited by U.S. Department of Justice: School Violence Resource Center, 2001.

Niang, Abdoulaye. "Bboys: Hip-Hop Culture in Dakar, Senegal." In *Global Youth? Hybrid Identities, Plural Worlds*, edited by Pam Nilan and Carles Feixa, 167–185. London and New York: Routledge, 2006.

Oddie, David. "Conquering Conflict." *the wee can* (Autumn 2005): 9.

Pankhurst, Donna. "The 'Sex War' and Other Wars: Towards a Feminist Approach to Peace Building." *Development in Practice* 13, no. 2 (2003): 154–177.

Pankhurst, Donna. "Mainstreaming Gender in Peacebuilding—a Framework for Action: From the Village Council to the Negotiating Table: The International Campaign to Promote the Role of Women in Peacebuilding." London: International Alert, 2000.

Pankhurst, Donna. "Women, Gender and Peacebuilding." Bradford: University of Bradford, Centre for Conflict Resolution, Department of Peace Studies, 2000.

Phillips, Coretta. "Who's Who in the Pecking Order? Aggression and 'Normal Violence' in the Lives of Girls and Boys." *The British Journal of Criminology* 43, no. 4 (2003): 710–728.

Phillips, Gerald. "Can There Be 'Music for Peace'?" *International Journal on World Peace* 21, no. 2 (2004): 63–74.

Porter, Elisabeth. "Women, Political Decision-Making, and Peace-Building." *Global Change, Peace & Security* 15, no. 3 (2003): 245–262.

Pough, Gwendolyn D. *Check It While I Wreck It: Black Womanhood, Hip-Hop Culture, and the Public Sphere.* Boston: Northeastern University Press, 2004.

Pratt, Mary Louise. "Arts of the Contact Zone." In *Profession 91,* 33–40. New York: MLA, 1991.

Pritchard, Eric Darnell, and Maria L. Bibbs. "Sista' Outsider: Queer Women of Color and Hip Hop." In *Home Girls Make Some Noise: Hip Hop Feminism Anthology,* edited by Gwendolyn D. Pough, Elaine Richardson, Aisha Durham, and Rachel Raimist, 19–40. Mira Loma, CA: Parker Publishing, 2007.

Prothrow-Stith, Deborah, and Sher Quaday. "Hidden Casualties: The Relationship between Violence and Learning." *Streamlined Seminar: National Association of Elementary School Principals* 14, no. 2 (1995): 2–5.

Ramirez, J. Martin. "Peace through Dialogue." *International Journal on World Peace* 24, no. 1 (2007): 65–81.

Ramsbotham, Oliver, Tom Woodhouse, and Hugh Miall. *Contemporary Conflict Resolution: The Prevention, Management and Transformation of Deadly Conflicts.* 2nd ed. Cambridge: Polity, 2005.

Rees, Stuart. *Passion for Peace: Exercising Power Creatively.* Sydney: University of New South Wales Press, 2003.

Rehn, Elisabeth, and Ellen Johnson Sirleaf. "Executive Summary—Women War Peace: The Independent Experts' Assessment." In *Progress of the World's Women 2002.* Washington, DC: UNIFEM, 2002.

Renew, Sandra. "The Social Construction of Gender, Violence and Schools." *Redress* (November 1995): 6–11.

Reynolds, Matthew W., Joanna Wallace, Tyra F. Hill, Mark D. Weist, and Laura A. Nabors. "The Relationship between Gender, Depression, and Self-Esteem in Children Who Have Witnessed Domestic Violence." *Child Abuse & Neglect* 25, no. 9 (2001): 1201–1206.

Rich, Emma. "Young Women, Feminist Identities and Neo-Liberalism." *Women's Studies International Forum* 28, no. 6 (2005): 494–508.

Richards, Paul. "Young Men and Gender in War and Postwar Reconstruction: Some Comparative Findings from Liberia and Sierra Leone." In *The Other Half of Gender: Men's Issues in Development,* edited by Ian Bannon and Maria C. Correia, 195–218. Washington, DC: The World Bank, 2006.

Rosenberg, Jessica, and Gitana Garofalo. "Riot Grrrl: Revolutions from Within." *Signs* 23, no. 3 (1998): 809.

Rycenga, Jennifer. "Lesbian Compositional Practice: One Lover-Composer's Perspective." In *Queering the Pitch: The New Gay and Lesbian Musicology,* edited by Phillip Brett, Elizabeth Wood, and Gary C. Thomas, 275–296. New York: Routledge, 1994.

Saldanha, Arun. "Music, Space, Identity Global Youth / Local Others in Bangalore, India." Brussels: Center for Media Sociology, 1998. Available at: http://www.snarl.org/youth/arun-msi.pdf.

Schäfer, Rita. "Masculinity and Civil Wars in Africa: New Approaches to Overcoming Sexual Violence in War." Edited by Jörg-Werner Haas. Eschborn, Germany: Federal Ministry for Economic Cooperation and Development, Program Promoting Gender Equality and Women's Rights, 2009.

Schell-Faucon, Stephanie. "Conflict Transformation through Educational and Youth Programmes." Berlin: Berghof Research Center for Constructive Conflict Management, 2001.

Schippers, Mimi. "The Social Organization of Sexuality and Gender in Alternative Hard Rock: An Analysis of Intersectionality." *Gender and Society* 14, no. 6 (2000): 747–764.

Schirch, Lisa. *Ritual and Symbol in Peacebuilding*. Bloomfield, CT: Kumarian Press, 2005.

Schirch, Lisa. *The Little Book of Strategic Peacebuilding*. Intercourse, PA: Good Books, 2004.

Schwartz, Stephanie. *Youth and Post-Conflict Reconstruction: Agents of Change*. Washington, DC: United States Institute of Peace Press, 2010.

Scott, Joan W. *Gender and the Politics of History*. New York: Columbia University Press, 1999.

Scott, Joan W. "Deconstructing Equality-Versus-Difference: Or, the Uses of Poststructuralist Theory for Feminism." *Feminist Studies* 14, no. 1 (1988): 33–50.

Senehi, Jessica, and Sean Byrne. "From Violence toward Peace: The Role of Storytelling for Youth Healing and Political Empowerment after Conflict." In *Troublemakers or Peacemakers? Youth and Post-Accord Peace Building*, ed. Siobhán McEvoy-Levy. South Bend, IN: University of Notre Dame Press, 2006.

Shepard, Ben. "The Use of Joyfulness as a Community Organizing Strategy." *Peace and Change* 30, no. 4 (2005): 435–468.

Shepherd, John. "Difference and Power in Music." In *Musicology and Difference: Gender and Sexuality in Music Scholarship*, edited by Ruth A. Solie, 46–65. Berkeley: University of California Press, 1993.

Slachmuijlder, Lena. "The Rhythm of Reconciliation: A Reflection on Drumming as a Contribution to Reconciliation Processes in Burundi and South Africa." Waltham, MA: Brandeis University Press, 2005.

Slobin, Mark. *Subculture Sounds: Micromusic of the West*. Hanover and London: Wesleyan University Press, 1993.

Sloboda, John. *Exploring the Musical Mind*. Oxford: Oxford University Press, 2005.

Smith, Dan. "Trends and Causes of Armed Conflict." Berlin: Berghof Research Centre, 2005.

Snyder, Anna C. *Setting the Agenda for Global Peace: Conflict and Consensus Building*. Aldershot: Ashgate, 2003.

Soja, Edward. *Thirdspace: Journeys to Los Angeles and Other Real-and-Imagined Places*. Oxford: Blackwell Publishing, 1996.

Sommers, Marc. "Fearing Africa's Young Men: Male Youth,

Conflict, Urbanization, and the Case of Rwanda." In *The Other Half of Gender: Men's Issues in Development*, edited by Ian Bannon and Maria C. Correia, 137–158. Washington, DC: The World Bank, 2006.

Sprague, Joey. *Feminist Methodologies for Critical Researchers: Bridging Differences.* Walnut Creek, CA: AltaMira Press, 2005.

Staub, Ervin, Laurie Anne Pearlman, Alexandra Gubin, and Athanase Hagengimana. "Healing, Reconciliation, Forgiving and the Prevention of Violence after Genocide or Mass Killing: An Intervention and Its Experimental Evaluation in Rwanda." *Journal of Social & Clinical Psychology* 24, no. 3 (2005): 297–334.

Steinberg, Donald. "Beyond Victimhood: Engaging Women in the Pursuit of Peace, Testimony to the House of Representatives Committee on Foreign Affairs, by Donald Steinberg, Deputy President, International Crisis Group (ICC), to Subcommittee on International Organizations, Human Rights and Oversight, 15 May 2008." Washington, DC, 2008.

Stewart, Shannon. "All-Ages Movement Project: Project Report." 2006. http://www.allagesmovementproject.org.

Stokes, Martin. "Introduction: Ethnicity, Identity and Music." In *Ethnicity, Identity and Music: The Musical Construction of Place*, edited by Martin Stokes, 1–27. Oxford, New York: Berg, 1994.

Storr, Anthony. *Music and the Mind.* London: HarperCollins Publishers, 1992.

Stuart, Graeme. "Conflict Resolution & Non-Violence Workshops with Young People." *Youth Studies Australia* 18, no. 2 (1999): 37–41.

Taylor, Charles. "The Politics of Recognition." In *Multiculturalism and the Politics of Recognition*, edited by Charles Taylor, Kwame Anthony Appiah, Jürgen Habermas, Steven C. Rockefeller, Michael Walzer and Susan Wolf, 25–73. Princeton: Princeton University Press, 1994.

The 14th Dalai Lama. "Nobel Lecture." Paper presented at the The Nobel Peace Prize Nobel Lecture, December 11, 1989.

Tickner, J. Ann. *Gendering World Politics: Issues and Approaches in the Post-Cold War Era.* New York: Columbia University Press, 2001.

Tickner, J. Ann. *Gender in International Relations: Feminist Perspectives on Achieving Global Security*. New York: Columbia University Press, 1992.

Tocci, Nathalie. "EU, Conflict Transformation and Civil Society: Promoting Peace from the Bottom Up?" In *Microcon Conference*. Brighton, UK: Institute of Development Studies, 2011.

True, Jaqui. "Reflexivity in Practice: Power and Ethics in Feminist Research." Brisbane: University of Queensland School of Political Science and International Studies Seminar Series Presentation, 2007.

Tulley, Angus. "Masculinities and Violence." *Changing Education: A Journal for Teachers and Administrators* 4 nos. 2 & 3 (1997): 1–6.

UNESCO. "Culture of Peace: Peace Is in Our Hands." http://www3.unesco.org/iycp/uk/uk_sum_cp.htm.

UNESCO. "Gender Dynamics of Conflict, Peace-Building, and Reconstruction." http://portal.unesco.org/shs/en/ev.php-URL_ID=7839&URL_DO=DO_TOPIC&URL_SECTION=201.html.

UNFPA. "Gender-Based Violence: A Price Too High." In *State of World Population*: United Nations, 2005.

UNFPA. "Homepage." http://www.unfpa.org/adolescents/index.htm; http://www.unfpa.org/adolescents/about.htm.

UNICEF. "Report Card 7: Child Poverty in Perspective: An Overview of Child Well-Being in Rich Countries: A Comprehensive Assessment of the Lives and Well-Being of Children and Adolescents in the Economically Advanced Nations." In *Innocenti Report Cards*. Florence, Italy: UNICEF Innocenti Research Center, 2007. Available at: http://www.unicef.org/media/files/ChildPovertyReport.pdf.

Valdez, Avelardo, and Jeffrey A. Halley. "Gender in the Culture of Mexican American Conjunto Music." *Gender and Society* 10, no. 2 (1996): 148–167.

van Tongeren, Paul, Juliette Verhoeven, and Jim Wake. "People Building Peace: Key Messages and Essential Findings." In *People Building Peace II: Successful Stories of Civil Society*, edited by Paul van Tongeren, Malin Brenk, Marte Hellema, and Juliette Verhoeven, 83–93. Boulder, London: Lynne Rienner Publishers, 2005.

Wade, Bonnie C. *Thinking Musically: Experiencing Music, Expressing Culture.* New York, Oxford: Oxford University Press, 2004.

Walby, Sylvia. "Gender Mainstreaming: Productive Tensions in Theory and Practice." *Social Politics* 12, no. 3 (2005): 321–343.

Wald, Gayle. "Just a Girl? Rock Music, Feminism, and the Cultural Construction of Female Youth." *Signs* 23, no. 3 (1998): 585.

Washington, Alesha Dominek. "Not the Average Girl from the Videos: B-Girls Defining Their Space in Hip-Hop Culture." In *Home Girls Make Some Noise: Hip Hop Feminism Anthology*, edited by Gwendolyn D. Pough, Elaine Richardson, Aisha Durham, and Rachel Raimist, 80–91. Mira Loma, CA: Parker Publishing, 2007.

Weekes, Debbie. "Where My Girls At? Black Girls and the Construction of the Sexual." In *All About the Girl: Culture, Power, and Identity*, edited by Anita Harris, 141–153. New York and London: Routledge, 2004.

Wise, Amanda. "Sensuous Multiculturalism: Emotional Landscapes of Interethnic Living in Australian Suburbia." *Journal of Ethnic and Migration Studies* 36, no. 6 (2010): 917–937.

Witherow, Jacqueline. "'The War on Terrorism' and Parading Bands in Northern Ireland." 2009. http://www.qub.ac.uk/sites/QUEST/FileStore/Filetoupload,25795,en.pdf.

Zelizer, Craig, and Robert A. Rubinstein, eds. *Building Peace: Practical Reflections from the Field.* Sterling, VA: Kumarian Press, 2009.

Zimbalist, Jeff, and Matt Mochary. *Favela Rising.* 80 mins. United States: Thinkfilm, 2005.

Index